STUDIES IN THE LITERATURE OF ASSAM

STUDIES IN THE LITERATURE OF ASSAM

SURYYA KUMAR BHUYAN

GYAN

Published by

Gyan Publishing House
5, Ansari Road
Daryaganj, New Delhi-110002
Phone: 011-47034999, 9811692060
E-mail: books@gyanbooks.com

Distribution Network
gyanbooks.com
India, USA, Canada, UK, Australia

ISBN: 978-93-6920-183-9 (PB)

First Published, 1956

2nd Impression 2025

Printed at: Gyan Press, Delhi.

STUDIES IN THE LITERATURE OF ASSAM
Author: SURYYA KUMAR BHUYAN

STUDIES IN THE LITERATURE OF ASSAM

STUDIES IN THE LITERATURE OF ASSAM

BY

SURYYA KUMAR BHUYAN

M.A., B.L. (CAL.), PH.D. (LOND.), D.LIT. (LOND.),

Formerly Vice-Chancellor, Gauhati University.

1962

FOREWORD

BY SHRI SRI PRAKASA, B.A. (ALLAHABAD), B.A., LL.B. (CANTAB.), BARRISTER-AT-LAW, THEN GOVERNOR OF MADRAS, FORMERLY GOVERNOR OF ASSAM, AND MINISTER IN CHARGE OF NATURAL RESOURSES AND SCIENTIFIC RESEARCH, GOVERNMENT OF INDIA.

It is an honour indeed that Dr. Suryya Kumar Bhuyan has done me in asking me to write a foreword to his learned book on the STUDIES IN THE LITERATURE OF ASSAM. I fear, like most of my countrymen, I had only a very distant idea of the fair land of Assam that nestles in our north-eastern mountain ranges and has, through the ages, lived more or less her life. As the home of the rhinoceros and the python, the tiger and the elephant, the British planter and the head-hunting Naga, we might have vaguely heard of her. As Kamrup that practises all forms of witchcraft and turns men into animals, we might even have imbibed some prejudices against her. Of her age-old history, her culture, her art, her beauty, her variegated life, her love of liberty, however, we had heard very little. The strange thing about it all is that the Assamese themselves seem never to have been anxious to make themselves known to the outside world, and they appear to have been ever satisfied as they were.

It is not that I had not known friends from Assam. I had a Barua as a fellow-students in the school; I had colleagues from Assam in later public life; but none of them ever spoke anything about their land; and so of Assam as such, I was blissfully ignorant. It was only when Shri Rajagopalachariar, as Governor-General, and Shri Jawaharlal Nehru, as Prime Minister, sent me to Assam as Governor early in 1949, that I found a new world opening before me, and myself coming in contact with the thoughts and activities, with the peoples and problems of which I had no idea before. The fair land of Assam just captivated me ; and though I was privileged to be there only for a brief space of fifteen months, I had opportunities of travelling extensively up-hill and down-dale, on the broad bosom of the Brahmaputra and in the interior of the densest forests ; and it was then that I realised what a variegated life our country presents, and what wonderful Unity in Diversity she stands for. Assam is very dear to my heart, and she always dwells there as a precious memory, as the symbol of a great heritage.

It was during those days that I first met Dr. Bhuyan ; and ever since then we have kept close contacts with each other both by correspondence and occasional meetings. I read his books with great avidity and eagerness while I was in Assam ; and from them I learn something of Assam through the centuries, her legends and her traditions, her history and her personalities, her great adventure in the realms of art, religion and politics. Dr. Bhuyan has an easy style of writing, and presents his figures in the most pleasing manner, narrating his facts with such lucidity and simplicity that one finds oneself reading his last page not very long before he had begun the first. The great work that he has done for the resuscitation of the past of Assam, and the books that he has written both in Assamese and in English, deserve to live as standing monuments to his great industry and scholarship and as an outward expression of the high patriotism that burns within. They should also give much information to those who seek to know; much food for thought to men and women who ponder over the problems of the country; and many directives as well, as to how these can be solved.

The Assamese, curiously enough, are a historical people; and the Buranjis that tell of their past, are not mere neglected chronicles, but active factors in their daily life. We, as a race, generally speaking, have little idea of or love for history. In Assam, however, dates are carefully preserved; and they will tell one approximately correctly the time when any particular events took place and particular personalities held sway. The task therefore of the historian and the chronicler becomes comparatively easy. Mahapurusha Shankar Deva, their greatest religious figure, and Lachit Barphukan, the great warrior, statesman and patriot, are remembered and honoured not as vague figures of some remote past, but as actual living human beings who have done great deeds; and the dates of their exploits and achievements are duly recorded. The people's love for freedom has always been intense. Muslim, Burma and British have alike known this, and when there was a talk of Assam going to Pakistan, the great patriot Shri Gopi Nath Bardoloi told Mahatma Gandhi that Assam will fight—and if she goes down, she will go down fighting—but never surrender. The stories of the great migrations from Kanauj or Cambodia are also known; and it is remarkable how very different types of peoples have lived there in comparative peace and amity through the ages without anyone trying to dusturb the life and thought of anyone else. India alone, I believe, can present a phenomenon such as this in the world in which we live ; and Dr. Bhuyan through his works, helps us to understand the process that has gone to make the Assam that she is at the present moment.

The present work deals with the literatures of Assam. A speciality of it is that it is not about literature *on* Assam nor the literature produced *in* the Assamese tongue. It is a study of literature as evolved in Assam through the centuries in various languages—Assamese, Khasi, Manipuri, Bengali and English. It has given a deservedly honoured place to the work of Christian missionaries who have made the literature of hill tribes of Assam available to us. A critical study is made of all these and it would certainly help us to enter into the heart of the Assamese people, and strike all the chords of sympathy and affection in our own. It is very essential that the people in the country outside Assam should carefully study Assam and her problems. Let it not be forgotten that it is our most strategic state. A narrow corridor, of only about forty miles, connects it with the rest of the country, while Tibet, Burma and Pakistan surround it on all sides. Between these and the main plateau of Assam, there are high mountains where innumerable strange tribes live their own lives to this day, following their own manners and customs and resenting any interference from anyone. They are our own countrymen and countrywomen, and we must understand them. They are integral parts of our Union and our Republic, and we have to know and realise that.

Nowhere else in the land I believe, does life present us so many facets as it does in Assam. No other State, to my thinking, contains in itself every possible problem that troubles anyone anywhere else in the land. I have a feeling that the way Assam solves her problems is the way that the country as a whole will solve all her own as well. To this great task of understanding and appreciating, as well as overcoming the various difficulties that assail us, Dr. Bhuyan gives a clarion call. His books will also help us to realise that fundamentally the whole country is One because alike in the North and in the South, we are bred up on the same traditions of thought and culture, and worship the self-same heroes of antiquity of legend or of history. That is the great bond between the past and the present, between the North and the South, between the East and the West. We have indeed a great task before us. We should be thankful that we live at a time when it is our high privilege to devote ourselves to these tasks; and help in the consolidation of the country, and by precept and example, in bettering the world in which we live.

Raj Bhavan, Madras,
November 25, 1955.

SRI PRAKASA
GOVERNOR OF MADRAS.

PREFACE

Essays written by the author on different occasions are brought together in the present book *Studies in the Literature of Assam*. They do not profess to constitute a history of literature which, as a rule, must do justice to every notable author, book, period or movement, and where the omission of an important trend or detail is regarded more or less as a tabu. The writer of an essay enjoys greater freedom inasmuch as he can emphasise on conspicuous landmarks, tendencies and developments in order to justify and support his thesis. Such a study, though not a substitute for literary history, is helpful in interpreting facts and achievements. It is for this reason that the essays in this book, though scattered heretofore, have been read by scholars and students with considerable interest and attention.

As will be seen, the scope of the book transcends the limits of the literature written in the Assamese language. Assam has been the home of diverse cultures : some of them are preserved in written records, while others are represented in orally transmitted folksongs, folktales and legends.

Through the medium of Sanskrit literature and the vast corpus of its translation work, Assam has maintained its cultural and religious contact with the Gangetic Valley, while the Ahom literature of Assam has served as the window through which it has gazed at the pastoral banks of the Chindwin and Irrawady rivers. The Khamptis and Phakials have, in their written records, preserved the message of Tathagata Lord Buddha ; they besides possess a secular literature of a realistic character.

The literature of Assam, written and oral, taken together, gives us a glimpse of the mind and soul of its people who have been living for ages under the same sky, breathing the same air, listening to the chirping of the same birds, watching the blossoming of the same flowers, sharing in the same realities of life, and rising and falling together. The volume and variety, and the reciprocal influences of the various offshoots of the literature of Assam are awaiting study and scrutiny at the hands of patient and industrious investigators.

The literature of the preliterate tribes of Assam has been formed comparatively recently mainly through the enterprising zeal of Christian Missionaries working in different fields and under different auspices. The folklore of these tribes should be collected, now, when there is time; it will form the nucleus and foundation of their national literature which will inspire creative and constructive works in future.

The literature of Assam has a bright prospect because the people are patriotic and alert. This trait may not be perceptible in ordinary times, but it comes to the surface very forcefully when national prestige and honour fall in danger of being undermined or destroyed.

I have included in this book the sketches of three modern authors U Soso Tham, Pundit Hemchandra Goswami and Dr. Banikanta Kakati—as they indicate some salient features of the present-day literature of Assam.

I have also added a chapter on the Assamese chronicle *Tripura Buranji*, for I feel that scholars in India and abroad should be acquainted with this monument of Assamese prose and of Assamese historical literature, and with the great purpose lying at the root of its compilation. It is significant that the dream of King Rudra Singha to bring Assam and Tripura nearer each other by ties of friendship is now reflected in the recommendation of the States Reorganisation Commission of the Government of India that the two States should be placed under one administration.

A list of books and articles about Assamese language and literature has been appended with the hope that scholars, students, librarians and publishers will find it convenient to trace the sources of information, to extend their range of study, to form a good collection, and to reprint the valuable and rare ones as the case may be.

I am deeply grateful to Shri Sri Prakasaji, formerly Governor of Assam, and now Governor of Madras, for kindly writing a

Foreword to this book and for the encouragement and sympathy he has been pleased to show to me all along. His love for Assam and its people, and for its history and culture, has contributed a great deal towards its proper understanding by our brothers and sisters in India, and this love has not been bedimmed by distance and time.

In conclusion, I embrace this opportunity to acknowledge my indebtedness to the institutions through whose kind instrumentality the studies were first brought to light :—Government of Assam ; University of Calcutta ; All India Radio, New Delhi and Gauhati Centres ; All-India Oriental Conference ; Indian History Congress ; Manipuri Sahitya Parishad, Imphal ; Asam Sahitya Sabha ; *Assam Review*, Silchar series ; and *Indian Historical Quarterly*, Calcutta. The relevant details are embodied in the bibliographical notes, appended to the book.

My thanks are also due to Sriman Bichitra Narayan Dutta Barua, Proprietor, Lawyer's Book Stall, Gauhati, for kindly undertaking to bring out this volume in pursuance of his patriotic and enthusiastic desire to publish Assamese classics and books relating to Assam ; and to Shri Kalicharan Pal, Proprietor, Nabajiban Press, Calcutta, for his personal interest and care and for the promptness with which he has executed the work of printing the book.

Gauhati, Dec. 1, 1955. S. K. BHUYAN

PREFACE TO THE SECOND EDITION

The first edition of the book was exhausted within a comparatively short time, and a second edition has thus become necessary to meet the demand for copies. I am thankful to students and teachers and the general reading public for according the book an appreciative welcome. Appendix A, *Aids to the Study of Assamese*, has been enlarged and brought up to date. I am grateful to Sriman Khagendra Nath Saikia, M.COM., LL.B., for his kind help in the revision of the proofs.

Gauhati, Sept. 1, 1962. S. K. BHUYAN

CONTENTS

FOREWORD, BY SHRI SRI PRAKASA
PREFACE

ASSAMESE LITERATURE : ANCIENT PERIOD ... 1
ASSAMESE LITERATURE : ANCIENT AND MODERN ... 15
ASSAMESE HISTORICAL LITERATURE 38
ASSAMESE MANUSCRIPTS 71
HEMCHANDRA GOSWAMI 96
MODERN KHASI LITERATURE 129
MANIPURI SAHITYA PARISHAD 138
BANIKANTA KAKATI 154
INDIAN HISTORY CONGRESS 160
ASAM SAHITYA SABHA 179
AN ASSAMESE CHRONICLE OF TRIPURA 195

APPENDICES

A. AIDS TO THE STUDY OF ASSAMESE 233
B. BIBLIOGRAPHICAL NOTE ON ASSAMESE HISTORICAL LITERATURE 246
C. BIBLIOGRAPHICAL NOTES ON THE STUDIES INCORPORATED IN THIS BOOK ... ... 251—54

TO

MY YOUNGEST SON

SRIMAN BIJOY KUMAR BHUYAN

WITH

AFFECTION AND LOVE

SURYYA KUMAR BHUYAN

January, 1956.

STUDIES IN THE LITERATURE OF ASSAM

ASSAMESE LITERATURE : ANCIENT PERIOD

The ancient period of Assamese literature represents the output from the earliest times down to the occupation of the country by the British in 1826, since when it came in contact with western ideas and western methods of literary treatment.

It is generally accepted that Aryan culture had taken its root in Assam since very early times, and that Assamese is a Sanskritic language directly connected with Prachya Magadhi Apabhramsa. The ancient kingdom of Kamarupa or Assam has accordingly been swept by a wave of Hindu civilization which has maintained its cultural homogeneity with the rest of India; and physically remote, Assam was not outside the cultural hegemony of Aryyavarta. The literature produced by a people like the Assamese is thus essentially Indian in spirit, and its individuality is derived from the impact of local circumstances, physical and political.

It is difficult to correctly estimate the time from when books in the Assamese language first came to be written, because a complete and exhaustive search for such writings has not yet been made. No state archives has been maintained in Assam in a continuous manner as there has been no unbroken succession of a single line or dynasty of rulers. Political upheavals have effaced the traces of any archives that might have been in existence before. In spite of the loss and damage to which Assamese manuscripts have been subjected through the ages past, we believe that some fortunate antiquarian in Assam may come upon a manuscript as momentous as the *Arthasastra* of Kautilya, the dramas of Bhasa and the *Samarangana* of King Bhoja.

Besides, the creation and growth of Assamese literature were hampered by the prevailing notion that all ideas and thoughts are to be written in Sanskrit, and it is believed that learning was mainly confined to the Brahmans. It was only during the period of Vaisnava revival and the centuries immediately preceding it that books were written in Assamese for the enlightenment and edification of the common people The realization of the utility of the vernacular medium thus opened the flood-gate of learning and we are amazed at the sight of the immense quantity of Assamese books which have come down to us. It is a tragedy that a conception of the wealth and variety of ancient Assamese literature has not yet been fully brought home to the people of Assam, and to our brothers and sisters in India, though efforts are in progress under the auspices of individuals and institutions to resuscitate the literary treasures.

The absence of early specimens of the vernacular literature of Assam is redeemed by the fact that its people were a highly intellectual and enlightened race, always in search of truth, and anxious to disseminate it in all possible ways. There were learned Pundits in the country; and owing to the encouragement given by the monarchs, scholars flocked to Assam from different places. The account of the Chinese pilgrim Hiuen-Tsang and the copper-plate inscriptions of the period bear testimony to the scholarship and patronage of the Assamese monarchs and the presence of learned men in Assam. "The king", wrote Hiuen-Tsang, "is fond of learning, and the people are so in imitation of him. Men of ability come from afar to study here". A similar statement is made in the copper-plate grants of King Vanamaladeva and King Ratnapala alluding to the presence of learned men, religious preceptors and poets in their respective capitals Haruppeswar and Durjaya.

Now the question is : were there no books written by the vast congregation of scholars and poets in the ancient kingdom of Kamarupa ? The literary remains of the great Pundits of Assam have been lost altogether, though in the field of Smritis we get occasional glimpses of the views they held, different from those expounded by the Smritikars of other parts of India. The literary genius and attainments of the Assamese people of yore are preserved in the texts of the copper-plates, for they were compiled with great care, in a sonorous and reminiscent style, in keeping with the dignity of the donor-sovereigns and the erudition of the scholarly composers. A few extracts are given below :

The spread of King Bhaskaravarma's warlike fame is thus eulogized in the Nidhanpur copper-plate : "As the portrait of the sun (Bhaskara) is seen simultaneously in numerous pots of water, the king's portrait, owing to his abundance of prowess, was seen uninterrupted in the palaces of his vassal chieftains".

In Harjaravarma's copper-plate, King Harshadeva is described as "a monarch who was endowed with numerous qualities, and who governed his subjects as if they were his own sons, and who desisted from ever oppressing them".

King Ratnapala is described in his copper-plate as "an Arjuna in fame, a Bhimasena in war, a Kritanta (god of death) in wrath, a forest conflagration in destroying his plant-like enemies, who is the moon in the sky of learning, the sweet jasmine of the Malaya mountain in the midst of the jasmine-like men of good birth".

The description of Ratnapala's capital Durjaya summarizes in a sense all the equipments of an ideal state, in profundity of learning, in steadiness of the mind, and in military strength. "The boundaries of Durjaya", runs the inscription, "were encompassed by a rampart, furnished with a fence strong like that used for the game birds of the Cakas, fit to cause chagrin to the king of Gurjara, to give fever to the heads of the untameable elephants of the chief of Gauda, to act like bitumen in the earth to the lord of Kerala, to strike awe into the Bahikas and Taikas, to cause discomfiture to the master of the Deccan country; and generally to serve for the purpose of discomfiting the king's enemies".

About the inhabitants of Durjaya it is recorded in the copper-plate : "Here dullness might be observed in necklaces, but not in the senses of the inhabitants;

fickleness in apes, but not in their minds; changefulness in the motions of the eyebrows, but not in promises, accidents happening to things, but not to the subjects".

The above passages are sufficient to give an idea of the existence of the intellect and humanism which lead to the production of literary masterpieces.

The plentitude of book-production in ancient Assam is borne out by the fact that several volumes of fine writing were presented by Bhaskaravarma to his friend and ally Emperor Harshavardhana of Kanauj. The presents also included a book of aphorisms, which was probably a collection of the proverbs and sayings in vogue in Assam.

The ancient records bear testimony to the musical aptitudes and talents of the Assamese people. In the Aphsad inscription of King Adityasena, a reference is made to songs sung on the bank of the Brahmaputra. Bhaskaravarma asked Hiuen-Tsang about the significance of a Chinese song sung in Assam describing the exploits of the Chinese prince Chin Wang Shihmin.

Such a musically-minded people like the Assamese could not but depict their feelings, experiences and traditions in a musical garb. We have in Assam a large mass of popular songs coming down from generation to generation, composed by unlettered rustic bards, mostly extempore, and sung by the people belonging to all sections of society. These songs are sung on occasions like marriages and spring festivals, for the appeasement of irate gods and goddesses, and for the inculcation of the evanescent character of human existence; and they are known as Biya Nams, Bihu Nams, Ai Nams and Dehabicharar Gits. There are also songs describing the different seasons, and the woes of boatmen whose profession keeps them constantly away from their dear ones. The stories of princes and nobles are also represented in these folk-songs of Assam. Curiously enough, some sentiments recorded in these songs find an echo in Buddhist literature. In an Assamese song about a prince named Phul Kowanr, his disconsolate sweetheart goes to the extent of threatening her mother that should she be disappointed in her love she will play the role of a co-wife with her mother. This novel, though repulsive, sentiment finds an expression in the Pali Therigatha, in the song attributed to Bhikshuni Utpalavarna. These songs are regarded as specimens of Assamese composition of the period of which we do not possess any recorded remains.

The most outstanding figure in the dark non-literary period of Assam is the natural philosopher Dak whose sayings are still held in high veneration like Vedic utterances—'Dakar bachan Vedar vani'. Aphorisms like Dak's sayings are in vogue in Bengal and Bihar. The Assamese claim him to be an inhabitant of Lehidangara village in Barpeta Subdivision in the district of Kamrup. Almost every Assamese family used to possess a manuscript containing the aphorisms of Dak, known popularly as *Dak-Bhanita* and *Dak-Charit*. Some of the sayings of Dak bear a striking resemblance to the literature of Buddhism. Like Aushadhikumar of *Maha-unmarga Jataka*, Dak at the moment of his birth, prescribes remedies for relief from the pains of child-birth. Dak also enjoins upon the observance of Dharma, as manifested in the construction of tanks and temples, centres of food-distribution, and the plantation of trees. He also dilates upon the futility of man-power, wealth and decorations as man's life is uncertain and short. He glorifies charity and gifts to which nothing else is superior. The methods of attraction mentioned by Dak as resorted to by women in alluring men find an echo in Buddhist literature.

Kamarupa is still believed to be the home of spells and charms, of magic and witchcraft—'Tantra-Mantrar Desh'; and stories are circulated all over India attributing to Assamese women the supernatural power of converting a man into a lamb. The charms and spells are still used, not to produce any thaumaturgic effect, but to cure certain ailments, and avert certain calamities, very frequently as a supplement to medicinal specifics. The language of the mantras is extremely archaic and the thoughts cryptic and mystic. The mantras embody specimens of the pre-formative period of Assamese literary diction of the age of which we have no recorded examples.

A book of songs and aphorisms written by a number of Tantric Buddhists between the eighth and twelfth centuries was discovered in Nepal by the late Pundit Haraprasad Sastri, and it has been published under the title "Bauddha-gan-o-doha". We get there the names of twenty-three poets, some of whom are believed to be men of Kamarupa, where the Vajrayana and Sahajayana forms of Buddhism were developed to some extent. The peculiar diction of the songs appears to bear some resemblance to the forms of Assamese poetic style in vogue till this day. Books of this kind may still be discovered throwing light on the very dark period of Assamese literature, when there was the needed scholarship and talent, but no visible performance in the direction of written Assamese literature.

As far as is known at present, Assamese literature in the strict sense of the term came into existence in the thirteenth century. The old Hindu kingdom of Kamarupa was dismembered about the twelfth century, and a new kingdom known as Kamata, came into being with its capital at Kamatapur, at a distance of some eighteen miles from Cooch Behar. Kamata extended from the river Karatowa on the west to Barnadi, opposite Gauhati, on the east; and it comprised the present districts of Rungpure, Cooch Behar, Goalpara and Kamrup. Eastern Assam was still then in a state of flux, being ruled at different places by the Chutiyas, the Bhuyans, the Kacharis and the Borahis and the Morans. The Shan conquerors from Northern Burma, generally known as the Ahoms, had established their dominion in a portion of Eastern Assam in the year 1228.

Being virtually a continuation of the old Kamarupa kingdom, though in a truncated form, Kamata became an asylum for the scholars and poets of Eastern India. The earliest Assamese poets on record, Hema Saraswati and Haribar Bipra, enjoyed the patronage of the Kamata ruler Durlabhanarayan, who has been immortalised in the colophons of their poems *Prahlad-charit*, *Lava-Kusar Yuddha* and *Babrubahanar Yuddha*. A third poet Kaviratna Saraswati wrote *Jayadrath-badh* under the patronage of the same enlightened sovereign Durlabhanarayan, and probably of his son Indranarayan as well. These four books are believed to be the earliest available specimens of Assamese poetry, though the perfection of the verses and the method of treatment presuppose several preceding generations of poetical endeavour.

The greatest figure in the firmament of Assamese poetry of this twilight was Madhab Kandali, who wrote under the patronage of Mahamanikya Raja who has not yet been definitely identified, though in all probability he was a non-Aryan ruler brought under the influence of Hinduism. Madhab Kandali translated the *Ramayana,* but only five out of the seven cantos are now extant. Another poem entitled *Devajit* is commonly attributed to Madhab Kandali. The diction of Madhab Kandali's poetry is elegant and refined, and difficult Sanskrit words have been rendered in mellifluous Assamese.

These early works bear definite traces of Vaisnavism in their attempt to glorify the heroes of the Vaisnava pantheon, Prahlad and Ramchandra. They however lack the insistence and emphasis on the worship of Vishnu which are predominant factors in the writings of the great Vaisnava reformer and poet Mahapurush Srimanta Sankardeva, 1449-1568 A.D. In a way they were precursors of the Vaisnava revival, and they paved the path for ushering in the great outburst of devotion, music and poetry of the age of Sankardeva, who, in humility, paid compliments to this preceding band of 'unerring poets'., *purva kavi apramadi,* and compared himself to a rabbit in the presence of an elephant.

The full efflorescence of Assamese poetry came however with Sankardeva and his devoted disciples and kindred spirits. The saint lived up to the age of one hundred and twenty years, and during his long span of life he gave to Assam a treasure-house of literary gems, all aiming at the glorification of Vishnu and his several manifestations. He based his teachings on the *Bhagavata-purana*, and hence his creed is known as Bhagavati Dharma. In his two pilgrimages to Aryavarta and the Deccan, Sankardeva contacted the saints of the age, acquainted himself with the various schools of thought, different media of literary expression and diverse melodies, dance-forms and song-patterns, and subsequently adapted them to the Assamese soil for the edification of his own countrymen. He himself translated several cantos of the *Ramayana* and the *Bhagavata*, compiled a number of episodes and wrote plays and songs. To perpetuate the recital of Vaisnava classics and the performance of dramas, and the spread of Vaisnava teachings, he established monasteries in Western Assam, and his disciples carried the torch of Sankardeva's gospel to different parts of Assam by the processes initiated by their master. The devotional routine of a monastery was also repeated in every Vaisnava village and household, with the result that Assam began to resound from one end to another with *nama* and *kirtan,* conferring upon the people the blessings of refinement, singlemindedness and a capacity for united action. Assam's religious fame reached far-off Rajputana, and the Rajput invader of Assam, Raja Ram Singha of Amber, received repeated warnings from his mother and his wife against the consequences of disturbing the peace of a country where there was universal *nama-kirtan* and where Brahmans and Vaisnavas were living in peace and happiness. The Satras or monasteries, are still in existence, and age has not staled their sanctity and popularity.

Poetry was not the only medium of propagating the Vaisnava cult. Brajabuli prose was introduced in the dramas, or *Ankiya Nats* as they were called. A saint named Bhattadeva, coming after Sankardeva, translated the *Gita* and the *Bhagavata,* into elegant and lucid Assamese prose, and the great scientist Dr. Prafulla Chandra Roy, after reading the *Katha-Gita,* the Gita in prose, admitted the development of Assamese prose literature in the far distant sixteenth century which no other literature of the world reached except the writings of Hooker and Latimer in England.

Sankardeva's cult became extremely popular in Assam on account of the equality which it preached, and the simplicity it enjoined upon in devotional matters. It did away with the barriers of caste by placing the highest and the lowest ranks of society in the same category provided the men were devoted, righteous and refined in manners. It made it easy for tribesmen to enter into the fold of Hinduism if they complied with some simple requirements after their initiation.

As a result of the spread of Vaisnavism, there was an enormous output of literature in Assam. The epics, *Puranas* and the classics were translated into Assamese, either in their entirety, or in the form of selected episodes therefrom. Dramas were also composed in large numbers, and they were staged on sacred occasions in *namghars* or congregation halls, in Satras and villages, and also in secular functions like marriages and the receptions of distinguished guests. There were two main impulses which led to this output :

First, it was realised very early that the high ideals and thoughts enshrined in Sanskrit books were not accessible to the general public. It was therefore necessary to translate them into the language commonly spoken by the people. This realisation comes out distinctly in the advice given by King Naranarayana of Cooch Behar, 1540-1581 A.D., when he commissioned the scholars, assembled in his court, to write popular treatises on grammar, astronomy and arithmetic, and translate the epics and the *Puranas*, "so that the books will be read by women and Sudras in the present age, and by Brahmans in later times." "It is only by this means", said Naranarayana, "that the scriptures can be protected from loss in this Kaliyuga". Ananta Kandali, a contemporary of Sankardeva, adopted the Assamese medium in preference to Sanskrit because he hoped "that women, Sudras and others will learn the true significance, and rejoice by listening to the books". Madhabdeva, the chief disciple of Sankardeva, said that the river of the nectar of love, which had shone forth formerly in Vaikuntha, has flooded the entire world, his master having broken open the banks.

Secondly, Assam being an independent kingdom there were a large number of princes and nobles in the country who could afford to give patronage to scholars and poets. This patronage emanated principally from the Ahom court in Eastern Assam and the courts of the ruling Narayani families in Western Assam situated in Cooch Behar, Kamrup and Darrang. Rama Saraswati, in his *Puspa-haran Vana-parva,* alluded to the gift of books, money and attendants to enable him to devote himself wholeheartedly to carry out the orders of King Naranarayana to translate the Mahabharata into Assamese.

Royal patronage in Eastern Assam became copious from the middle of the seventeenth century when the Ahom kings were converted into Hinduism. This patronage reached a highwater-mark during the reigns of King Rudra Singha and his two sons, Siva Singha, 1714-44, and Rajeswar Singha, 1751-69 A.D. The most outstanding figure of the period was the court-poet Kaviraj Chakravarty who translated *Brahmavaivarta-purana* and Kalidasa's *Sakuntala.* King Rudra Singha and his son Siva Singha were themselves song-writers of no mean order; and Rajeswar Singha wrote a drama entitled *Kichak-badh.* A poet named Kavi-sekhar Bhattacharyya wrote a book named *Hari-vamsa* dealing with sexology for the entertainment and education of King Rajeswar Singha's son Yuvaraj Charu Singha and the latter's consort Princess Premada Sundari. Many manuscripts of the period are profusely illustrated in colour, the notable examples being *Gita-Govinda, Hasti-vidyarnava, Sankhachura-badh* and *Dharma-puran.* The death of Rajeswar Singha was followed by convulsions and strifes till the first quarter of the nineteenth century, and literary patronage began to dwindle in consequence.

Vigilance is the prince of freedom, and Assam being an independent state it had to remain perpetually alert in order to ensure the efficiency of its internal administration and its immunity from foreign aggression. All useful information was therefore recorded, and precedents and past events were enscrolled in chronicles or Buranjis, which throw light on the past history of Assam and also of India, and on the customs, manners and the economic condition of the people. The Buranjis of Assam have imparted a unique distinction to its literature in view of their practical absence in the vernacular literatures of other parts of India.

Besides the Burnajis, treatises were also compiled, under the auspices of the government, on the art of warfare, on the construction of forts and ramparts, royal palaces and on the ailments of elephants, horses and hawks and on all subjects, mastery over which was necessary for efficient administration.

April 27, 1955.

New Delhi Centre, Talk broadcast from All India Radio. Published in *The March of India* for March 1956.

ASSAMESE LITERATURE : ANCIENT AND MODERN

Ancient Assamese Literature : To those who have had the opportunity of critically examining the manuscript specimens of Assamese literature, its antiquity, richness and variety appear as outstanding features. The superficial observer who draws his conclusions from the limited output of printed books, losing sight of the immense mass of manuscript remains, will not readily believe how a numerically inferior, and at present, a backward race like the Assamese could possess such a varied store-house of literary treasures.

The Assamese were intellectually an alert and active race. They responded magnificently to the new waves of thought evolved within their country, or imported from outside, provided they were communicated in the form traditionally acceptable to them. Politically isolated from the rest of India, the Assamese received with open arms those foreigners who had something new to teach and who contributed to the appeasement of their intellectual curiosity. These ambassadors of culture were ordinarily brought to Assam under express commissions of the state, and were given full facility and encouragement to settle in the country becoming one with the children of the soil in language and manners after a few generations. The farsighted sovereign King Rudra Singha, 1696-1714 A.D., created a new order in society, the Khaunds and the Bairagis, whose function was to visit important centres in India and bring back to their country beneficent foreign customs and manners which might be usefully transplanted in the Assamese soil.

The numerous Vaisnava monasteries, each presided over by an abbot or Satradhikar, and attended by a permanent body of Bhakats or monks, disseminated to the literate and illiterate laity the knowledge of the epics and the Puranas. A manuscript, sometimes alone, and sometimes in the company of an image of Vishnu or Srikrishna, was the object of worship in every Vaisnava sanctuary; and the ceremonies of the day required musical recital of the religious and semi-religious classics. On important occasions like the anniversary of a saint or the inauguration of a new pontiff there were dramatic performances accompanied by copious music. Every lay disciple erected in his house a small tabernacle of his own in imitation of the elaborately instituted chapel of a Satra. Every village had a Namghar where dramas were performed and chapters read now and then from the scriptures. "There is universal *nama-kirtan* (religious music and recital) in the country of Assam. By invading it how long could Mir Jumla thrive? So take heed, and do as you think proper",—thus wrote the mother and wife of Raja Ram Singha of Amber, who was afterwards defeated by the Assamese general Lachit Barphukan in the battle of Saraighat in 1671.

Through the network of Satras and Namghars, spread all over the country, knowledge permeated the masses of Assam. Illiteracy was no handicap to the acquisition of this knowledge as there were arrangements everywhere for reading aloud portions of the scriptures and explaining their purport to audiences of household members and large congregations of villagers. Every family of some consideration had a cluster of manuscripts in the bamboo loft in the family chapel. The family priest or a literate relative occasionally read out the manuscripts. The reading out of portions of the classics was regarded as a preventive or curative remedy for many domestic calamities. Every pontiff before being formally installed had to give evidence of his literary and musical attainments by composing a drama.

The scriptures and classics of the Assamese were available to them in translations. The Ramayana, the Mahabharata, the Puranas, and other semi-religious treatises were all translated into Assamese between the fifteenth and the eighteenth centuries, either in their original complete form or in the form of detached episodes. The demand for this translation was so great that if an auther left one portion unfinished, or if it was lost, a subsequent author was always found to complete the incomplete or lost portion. Five cantos of the *Ramayana* were translated by Madhab Kandali, and the remaining two by Sankardeva and Madhabdeva. Sankardeva also translated several cantos of the *Bhagavat Puran* into Assamese; the first part of the tenth canto was translated by him and the last part by Ananta Kandali. The entire *Mahabharata* was translated by Ram Saraswati, the court-poet of King Naranarayan of Cooch Behar; the voluminous *Brahmavaivarta Puran* by Kaviraj Chakravarty, the court-poet of King Rudra Singha and King Siva Singha; and the *Naradiya Puran* by Bhubaneswar Bhattacharyya, court-poet of the Kachari Raja Suradarpanarayan. The Assamese nobles, including Ahom Dangarias, Phukans, and other grandees, maintained poets and scholars in their staff, and inspired the translation of numerous classics.

The intensive and wide-spread stimulus given to translation work was due to the realisation of the fact that knowledge must be rescued from the sybilline leaves of Sanskrit books and delivered to the people in the popular vernacular garb. King Naranarayan summoned the Pundits of Kamrup and ordered them to translate the classics when he stated his object as follows: "These translations will first be read with eagerness by women and Sudras, and after some time by the Brahmans as well". The masterpieces of Indian literature were thus brought home to the Assamese through the translations of the Assamese poets. The *Bhagavat Puran,* in addition to the translation in verse, was translated by Bhattadeva into elegant Assamese prose in the sixteenth century. The *Gita* was translated early into Assamese by Govinda Misra; the *Hitopadesa* by Ram Misra; Jaydeva's *Gita-Govinda* by Kaviraj Chakravarty; Kalidasa's *Sakuntala* by Kaviraj Chakravarty; *Lanka-kanda Ramayana* by Srikanta Suryya-vipra.

If an exhaustive search is made for Assamese manuscripts, or even if the manuscripts hitherto discovered and traced are thoroughly catalogued, we have a firm belief, that a far greater percentage of the Indian masterpieces will be found translated into Assamese than in any other Indian vernacular literature including Maharatti, Gujrati and Hindi, which appear to have beaten Assamese in the output of modern books. The cultural situation in Assam was exactly like that of England and Europe after the Renaissance or the Revival of Classical Learning, born in which atmosphere it was possible for Shakespeare, with his "little Latin and less Greek", to assimilate the classical spirit and transmit it to the Elizabethans through the medium of his immortal dramas. There grew in Assam what we may conveniently term "illiterate literacy" of a form unknown in any part of India. An Assamese villager of the older type still carries this tradition about him ; and if we can make him speak freely we shall see that he possesses a fair acquaintance with the general contents of the epics and the Puranas.

My object in dilating on this point is to show that there was the receptive intellectual atmosphere in Assam which led to the production of books. The vast mass of manuscripts bear testimony to the existence of this atmosphere.

Another reason why the Assamese mind was always alert was because their brain was constantly stirred and stimulated by the interest which they took in the political affairs of their country. Every Assamese adult in the olden days, except when his profession did not allow him to be detached from his work, had to put in three months' service to the state, either at the metropolis or at any other appointed place. He was replaced by his brother, nephew, or a trusted co-villager. On return from service the Assamese villager came with his budget full of news which was listened to rapturously by his home-keeping relatives and companions. "The news of Gargaon", the Ahom capital, as it reached the masses through the lips of those periodic servitors had its own characteristic odour being in the semblance of "travellers' tales". Through these agents court politics came frequently to be discussed in the villages. This interest in politics sometimes assumed a vital shape, as these very same villagers might have been asked to supply a contingent for an expedition to Cachar and Jayantia, or against the Moguls. The villagers had to know something about the political institutions of the country, as every one of them, if not otherwise employed, was a worker for the state; and instances are recorded of ordinary servitors rising to eminence by their superior knowledge and efficiency.

This preliminary knowledge of the court and the metropolis, imparted to the distant villages by the *paiks* or servitors, prepared their minds for receiving the vast mass of political literature that was in circulation in the country. The chronicles dealing with complete dynasties, chosen events, or isolated episodes formed the most important part of this political literature. There were also staff manuals for the use of engineers, hawk trainers, elephant and horse specialists, military experts, communication experts, and fort experts. Treatises were compiled laying down the duties of princes, the rules of precedence at court, the functions of the various officials, the process of gold-washing, of extraction of iron from ores and tank excavation, names of different khels or political units, names of ancient families, etc. The courtiers and nobles lived in an atmosphere of literature. Their *Ligiras* or lackeys, like the slaves of ancient Athens, occasionally played the part of pedagogues, painters, physicians and poets. The court literature of Assam was secular in tone and character, and it ministered to the practical necessities of life and government. A versified treatise on sexology was compiled by the poet Kavisekhar Bhattacharyya for the entertainment and instruction of

Yuvaraj Charu Singha Gohain, son of King Rajeswar Singha, 1751-69 A.D., and of his amiable consort Princess Premada Sundari Aideo. Bengali literature is conspicuous by its absence of any political literature, as there was no national court in Bengal since the twelfth century when the country was occupied by the Muslims; and there was no need of political education in Bengal, whereas in Assam it was an inseparable element of culture and ambition; and in the case of officials and courtiers, political education was an essential corollary to the maintenance of their position and bread.

In addition to the Vaisnava literature and political literature there was in Assam a literature of romance "in fairy fiction dressed". Rama Dwija's *Mrigavati-charit* depicts the adventures of a prince on his way to the fairyland in quest of his sweetheart Mrigavati who was a fairy. The prince wins his beloved after a series of struggle with adversaries. *Teton Tamuli* is a picaresque romance describing the adventures of a Teton or rogue. More books of this type will surely come out when a diligent search for manuscripts is instituted.

The Vaisnava literature of Assam is idealistic in tone. The characters and surroundings are remote from the immediate experiences of the Assamese, and frequently they transcend the limits of possibility. But the ethical principles which they enunciate, illustrate and uphold are imbued with universal interest. Their quality is, therefore, of a superior order, inasmuch as high ideals are couched in a popular garb, divested of their matephysical and esoteric intricacies, like Plato explaining the abstruse philosophy of

Socrates in the popular expositions of his *Dialogues*. The Assamese translations of the Sanskrit classics and scriptures were of an interpretative character. The translator took up the essence of the original Sanskrit passage and explained it in pure literary Assamese, simplifying those phrases and expressions the ideas of which did not come within the ken of the ordinary Assamese reader. The Assamese translations developed a very simple process of translating long strings of Sanskrit epithets and compounds, by which even the most uncouth ideas could be rendered in simple Assamese. Their sole object was to render their translations understandable to the uninitated laity, and "to women and Sudras presently and to Brahmans at a later age". Man's obligations to his neighbours, to his fellow human beings, to the state, as well as the duties of rulers to their subjects, are to be found in some place or other in the voluminous mass of the translation literature of the Assamese.

The diction of Assamese Vaisnava literature was of a peculiar character. The structure and vocabulary were Assamese no doubt, but it gradually developed certain mannerisms tending towards an approach to the diction of other vernacular Vaisnava literatures. The dramas were avowedly written in the Brajabuli dialect, and the Vaisnava songs had their characteristic outlandish tone. But the translations and songs being dinned into the ears of the Assamese through individual or congregational worship attained the position of a second natural language, and even the realistic prose of the Buranjis occasionally indulged in the artificial diction of the translations. This literary diction, natural to the Assamese in the sense that their ears were attuned to it, has the advantage of being understood by the speakers of Bengali, Oriya and Hindi languages. Dr. Dineschandra Sen, the historian of Bengali literature, led by the understandibility of the ancient Assamese classics, has included several of them within the fold of Bengali literature. Such mistakes are lamentable no doubt, but they point invariably to one conclusion that the Vaisnava literature of Assam is cosmopolitan in character, and its meaning can be comprehended by all who speak languages allied to the Assamese. It may be added that numerous Sanskrit classics are yet untranslated in several Indian vernaculars, but they were translated into Assamese centuries before. In these days when patriots and reformers are exploring the possibility of a common language for India, the Vaisnava classics of Assam can be made acceptable to the Bengalis, Oriyas, Biharis, Hindusthanis and Mahrattas, for the purpose of study and investigation, if not for adoption.

For a proper comprehension of Assamese society and the growth of their institutions and political ideas we must turn from the domain of Vaisnava literature to the Assamese Buranjis. Crude though they may be they have faithfully recorded the political ideals and social sympathies of the Assamese people, as they actually operated themselves in their dealings and actions ; and as such they are accurate barometers of the Assamese mind. I will cite a few illustrations from the ancient chronicles of Assam :

During the invasion of Mir Jumla many Assamese subjects joined the ranks of the foreigners. The Ahom king Jayadhwaj Singha, after regaining his throne, proposed to inflict exemplary punishment upon all such recalcitrants. Rajasahur Rajmantri Phukan, the father-in-law of the king, dissuaded him from adopting such a measure, saying,—"When there are a few streaks of gray hair on the head it is soothing to pluck them one by one; but when the whole head has turned gray no body thinks of undergoing such a painful operation."

Assamese kings were reminded of their relations with the ministers,—"When ministers became too old in service replace them by new ones, lest the old ministers become too strong by securing powerful adherents. Never appoint young and immature ministers lest they mislead you by their emotion and enthusiasm. Accept the secret counsel of a solitary minister in preference to the collective opinion given to you by ministers deliberating in a body."

Kirtichandra Barbarua, the chief executive officer of King Lakshmi Singha, 1769-80 A.D., imparted the following advice at the outbreak of the Moamaria hostilities,—"When enemies occupy your country you should procure their departure from the land by promises of indemnity and tribute. Having emptied your country of the vestiges of foreign occupation you should increase your military resources. Then you should fall upon your enemy and recover your lost grounds."

Kekeru Kalita Phukan, Secretary for Commerce and Foreign Affairs in the reign of King Lakshmi Singha, sent a messenger to the Barpatra Gohain Dangaria, to persuade the latter to accept the Sakta faith and become a disciple of the Sakta priest Parvatia Gosain as other nobles had done. The Barpatra Gohain who was one of the three cabinet members and superior in rank to the Kalita Phukan realised very well that Saktaism and state duties cannot go hand in hand, and sent the following reply to the Kalita Phukan,—"I am an Ahom by birth. What have we to do with Sakta mantras ? We are tied to the hook of worldiness and servitude. If we accept Saktaism just see what will happen to us.—When we shall commence uttering the *mantras* the children in the house will begin to shout, our women will join the children creating disturbance all around, our retainers will also create a vociferous noise, and orders will come from His Majesty to go and see him at once. How will it be possible in these circumstances to perfect our *mantras* ? We are after all Ahoms, and we have in one accord accepted the religion of Bhagavati Vaisnavism as the path of our salvation. Why should the Parvatia Gosain propose to convert us Ahoms to Saktaism ? Please tell the Kalita Phukan that Gauhati and Marangi are in a disturbed condition still ; Sadiya has not yet become perfectly quiet ; we know well the attitude of the Bare-Sirings ; and besides we have received reports of disloyal moves on the part of Prince Tipamia Gohain. Why should not the Phukan exert himself in these urgent matters of state ? If state duties do not receive prior consideration at our hands it is desirable that we should renounce our offices and sit quietly at home. Why should the Phukan talk with a man like this messenger ? It is my clear order that he should not do it in future ; and if he does he will be guilty of misdemeanour."

Passages could be multiplied from the Buranjis sufficient to evolve a code of Assamese political thought. In many instances these thoughts constitute anticipations of modern ideas.

I shall quote a few random passages from Govinda Dasa's *Santa-samprada* to show the height of Assamese idealism in social outlook. This book was compiled in the early years of the eighteenth century during the reign of King Rudra Singha. Speaking of the asceticism of Gopaldeva, the founder of Kuruavahi Satra, a premier monastery of Assam, Govinda Dasa says,—"Gopal's sister made arrangements for the marriage of her brother. But Gopal did not marry, and he became a Brahmachari or celibate. He took only one meal a day consisting of *Atap* rice. He abandoned the use of fish, meat and *Ushna* rice. He did not give any comfort to his body and slept on the bare ground by spreading a single sheet of cloth. He bathed both in the morning and in the evening. He regarded earthly possessions and honours as trifles. He had no vanity whatsoever. He always took the name of Hari and sang His praises. He never looked at a woman, and never talked with a wicked man. He used to observe silence by ceasing from speaking to others. He never indulged in unnecessary utterances." Govinda Dasa continues in the same strain when he speaks of Gopaldeva after he had been formally installed as a Dharmacharyya,—"Gopaldeva sent the Bardeuri Bapu with a number of attendants to Orissa to bring the image of Govinda Thakur from Jagannath. The image was placed on the altar by Gopaldeva and offered due worship. One Brahman of Dhoalor Satra found the image of Madangopal which had formerly belonged to Sankardeva. This image was also placed on the altar along with Govinda Thakur, and it received the customary worship from Gopaldeva. From that day the prosperity of Gopaldeva knew no bounds, but he was not at all interested in his worldly belongings, because prosperity is regarded by a saint as a hindrance and by a fool as a source of pleasure. But just see what Devagopal did when he was placed in the midst of such fortune and prosperity. He used to sit on a sheath of betel-nut tree, never wore a gay apparel, never tasted sweet things, never glanced at women and gold. At night he used to sit inside a curtain four cubits square, and he averted his sleep by being engaged in the counting of the beads in his rosary. Such was Devagopal. There was never a saint like him and there will be no one like him in future." This picture of Gopaldeva recalls to our mind the description of Marcus Aurelius "sleeping on the bare ground on a bed upon which were stretched sheepskins."

Govinda Dasa thus concludes his history of the saints,—"In dealing with the history of the saints some have been dealt with earlier than the rest. This precedence is accidental and not wilful, and does not imply any order of superiority or inferiority. In the sphere of spiritual greatness all are equals. Some may be superior in fortune and others inferior; but that should not indicate any difference in their spiritual eminence; as Fortune is evanascent whereas Faith is eternal. The poor are the beloved of God and the rich are not His favourites. So bow down to the saints, then only you will get salvation; as in this Kaliyuga the saints are in the position of God".

It should be noted that Govinda Dasa's *Santa-samprada* is one of the numerous books dealing with the lives of saints and reformers, either individually or collectively. Gems can be extracted from them which will adorn the thoughts of all mankind.

In addition to the written literature of the Assamese, account must be taken of the extensive mass of folk-literature which has treasured in an unsophisticated form their joys and sorrows, their worldly wisdom and idealism. Their ballads, marriage songs, and other species of folksongs are tuneful repositories of the life of the nation as it has evolved through the processes of the centuries. Their proverbs and riddles have served as guides in the solution of difficult situations. Some of this folk-literature has been reduced to writing, and the rest are bound to come out as people realise that they contain truths and imageries which will be appreciated all over the world, as folk-literature emanates from certain basic conceptions of the human mind which is the same everywhere.

It is not possible to convey within the compass of an article a sufficient idea of the profusion and quality of ancient Assamese literature. A very large portion of the books is not available in print, and very few educated Assamese can even read the old Assamese script. Their value has not been realised at present. Even those who have realised their charm and hold upon the mind have not been able to communicate the same to others due to the absence of the atmosphere of critical study carried on for the purpose of transmission. But we can safely predict that when the wealth of old Assamese literature will be brought home to the world they will see that the Assamese of old could dream mighty dreams, formulate high ideals and imbibe and assimilate the vitalising elements of cultures not directly their own. The Renaissance was a mere accident, the result of the expulsion of the Greeks from Constantinople in 1453; but for this accident the mighty treasures of Greek literature would have remained sealed books to us, and we would have still been muttering with the Schoolmen the half-digested logic of Aristotle. To this I will add what I had said in my *Note on Assamese Manuscripts* prefixed to Hemchandra Goswami's *Descriptive Catalogue of Assamese Manuscripts* : "Some manuscript-hunter in Assam may come upon a manuscript, which will be as momentous as the *Artha-sastra* of Kautilya, the dramas of Bhasa, and the *Samarangana* of King Bhoja."

Modern Assamese Literature: The student of Assamese literature will be surprised at the comparatively smaller output of modern books as contrasted with the profusion and variety of the literature of the earlier periods. The reason is not far to seek. The economic structure of the Assamese society of the olden days was based on personal services reducing the expenditure of money to a minimum. If a village Namghar had to be constructed the people of the constituent villages supplied the wood, the bamboo, the thatch and the cane. The villagers had to take part in the building operation by batches and by rotation. The old roads and tanks were similarly constructed by relays of people who had to render personal service to the state in lieu of the revenue which they had to pay for the lands they cultivated. Their domestic economy was also run on the same principles. All the needs of the family,—food, clothing and intellectual and spiritual enlightenment, were obtained in return for the products of the field acquired by the labours of the members of the family or of their retainers and servitors. Abundance of leisure coupled with the amenities of an agricultural society made this system workable.

The principle of book-production was also based on the same conditions in society. With abundance of leisure and with very little cost of money the Assamese could produce in ancient times books and treatises of all grades of interest and importance. Authors generally lived under the patronage of nobles and pontiffs who gave the writers all the necessaries of life, and placed libraries of manuscripts at their disposal, enabling them to devote themselves wholeheartedly to the composition of books. The manuscript materials could be procured readily for a few bags of paddy. Villages like Siripuria specialised in the manufacture of manuscript leaves, in addition to the numerous amateurs in every village having knowledge of the processes of making Sanchipat from the bark of aloe wood. Costly manuscripts containing paintings and illuminated folios could be produced only under the patronage of princes, nobles and Gosains. The manuscripts which passed from hand to hand and thus contributed to the diffusion of knowledge and culture could be produced in a very inexpensive form. The only materials necessary for book-production in ancient times were the learning and willingness of the author, provision of life's necessaries to him which were readily procurable as life itself was shorn of the complications of modern times, and the writing kit in the shape of manuscript leaves, a pot of ink and a number of goose quills or reed pens. King Naranarayan of Cooch Behar while ordering Ram Saraswati to translate the Mahabharata into Assamese sent to the poet's house several bullock-carts laden with manuscripts, and supplied him with a contingent of servants and maids so that the poet might be free from worldly anxieties and devote himself entirely to the work of translating the epic. The colophons of the older books indicate in almost all cases that their authors undertook their compilation "having received on their heads the garland of orders of so and so, great in the admiration of the learned".

But conditions in society have vastly changed, and the handicaps in book-production at the present time are numerous and almost of an insurmountable character. Where is the patron who will send to the poet's house manuscripts, servants and maids? A whole-time author is a rarity in Assam. Authorship is joined to the profession of a lawyer, a judge, a teacher, a physician, and even a land-measurer and a red-tapist. Even when a book is written the author thinks it thrice before he undertakes its publication which involves actual loss of cash without any positive assurance of return within a reasonable length of time. How many men there could be among the Assamese who would throw away two hundred or three hundred rupees of their hard-earned money? Book-production in ancient days meant only the employment of an author to transcribe his thought on the readily procurable leaves of Sanchi bark. One manuscript was quite enough as it was copied by a book-lover when he felt interested in it. In the establishment of a Satradhikar, of a noble, or officer of considerable importance, there used to be always a handy congerie of scribes who prepared and transcribed manuscripts for themselves and for their patrons. No author of the present time can ever dream of producing a book in return for the products of the paddy field. It may be added that several voluminous Assamese compilations involving years of labour to their authors have been lost or are going to be lost to the world because no arrangement could be made for publishing them, *e.g.*, Jaduram Deka Barua's *Assamese Dictionary,* Maniram Dewan's *Assam Buranji,* Padmeswar Naobaicha Phukan's *Assam Buranji**, Chandrahas Bhuyan's *Commentaries on the Gita,* Hiteswar Barbarua's *Ahomar Din,* Kamalakanta Bhattacharyya's *Ashtavakra Rishi.* It should be pointed out that but for the timely intervention of Sir Edward Gait and the Assam Government, Hemchandra Barua's *Hema-kosha* would have swelled the ranks of forgetten treasures.

The situation with regard to modern Assamese literature was summarised by me in my article *The Assamese* published in "The Assam Review" of April 1928 :

"The progress of Assamese literature has been seriously hampered by the numerical inferiority of the reading public. For several decades after the British occupation of the country, Bengali was the language of the schools and the courts ; and the influence of Bengali literature thus introduced has not been entirely eradicated from the land. The Assamese author publishes a book at a loss, and he is naturally shy in repeating his financially unprofitable experiment by publishing another book. The Assamese are not whirled by the remote traces of any world-movement and hence no Assamese litterateur of the present day has occupied a position in the world-wide republic of human letters. To ensure a large circulation of his book the Assamese

*The Department of Historical and Antiquarian Studies in Assam has, however, retrieved Maniram Dewan's *Assam Buranji* and Padmeswar Sing Naobaicha Phukan's *Assam Buranji.*

author has to adjust the manner and matter of his writings to suit the mind of all readers ranging from the most highly educated scholar down to his semi-illiterate countrymen. Every man has to struggle hard for bread and cannot participate in the economically unprofitable amenities of a cultured life, by expanding the scope of his knowledge, or by "voyaging through the realms of thought alone." The only effective remedy will be the establishment of a central publishing organisation with a network of branches all over the Assam Valley. The cumulative effect of all the handicaps has been the concentration of Assamese literary activities in Assamese periodicals."

To the impediments mentioned above we must add the absence of a city containing a large population in a concentrated form. An author or publisher in Calcutta can expect a fair sale of his book if it be catered from house to house. Many will not buy it, but there will be always a section whose patronage will be sufficient to secure a fair return for the expenses of publication. The Bengali press can confer a publicity upon the book which can never be obtained for a book in Assam. In Assam the book trade is mainly carried on by the V.P. system. So, for a man to get a book of eight annas delivered to him at his door, he will have to spend on postage alone an additional sum of six annas, thus raising the cost of the book from eight to fourteen annas.

But in spite of the difficulties the total volume of Assamese literary production at the present time is not a negligible quantity. Several decades had passed before the Assamese thought it worthwhile to write in their mother tongue as it was branded as a mere patois of Bengali. The Assamese took to their literature seriously only when this ignominy was removed by the sustained efforts of their literary champions and protagonists, during the eighties and nineties of the last century. The total output during this short interval is quite respectable and praiseworthy. Independent volumes in book-form have been published representing different branches of literature.

Modern Assamese literature is particularly rich in dramas because a good drama will be staged all over the country, and a part of the money realised may go to the pocket of the author. Besides, a successful drama confers more popularity upon an author than a serious treatise or dissertation. We have a very good literature of short stories depicting all phases of Assamese life. Modern poetical literature is also respectable in quality and quantity. In fact, almost every Assamese author commences his literary career by offering oblations to the Muse of Poetry. The Assamese have produced a sufficient quantity of biographical literature, dealing with eminent personages not only of their own country but of other countries as well. We possess a goodly number of books wherein the authors have tried to introduce their countrymen to the new ideas and movements now agitating the world. Books on scientific subjects are coming out in rapid succession due to individual labours and under the auspices of the Asam Sahitya-Sabha. The Chandradhar Barua Trust Fund, administered by the Education Department, is also responsible for the compilation and publication of a number of valuable anthologies.

To understand the quantity and quality of modern Assamese literature we must turn to the reviews and periodicals wherein are published articles of all shades of interest. A large number of articles of permanent value have been published in the pages of the *Arunoday, Assam Bandhu, Jonaki, Bijuli, Usha, Banhi, Milan, Asam Sahitya-Sabha Patrika, Awahon,* etc. The few Assamese anthologies that have come out are more or less collections from periodical literature. There is room for several more anthologies if we ransack all the periodicals and make a judicious selection from them.

Elsewhere, when an author contributes articles to the papers he collects them afterwards in book-form. The works of Matthew Arnold, Carlyle, Frederic Harrison, Morley and Dowden are mostly of this character. An Assamese author goes on writing throughout his life and can never dream of putting them together under one cover. In course of time the very traces of his articles are lost and forgotten due to the absence of the custom of compiling authors' bibliographies. The copious contributions of authors like Anandaram Dhekial Phukan, Gunabhiram Barua, Ratneswar Mahanta, Hemchandra Goswami, Kamalakanta Bhattacharyya are buried in the pages of magazines. What Lakshminath Bezbarua has published in book-form represents only a fraction of what he has written during his life as most of his writings are scattered in the newspapers and magazines of the last half-a-century. Some of Mr. Bezbarua's contributions in the periodicals are as interesting and attractive as those he has published in books. The publication of anthologies is also a lukewarm business in Assam, due to the paucity of publishing firms prepared to advance money in ventures of a precarious character. The late Srijut Hemchandra Goswami's monumental work

Typical Selections from Assamese Literature was possible on account of a combination of circumstances,—Sir Asutosh Mukherjee's zeal for the promotion of vernacular studies in his *alma mater* and the generous patriotism of Assam's premier merchant and philanthropist Bholanath Barua.

Thus, if we take into consideration the volume of work in book-form, and the total output in periodical literature, the quantity and quality of modern Assamese literature will be quite a respectable one. The next decade will see a perceptible increase in the volume and variety of this literature in view of the new consciousness which has swept the mind of the Assamese. It is only a hundred years since the Assamese came in touch with western civilization; but the real force of the contact was felt sometime in the eighties of the last century. More than four decades have been spent in imbibing and assimilating the new mass of ideas which have reached Assam in the wake of her contact with the outer world. The modern outlook is a resultant product evolved in the process of time taking its own course in crystallising itself; his outlook cannot be bodily transplanted or grafted on a society to which it is not germane. The Assamese have naturally taken time to adjust themselves to the tupendous changes through which they have passed, and in fully developing the new outlook, the manifesations of which have been perceived only very recently.

The Assamese have now learnt to review their urroundings critically in the light of this new outlook. As a result there has been a remarkable growth in recent years of literary activities, publication of newspapers, formation of associations and institution of presses. The mainspring of this awakening has been to communicate to the world the greatness of Assamese culture and civilisation which are frequently misrepresented, to protect this culture and civilisation from encroachments from other quarters, and to imbibe those ideas which will enrich the blood of Assamese culture. The growth of newspaper literature has brought knowledge to those who had not the opportunity to go to schools and colleges. Women and villagers are now taking interest in things which were hitherto unknown and foreign to them. The general inquisitiveness of the Assamese of the present day are on a much higher level than that of their brothers and sisters ten years before.

The Assamese have just learnt to take interest in things. The result of this great change will be the automatic increase of the reading public which will certainly contribute to the advancement of Assamese literature the foundations of which are laid on solid rocks, formed of the deposits of centuries of ideas noteworthy for their capacity for endurance and rapprochement.

January, 4, 1936.

ASSAMESE HISTORICAL LITERATURE

The talented compiler of the Gupta inscriptions penned the following lines deploring the absence of ancient historical compilations in India: "Rich as have been their bequests to us in other lines, the Hindus have not transmitted to us any historical works which can be accepted as reliable for very early times. It is, indeed, very questionable whether the ancient Hindus ever possessed the true historical sense in the shape of the faculty of putting together genuine history on broad and critical lines."[1] This statement would have been qualified to a great extent if it had known that the Assamese people have preserved regular chronicles of their country from very early times. This claim is substantiated by what Sir George Abraham Grierson said several years ago in the *Linguistic Survey of India*: "The Assamese are justly proud of their national literature. In no department have they been more successful than in a branch of study in which India, as a rule, is curiously deficient. ....The historical works, or Buranjis as they are styled by the Assamese, are numerous and voluminous. According to the custom of the country, a knowledge of the Buranjis was an indispensable qualification to an Assamese gentleman."[2]

[1] Dr. J. F. Fleet's *Indian Epigraphy*, reprinted from the *Imperial Gazetteer of India*, Vol. II, pp. 3 and 5.

[2] Linguistic Survey of India, Vol. I, Part I, Introductory, p. 156.

Anandaram Dhekial Phukan, the first Assamese to receive the light of western culture, and to rise to the rank of a District Magistrate at the age of twenty-seven, wrote so early as 1855 : "In no department of literature do the Assamese appear to have been more successful than in history. Remnants of historical works that treat of the times of Bhagadatta, a contemporary of Raja Yudhisthira, are still in existence. The chain of historical events, however, since the last 600 years, has been carefully preserved, and their authenticity can be relied upon. It would be difficult to name all the historical works, or as they are styled by the Assamese, Buranjis. They are numerous and voluminous. According to the custom of the country, a knowledge of the Buranjis was an indispensible qualification in an Assamese gentleman, and every family of distinction, and specially the government and public officers, kept the most minute records of historical events, prepared by the learned Pundits of the country."[3]

Of these Buranjis, a few have been recovered, while many others are still in the possession of ancient families. They are written in fast-coloured ink on polished strips of the bark of Sanchi (*Aquilaria Agallocha*) tree. We may classify these chronicles under three main heads, confining our remarks to those which we have ourselves seen and gone through :

(1) Desultory chronicles of the Hindu kings of Kamarupa, from Bhagadatta to the conquest of Assam by the Ahoms, a Shan tribe, in 1228 A.D.

[3] Anandaram Dhekial Phukan : *A Few Remarks on the Assamese Language*, 1855, p. 45.

(2) Chronicles of the Ahom kings of Assam from 1228 to the termination of their rule in 1826, continued up to 1838 A.D., or even later, and,

(3) Chronicles of countries other than Assam.

Besides the above three classes there are other chronicles supplementing and amplifying the information found in the former, *viz.*, dynastic chronicles, family histories or Vamsavalis, chronicles of the religious institutions or Satria Buranjis, and metrical chronicles dealing with the lives of religious pontiffs and founders of the numerous religious institutions and monasteries of Assam.[4]

(1) *Chronicles of early Kamarupa rulers.*—History and tradition are interwoven in the texture of these chronicles, and none of them gives an exhaustive survey of all the rulers, though attempts are made to indicate the chronology by the mention of succeeding dynasties with the names of their prominent representatives. One feels that the crude chroniclers have committed "the fault of treating contemporaneous dynasties as successive ones". Some names occurring here are to be found in the inscriptions of Kamarupa kings published from time to time in the *Journal of the Asiatic Society of Bengal* and the *Epigraphia Indica.*[5]

According to these chronicles, the earliest king of

[4] For a detailed classification of Assamese Buranjis see S. K. Bhuyan's *New Lights on Mogul India from Assamese Sources*, published in the *Islamic Culture*, July, 1928, pp. 324-27, since published in book-form under the title of *Annals of the Delhi Badshahate*, 1947.

[5] The copper-plate grants of the following kings of Kamarupa were published in the *Journal of the Asiatic Society of*

Assam or Kamarupa was Mahiranga-danava, son of Brahma, who had his capital at Moiroka near Gauhati. He was succeeded by Hatakasur, Sambarasur and Ratneswar. The last king was killed by Vishnu, who installed Narakasur on the throne of Pragjyotisha. After the death of Naraka at the hands of Srikrishna, the great Bhagadatta of Kurukshetra fame sat on the throne of Kamarupa. Discrepancies are noticeable in the enumeration of the successors of Bhagadatta, and we come across the following names : Bhagadatta's son Dharmapala, his son Kamapala, his son Prithvipala, and numerous other kings of the Bhagadatta line, extending over nineteen generations, each ruler reigning for a period of 105 to 125 years.

Then came a king of another dynasty, named Madhava, whose son Lakshmipala invaded Gauda, and died after a reign of 74 years. Lakshmipala's son Subahu, Savanga in some chronicles, detained the horse let loose by Raja Vikramaditya in connection with his Asvamedha sacrifice. Vikramaditya invaded Pragjyotishpur, and rescued his sacrificial horse after vanquishing Subahu, who then retired to the Himalayas with his wife and children. He was succeeded by the minister Sumati, though he had a son, Subala, who joined his father in his penances. There were 21 kings of the dynasty of Madhava.

Then a Kshatriya named Jitari, who belonged to the Dravida country, occupied the throne of Kamarupa and assumed the name Dharmapala and brought to

Bengal for 1840, 1894, 1897 and 1898 respectively :—Vanamaladeva, Balavarma, Indrapala and Ratnapala : those of Vaidyadeva, and Vallabhadeva, were published in the *Epigraphia Indica* of 1894, 1898, 1899 and 1914.

Assam several families of Brahmans and Kayasthas from Gauda and Kanauj. Dharmapala's son Satanik, also known as Ratnapala or Raktasingha, invaded the Gauda kingdom, and was succeeded by his son Somapala. The Kshatriya dynasty founded by Jitari ruled for eight, and according to some manuscripts, for seventeen generations, the last monarch being Ramchandra or Pratapsingha, whose son through Chandraprabha, named Sasanka or Arimatta, became ruler of all the four *pithas* of Kamarupa,—Ratna, Kama, Swarna and Saumara. Arimatta constructed a huge rampart, which is known as Vaidyargarh up to this day; he was defeated by the invader Phingua of the royal family of Kamata, who had learned the vulnerable point in the war-methods of Arimatta from the latter's wife Raktamala. Phingua murdered Raktamala, but was himself killed by Arimatta's son Raktasingha or Gajanka, who then ascended the throne of his father. Gajanka was succeeded by his son Sukaranka, and the latter by Mriganka. Arimatta's descendants ruled for four generations, for the period of 240 years, from Saka 1160 to 1400. Mringanka was childless, and he died of consumption as a punishment for carrying on secret liason with a Brahman woman. With Mriganka, the long line of Hindu rulers of Assam came to an end. Kamarupa then became divided into numerous principalities, governed by the Bara-bhuyans and others who were gradually subdued by the Ahoms. The kingdom was invaded by Hussain Shah, Badshah of Gauda. Cooch Behar then rose into prominence under Viswasingha in the first half of the sixteenth century.[6]

[6] This account of the early Kamarupa rulers is based on two India Office manuscripts, transcripts of which are in the library

The above synopsis, which has been based on manuscript chronicles, without any attempt to divest the narrative of its native crudeness, will convince the reader that a systematic attempt was made in old Assam to record at least the traditions, which have been regarded as a subsidiary source of history, specially when they receive corroboration from other authoritative records, such as inscriptions. The original narrative of the Buranjis might have been drawn from written records which have now been lost, and which may eventually come to light when a more systematic, vigorous and organised attempt is made to recover and examine all the manuscripts lying in the archives of Assamese families. Epigraphic records, hitherto discovered, tend more to corroborate in substance than to contradict the account given above, making ample allowance for the absence of the critical spirit which is mainly a modern product. At least, it has not been proved that any of the facts is of doubtful authenticity.

Inscriptional evidence helps us to trace the following rulers of Kamarupa : Naraka, Bhagadatta, Vajradatta, interval,[7] Pushyavarman, Samudravarman, Balavarman I, Kalyanavarman, Ganapativarman, Mahendravarman, Narayanavarman, Mahabhutivarman,

of the Kamarupa Anusandhan Samiti, Gauhati. I have also consulted Haliram Dhekial Phukan's *History of Assam* in Bengali, published in 1829. Phukan appears to have drawn his materials from manuscript chronicles of the class described in this paper. a

[7] According to Yuan-Chwang, the dynasty of Bhagadatta had been ruling for 3,000 years when he visited Kamarupa ; so the interval between Vajradatta and Pushyavarman may be roughly computed at 2,600 years.

Chandramukhavarman, Sthitavarman, Susthitavarman *alias* Mriganka, Suprasthitavarman, Bhaskarvarman, interval, Salastambha, Vigrahstambha, Palakastambha, Vijayastambha, interval (?), Sri-Harish, interval, Pralambha, Harjjara, Vanamala, Jayamala, Balavarman II, interval, Tyagasingha, Brahmapala, Ratnapala, Indrapala, interval, Tisyadeva, and Vaidyadeva. The non-recurrence of most of these names in the chronicles may be due to the following reasons :

First, the epigraphic texts were composed by learned scholars under the strict supervision of ministers, and in consultation with authentic records, where laudatory exaggerations may creep in, as in the case of the Mandasor Inscription of Yasodharman[8]; but never an inaccuracy with regard to the names of persons or places. As a reward for his labours the composer's name occasionally goes down to posterity being engraved in the concluding part of the inscription, like Mahadandanayaka Harisena of the Allahabad Inscription of Samudragupta. The kings are mentioned by their honorific appellations, rather than by their popular names, except on very rare occasions, when the popular name had some widespread significance as in the case of Bhaskaravarman's father Susthitavarman, whose alternative name Mriganka also figures in the Nidhanpur copper-plate, a title which Hamsavega also mentions before Emperor Harsavardhana.[9] The chronicles of the early period which were mainly written for popular information and instruction generally inserted the names by which the monarchs were known widely among their subjects. Arimatta, who like King

[8] Vincent Smith's *Early History of India*, p. 328.

[9] Bana's *Harsha-charita*, translated by Cowell and Thomas.

Arthur is the central figure of an extensive cycle of legends, is also known as Sasanka, which name occurs curiously in one chronicle only. So we believe some of the chronicle kings of Kamarupa may be identical with the sovereigns of the epigraphic records.

Secondly, the inscriptions hitherto discovered do not help us to trace the missing links; and intervals of hundreds of years, as in the case of Vajradatta and Pushyavarman, remain still unbridged. The chronicle kings might have reigned in these intervals.

Now let us turn to the epigraphic corroborations of the chronicle account. In all the inscriptions and Hindu classics, Bhagadatta is regarded as the founder of the dynasty of kings known after his name, and known also as the Bhauma or Kaumra dynasty.[10] The chronicles give Dharmapala as the name of Bhagadatta's successor, against Vajradatta in the inscriptions. Dharmapala is a generic title, being assumed also by Jitari, the first Dravidian king of Kamarupa. Vajradatta might have been known also as Dharmapala, which has been used by our traditionalist chronicler, leaving the more accurate dynastic name Vajradatta to the official composer.

Another king of Kamarupa, Subahu, is said to have intercepted the sacrificial horse of Vikramaditya, evidently a powerful ruler of Northern India. As this tradition has a more general interest we shall scrutinise

[10] *Bhauma* is applied in Ratnapala's grant to a ruler of Naraka's race; while *Kaumra* is used in Indrapala's grant as the name of the dynasty to which Vajradatta belonged. Vide, JASB, 1897, p. 124.

it somewhat minutely. The generic character of the name Vikramaditya has now been established beyond question. But who was this particular Vikramaditya who vanquished the Kamarupa king Subahu, the last king of the post-Bhagadatta dynasty? There are four recorded conflicts between Kamarupa and the rulers of Northern India.

(*a*) Kamarupa was one of the kingdoms whose rulers, *Pratyanta-nripatis*, fulfilled the imperious commands, and obeyed the orders of the Indian Napoleon Samudragupta, as we learn from the Allahabad Inscription, which however does not give any account of the conquest or subjugation of Kamarupa beyond a mere reference to the event. It is a well-known fact that the Imperial Guptas favoured the recrudescence of Hinduism, and that Samudragupta, who has been styled *Asvamedhaparakrama* in a coin, restored the Asvamedha sacrifice, which was in abeyance perhaps since the time of Pushyamitra. The conqueror performed the ceremony with great splendour, and millions of gold and silver coins were distributed among Brahmans. An inscribed stone figure of the horse is now in the Lucknow Museum, though the inscription which was visible before is now almost effaced.[11] Samudragupta's son Chandragupta II is regarded as one of the Indian Vikramadityas, during whose reign Kalidasa is supposed to have flourished. The poet's description of Raghu's victory over the Kamarupa king, who was vanquished in his own territory by the imperial invader, might be an echo of the actual defeat of the ruler of Assam at the hands

[11] Smith's *Early History of India*, p. 288.

of the father of the poet's patron.[12] It is one of the most rational historical mistakes in record that our chroniclers transferred the title *Vikramaditya* from son to father; and besides, who knows that the Indian Napoleon himself was not a Vikramaditya?

(*b*) According to the Mandasor Stone Inscription, Yasodharman extended his territories up to Lohitya. The achievements of this ruler as recorded in the inscription have been held as an instance of panegyric grandiloquence; and his name is not mentioned in any other contemporary document, except a few inscriptions which would be impossible if he had been a Vikramaditya.

(*c*) The Aphsad Inscription refers to the victory of Mahasenagupta of the Later Gupta family over Susthitavarman, the fame of which heroic deed was heard on the banks of the Lohitya during the reign of Mahasenagupta's grandson Adityasena, some seventy or eighty years later. Discarding the theory that Susthitavarman was a Maukhari king, and taking him to be a Kamarupa ruler, father of Bhaskaravarman, we have no additional data to connect the Mahasenagupta-Susthitavarman contest with our chronicle's Vikramaditya-Subahu conflict.[13]

(*d*) According to the account of the chronicles, the last king of Naraka's line was ousted by Madhava, who had twenty successors, the last being Subahu who was defeated by a Vikramaditya. The copper-

[12] *Raghuvamsa,* canto 4, verses 81-85.

[13] The name Susthivarman does not occur in any Maukhari coin or record.

plate of Ratnapala (JASB, 1898, p. 114) states that Naraka's dynasty was overthrown by Salastambha, a great king of the Mlecchas. Salastambha had twenty successors, the last being Tyagasingha. The grant of Vanamaladeva (JASB, 1840), says that Pralambha, father of Harjjaravarman, destroyed his enemies and took action against those who were enemies to his ancestors, from Salastambha to Sriharsha.[14] In the inscription of Jayadeva Paracakrakama, the Licchavi king of Nepal, Harshadeva is mentioned as father of Rajyamati, born of the royal family of Bhagadatta, a compliment which has not been paid to her father Harshadeva, probably because Rajyamati's relationship with the Bhagadatta family was derived from the female line.[15] One thing is clear from this inference, that Rajyamati's mother being of the family of Bhagadatta, Harshadeva must be of a non-Bhagadatta family, a conclusion which agrees with the evidence of the chronicle account and Vanamala's grant read with that of Ratnapala. Prof. S. K. Krisnasvami Aiyangar surmises that Harshadeva of the Nepal inscription is the same as Sri-Harsha of Vanamala's grant. The learned historian points to the possibility of Harshadeva of Kamarupa and Lord of Gauda, Odra, Kalinga and Kosala, being the Gupta ruler who was defeated by Yasovarman of Kanauj, as described in the Prakrita poem *Gaudavaho*, *i.e.*, Gaudavadha or slaying of the

[14] In the rock inscription at Tezpur, of the reign of Harjjaravarman where the Gupta year 510 has been used, corresponding to 828-29 A.D.

[15] The inscription was deciphered by Dr. Bhagawanlal Indraji, *Indian Antiquary*. Vol. IX. The date of the inscription corresponds to A.D. 758-59.

Bengali ruler.[16] Yasovarman was a veritable Vikramaditya, being the patron of Bhavabhuti and Vakpatiraja, the author of the *Gaudavaho*. May we not take the Vikramaditya-Subahu conflict to be identical with the Yasovarman-Harshadeva war?

The chronicles have preserved a large mass of folklore which is still to be found in oral traditions among the people, some being associated with many ancient sites and ruins of the Assam Valley. We hesitate to dismiss the account as untrustworthy for the paucity of data with which they can be verified, and which may be forthcoming when long-continued investigations will place at our disposal a larger volume of facts. There are instances where tradition has preceded history. I will cite only one instance. A historical ballad, procured by me from a villager, dealing with the adventures of Badanchandra Barphukan, the Ahom viceroy of Gauhati, who brought over the Burmese to Assam in 1817, gives the picture of an Assamese princess named Rangili, who was the queen of King Bodowapaya of Burma.[17] According to the ballad, Rangili was responsible for securing for the supplicant a strong Burmese detachment with which he returned to Assam. This episode was never before known, not being mentioned in any history published up to date. Subsequent investigations proved that Rangili's intercession was a historical fact, which

[16] *Forgotten Episodes in the History of Medieval India*, Journal of Indian History, Dec. 1926, p. 327.

[17] *Barphukanar Git*, edited by S. K. Bhuyan, reviewed by Lt. Col. P. R. T. Gurdon, J.R.A.S. Oct. 1925, pp. 763-768.

received further corroboration from the Diary of Capt. Hiram Cox, the British Resident at Ava.[18]

With regard to these chronicles, the duty of the future investigator, will be to extricate the historical substance from the large mass of narratives of a traditional character. Whatever might be their value, they at least help us to sketch the outline of the ancient history of Kamarupa provisionally, and not entirely, in an unconnected form.

(2) *Chronicles of the Ahom rulers, 1228-1838.*—Our claim that Assam is an exception to the complaint made by western scholars regarding the paucity of historical literature among the Hindus is based upon the chronicles dealing with the events of the Ahom period. The Ahoms were a member of the great Tai race, to which the peoples of Burma and Siam also belong. The Siamese and the Burmese have maintained voluminous chronicles of their countries, known as *P'ongsawadans* and *Azawins* respectively, which show their historical instincts, though not critical according to our modern conception. The introduction of historiography into Assam by the Ahoms is one of the greatest cultural contributions which they made to their land of adoption. At the same time, there may be some room for the supposition that the contact of Assam with Kashmir, the only other Hindu country which can boast of any historical literature, through King Meghavahana, the husband of the Kamarupa princess Amritaprabha, and through the invasion of Muktapida Lalitaditya, might also be responsible for

[18] *Rangili,* by Benudhar Sharma, published in *Banhi,* Vol. XV, p. 492.

the historical predilections of the Assamese people. The question has not yet been fully examined.[19]

Whatever may be the contributory factors, Assam possesses a voluminous mass of chronicles. They are known as *Buranjis,* which is an Ahom word, literally meaning 'a store that teaches the ignorant.' They were compiled under the supervision of government officials, and the chroniclers were given free access to all necessary state papers, including despatches from local administrators and commanders, diplomatic correspondence, court minutes recorded from day to day, as well as proceedings of important judicial trials. Attached to the secretariat there was an army of scribes under an officer called Likhakar Barua, or superintendent of the department of writers. Buranjis were also compiled by the nobles under their immediate supervision or by themselves. Copies of chronicles were taken by persons who wanted to preserve in their family archives a representative collection of *puthis* or manuscripts. The result was that every family of distinction managed to have a Buranji in its possession.[20]

A knowledge of history was an indispensable factor in the cultural equipment of an Assamese gentleman. It was a part of the training imparted to the children of princes and nobles. It was even believed that the future could be ascertained by consulting hand-written chronicles. All this tended to convert

[19] *Rajatarangini,* translated by A. Stein, Book II, verses 147-150; Book III, verses 9-10.

[20] The subject of Assamese historiography has been discussed in S. K. Bhuyan's *Ahomar Din,* pp. 89-92.

the secular Buranjis into religious scriptures. In A.D. 1803, an Ahom officer named Srinath Duara Barbarua, compiled a history of the kings of the Tungkhungiya dynasty, who reigned from 1681 to the termination of Ahom rule. The preamble to this chronicle testifies to the esoteric veneration with which Buranjis were looked upon in old Assam :

"Salutation to Srikrishna. Salutation to Ganesa. Salutation to Parvati. This is the Buranji compiled in *saka* 1725 under the orders of the Duara Barbarua. Keep it secretly. Do not give it to your son if you have no confidence in him. Pundits have prohibited the betrayal of princes, and if trust is violated it amounts to an insult shown to one's mother. So keep it confidentially; more specially it is an unfathomable *Sastra;* who ever finds its bottom? Even great sages become victims of mistakes; so Pundits should not at random find fault with this book; if one is bent upon detecting blemishes he will find many. This is the chronicle of the Swargadeos or kings of the Tungkhungiya dynasty. This history was written on Thursday, the twenty-second day of Phalgun, on the Panchami Tithi".[21]

The chronicles are mutually corroborative and supplementary, and inaccuracies and mis-statements are rare except those arising from scribal ignorance or idiosyncrasy. The portions relating to the conflicts with the Muhammadans are materially corroborated

[21] This chronicle is being translated into English by S. K. Bhuyan for the Assam Government. Since published by the D.H.A.S. in 1933.

in the corresponding Persian chronicles.[22] Facts are mentioned accurately to the hour and the minute. We cite two instances from a manuscript chronicle, part of which was pubished in the first Assamese magazine *Arunodoi* in 1852;

(*i*) "On Saturday, the 13th of Sravan, in the year 1565 *saka*, on the sixth *danda* at night, the queen said to the brother of the king—'It is your son who killed my son. I will slay him in turn. So bring him out.'

(*ii*) "Not being able to disregard the request of the Dangarias, the Baruas and the other officers, the Nuaria prince ascended the throne on the morning of Saturday, the 13th of Bhadra, *saka* 1566".

In the process of conserving the deeds of the people with a remarkable touch of realism, the Buranjis have become endowed with human interest, instead of being dry-as-dust chronicles of court events. We shall quote an example from a voluminous chronicle of the reign of Lakshmi Singha, 1769-1780. A worldly-minded Vaisnavite Ahom noble, being importuned to accept initiatory *mantras* from a Sakta Gosain, replied as follows :

"I am the son of an Ahom, what *mantras* have we got? We are all bewildered by the bait of worldliness. If we take *mantras* and sit down for a moment to utter them, the children will cry, the womenfolk

[22] Some instances of the confirmation of Assamese accounts by Persian chronicles were mentioned in S. K. Bhuyan's *Mir Jumla and Ram Singha in Assam*, published in the Journal of Indian History, December, 1926.

of the house will break the silence of the atmosphere by their gossips, our retainers and tenants will give out a vociferous howl, and commands will come from the king to proceed to his presence at once. So, how will one bring his *mantras* to perfection ? So we, the sons of the *Ahoms,* have all agreed to cherish the religion as propounded in the *Bhagavat.* So, why should we be offered the *mantras* ?"

Patriotic utterances are not rare in these chronicles. The Moamarias, a Vaisnava sect, were once insulted by a Sakta sovereign, Queen Phuleswari Devi, consort regnant of King Siva Singha. They marshalled their forces and raised the standard of revolt, and thereby caused a civil war in the country which had very disastrous consequences. Lakshmi Singha fled from the capital, and took shelter in an old rampart with his ministers and dependants. The nobles suggested two alternatives, one to surrender to the rebels and the other to proceed to Lower Assam with a view to collect an army to oust the insurgents. Kirtichandra Barbarua, the chief executive officer, championed the second proposal, and said :

"The duty of a Kshattriya is to fight as long as there is life in his body. If victorious, he enjoys the powers and blessings of sovereignty ; if dead, he goes to heaven. If he desists from fighting he earns disgrace in a life hereafter, while in this world he has to lead a life of subservience to others. As he has perpetually to carry out the commands of others, he becomes subjected to fright, humiliation and pain. He has to live in eternal solicitude of death. This is certainly a dire distress. When a king becomes subjected to the monarch of another country, diplomatic measures should be adopted so that the conqueror may return to his own kingdom. On his retirement, the subdued prince should remain in preparedness with his army; and when opportunities present themselves for action he should act promptly and reinstate himself in his lost suzerain power......The wicked have never consistenty maintained their vows of friendship with the pious. The wicked have no forgiveness and piety. So none of the king's adherents will be spared by the rebels. If nothing untoward happens to His Majesty, he will at least have some mental anxiety and discomfort; his nobles and followers will also share the same; it will then be impossible for the king to collect adherents like ourselves. A person acquires a petty job which he tries to retain by parting with large sums of money. He is reluctant to give it up. If anybody asserts that the Moamarias will retire to the forest after attaining the position of a *Raja-chakravartin*, Your Majesty should by no means believe in such words."[23]

The warning of the Barbarua was ignored, with the result that the rebels seized the persons of the king and his nobles, and ran the government in their name for sometime. Kirtichandra was pressed to death under two wooden cylinders; and the country became plunged in anarchy and confusion.

Let us quote a patriotic speech uttered under more favourable circumstances. The western limit of the ancient Kamarupa kingdom was extended up to the river Karatoya. In course of time Kamarupa became

[23] Manuscript chronicle of the reign of Lakshmi Singha, 1769-80.

much reduced in size. In the first half of the sixteenth century, the victorious Ahoms chased the Muslim invaders upto the Karatoya, but for diplomatic reasons the boundary was retracted further east, and it rested on the river Manaha, opposite Goalpara. The greatest of the Ahom rulers, Rudra Singha, 1696-1714, cherished the ambition of restoring the limits of the once extensive kingdom of Kamarupa, and made colossal preparations for the same enterprise. We shall quote an extract from the proceedings of the war-council, convened specially to discuss the scheme, as we have got them recorded in a manuscript :

"Barpatra Gohain's speech : The territories bordering on the Karatoya are ours. The enemies have got possession of them only on account of our indifference and inaction. The duty of a king is to destroy the enemy, and to recover his lost possession with a view to preserve the ancient boundaries of his kingdom. We have a large fleet and naval soldiers, and abundance of war-materials. If the king orders, the enemy will be crushed and destroyed.

"The Buragohain then added : The king's proposal is reasonable, and what the Barpatra Gohain says is equally reasonable. The ancestors of our king had, by virtue of their prowess and courage, crossed the boundaries of Rangamati, and washed their swords at the Karatoya-Ganga. They found it inconvenient to fix the boundaries of Assam at the Karatoya, so they made the river Manas the western limit of Assam, and established a garrison at Gauhati. In the reign of Jayadhwaja Singha, there was an abundance of provisions and men, and still he earned the name of the

Deserting King.[24] Arms and ammunitions, materials and supplies are torpid and impotent; the followers and subordinates of the king are symbols of life and animation, they alone can infuse into the immobile war-provisions a dynamic force."[25]

The Ahom conception of sovereignty is nowhere better illustrated than in the speech made by Sonai Buragohain, the prime minister, at the coronation of Pramatta Singha, 1744-51 :

"The Barphukan led the new king by the hand to the throne, and said :—'The king's brother has become the king. All people assembled here, including the Baruas and the Phukans, should now bow down before the newly anointed king'. Then the assembly knelt before the monarch, and paid their homage to him.

"The Buragohain then turned to the king and said,—The Almighty God has conferred upon you the exalted office of a monarch. The affording of shelter to the pious, punishment of the wicked, and vigilant investigation into the happiness and misery of your subjects, have now become your sole duty. Just as one sheltered by a huge tree becomes free from heat and rain, so during the kingship of your elder brother [Siva Singha] Your Majesty was not affected by the piety or sin of your subjects. From to-day God

[24] Jayadhwaja Singha was the king of Assam during whose reign the country was overrun by the Moguls under Mir Jumla. The king left the capital and took shelter in the hills of Namrup.

[25] This extract was embodied in S. K. Bhuyan's *Mir Jumla and Ram Singha in Assam*, published in the Journal of Indian History, 1926, pp. 372-73.

will hold you responsible for the virtue and wickedness of the creatures under your sway. Your Majesty will have to discriminate between actions which are good and those which produce evil."

The chronicles contain many accounts which are valuable to historians of Assam-Muhammadan conflicts of the sixteenth and seventeenth centuries. Some of them are interspersed with copies of diplomatic letters that were exchanged between the Ahom and Mogul courts. Mir Jumla wrote to Aurangzeb from Dacca :

"Assam has occupied Kamarupa, and is contemplating to invade us. My plan of subduing the country of the Maghs cannot be completed within a short time. So in the meantime I propose to invade Cooch Behar and Assam. I am awaiting the orders of the emperor". Aurangzeb replied as follows,—"I want you to invade Cooch Behar and Assam and to consolidate our supremacy there".

I shall now reproduce an extract illustrating the diplomatic negotiations between the Mogul general Ram Singha and the Ahom commander Lachit Barphukan. According to the treaty concluded between Allah Yar Khan and Momai Tamuli Barbarua during the reign of Emperor Shah Jahan, Gauhati had belonged to the Moguls. After the departure of Mir Jumla, Gauhati was wrested back by the Ahoms. Ram Singha sent a message to Lachit Barphukan to the following effect :

"The Phukan should remember the old treaty and give us back the fort of Gauhati. Then only the cows and the Brahmans will be saved. I am a descendant of Raja Mukunda, and the Phukan is an exalted personage being the son of the Barbarua. If he has no war-provisions, let him write to me, and I shall furnish him with the necessary materials. Anyhow our brother Phukan should give us a fight at least for an hour".

Having received the above message Lachit Phukan sent the following reply through the Mogul messenger Firuz Khan :

"Well Firuz Khan, tell my friend the Raja of Amber, that though he cites the authority of the treaty between Allah Yar Khan and my father the Barbarua, yet Gauhati and Kamrup do not belong to the Moguls. We have taken possession of the place by turning out the Koches. It was through mere chance that it fell into the hands of the Moguls for a few seasons. Now God has given it back to us. When He pleases to give it to our brother-sovereign he will then get Gauhati, otherwise not. To his request for a fight for one hour, I would like to say that we are prepared to fight as long as there is life in our body. He has besides expressed his willingness to give us war-materials ; he has come over a long distance undergoing fatigue in his journey, and the provisions may be inadequate for his own purpose. Our Heavenly King has nothing unavailable to him. If the Rajput Raja has fallen short of articles, let him ask me and I will try to oblige him".

The engagements which ensued between the Moguls and the Ahoms did not prove advantageous to the invaders. The battle of Saraighat witnessed the crushing defeat of the Mogul forces. Lachit Phukan, though in high fever, personally conducted the operations, and Ram Singha could not but give vent to his admiration for the manner in which the war was conducted by the Assamese forces.[26]

The above extracts translated literally from manuscript chronicles will convey some idea of the nature of their contents. They are written in Assamese prose of a very racy character, though Buranjis written in the now practically obsolete Ahom language are also met with here and there. The Vaisnava literature of Assam is artistic in its style and subject-matter, but it does not throw much light on the actual life of the people except in an indirect manner. The Buranjis have enshrined the sorrows and sufferings of the people, which, when widely read, will be a revelation. There are amorous intrigues and courtly romances, idylls of pastoral life, outbursts of patriotism and valour, critical analysis of complex political situations, and epic descriptions of war and triumph. We only wish that our fellow-workers in and outside Assam had known more of these Buranjis of which, not only the Assamese but all people of Hindusthan may rightly feel proud.

Recently, a list of the Buranjis was made, and their number came to one hundred and fifty. Besides, there are many more in the possession of the ancient families. Many Buranjis have been destroyed by fire and water. Kirtichandra Barbarua destroyed numerous Buranjis suspected to have reference to his obscure descent.[27] The civil war of the Moamarias as well as the depredations of the Burmese devastated the country, and people left their homes and took shelter in forests

[26] Vide J.I.H., 1926, pp. 373-4.

[27] This subject has been elaborately dealt with in S. K. Bhuyan's *History of Rajeswar Singha, Banhi*, Vols. XV and XVI.

or remote unaffected areas. This dislocation was responsible for the loss of many manuscripts and relics including chronicles. The numerous Buranjis which have survived these disasters only point to the very extensive scale on which they were used in the country.

(3) *Chronicles of countries outside Assam.*—The historical instincts of the Assamese people led them to take interest in the events of countries other than their own. So we have in Assam many chronicles throwing light on the history of neighbouring and remote countries. A chronicle of Burdwan was recovered some years ago and exhibited in a literary conference wherefrom it disappeared mysteriously.

By far the most noteworthy chronicles of this class are the Assamese accounts of the Delhi Badshahate, dealing with the reigns of the greater Timurids, and their predecessors. They are commonly known as *Padshah-Buranjis*, and of them I have seen two and heard of two others. One of them is a manuscript in the possession of Lady Buckingham, the widow of Sir James Buckingham, sometime Superintendent of the Amguri Tea Estates in Upper Assam. A transcript was prepared by Srijut Benudhar Sharma some years ago for the Kamarupa Anusandhan Samiti, Gauhati; and the other was found by me in 1925 in the godown of the Gauhati branch of the American Baptist Mission along with other chronicles of the Ahom period.[28]

[28] For a very detailed examination of the *Padshah-Buranjis*, see S. K. Bhuyan's *New Lights on Mughal India from Assamese Sources*, published in the Islamic Culture, Hyderabad, Deccan, July 1928 to July 1929. The articles have been embodied in *Annals of the Delhi Badshahate* published by the D.H.A.S. in 1947. The original Assamese version was published in 1935.

For historians of Muhammadan India the *Padshah-Buranjis* present an unexplored field of materials. They were mainly compiled in the seventeenth century when Assam was invaded by the Moguls more frequently than before. The primary object was to acquaint the Assamese with the history and manners of the invaders, an intimate knowledge of which was an essential factor in encountering the enemy with success. The authors took as their materials the reports of reliable witnesses as well as written records. There is only one date mentioned, and the chronology is maintained by reference to the reigns of successive sovereigns, and the chain of events is thus maintained with precision. One of the reporters whose testimony is embodied by the chronicler was Muhammad Ali of the territory of Siliman Padshah of Farranga-Bundar.[29] He was a great scholar, being highly proficient in Arabic and Persian *loghats* or vocabularies. He was tutor to the children of Nawab Mansur Khan, who was Fauzadar of Gauhati from 1679 to 1682. Another reporter was Paramananda Bairagi of Gokulpur in Brindaban, who exercised almost a supernatural influence upon the Assamese king Udayaditya Singha, 1670-73, during whose reign the Rajput general Ram Singha was defeated in Assam. The author refers to some chronicles of the reign of Shah Jahan in the chapter devoted to that emperor.

The language of the book is Assamese, but unlike

[29] The chronicle gives a detailed account of Secunderabad and its conquest by Siliman Padshah of Farranga-Bundar, who can be identified with Manucci's Siliman Khan, Governor of Porto Novo. Vide William Irvine's edition of *Storia do Mogor*, Vol. III, p. 370.

other Buranjis, there is a large admixture of words of Arabic and Persian origin, which have been all used in their appropriate context, such as, zabah, gor, khuda, nikah, tamam, vilayat, haramzada, haramkhor, takhth, fatiha, doa-sapasi, takid, muzra, baghal, dakhil, Padshah-hazrat, behaya, amal, inam, loghat, zahar, waqayanavis, khan-khana, siparsalah, amirul-omrao, mansabdar, darbar, wazir, qazi, hazurnavis, panch-hazari, dewan-khas, am-khas, farman, sirpao, etc.

The chronicle shows a wonderful knowledge, on the part of the author, of the traditions and customs of the Muhammadan world, which tempts us to think that he was either a Muhammadan scholar or a Hindu ambassador who had visited Mogul courts in connection with the numerous embassies and diplomatic missions.

The *Padshah-Buranjis* deal with the establishment of Muhammadan supremacy in India after the defeat of Pithor Raja. The conqueror introduces reforms into the system of administration, though he leaves social problems alone. The army is properly organised on the mansabdari system. During the reign of his successors, Timurlane having risen to power through the mediation of a *faquir* invaded India. The chronicle gives a picturesque account of Timur's life as a shepherd in Central Asia. Not much is written about Babar. Humayun's throne is usurped by Sher Khan, afterwards Sher Shah. The emperor flees to Persia, where the ruler of that country takes the fugitive into his confidence only after a series of trials which are fully described. The magnanimous Sher Shah permits the ex-emperor's wife Hamida Banu Begam or Miriam-Makkani, and prince Akbar to live in their accustomed splendour. Humayun fails to regain his throne even with the help of Persian soldiers. Sher Shah invites Humayun to reoccupy his lost throne at Delhi, while he himself retires to Agra. The details of Akbar's reign are omitted. Jahangir conquers Secunderabad after long efforts. Its forts are impregnable, being surrounded by a moat as wide as a river where monstrous crocodiles and sea-horses were let loose which devoured the imperial soldiers. Shah Jahan interviews Prithivi Shah of Kandour, whose country was one of the most prosperous kingdoms of India. The emperor peacefully distributes power among his four sons, but they subvert the arrangement in no time. Mumtaz Mahal, afraid of the inevitable sight of a fratricidal conflict among her spirited sons, dies by self-immolation. Aurangzeb slays Dara and Murad and ascends the throne. His chief helper in his ambitious design was Mir Jumla who had given the prince 18 crores of Rupees. Mir Jumla, son of Mirza Hazru, exasperates his master, the Sultan of Golkunda. The Nawab flees from the Deccan and joins Aurangzeb. On the latter's accession to the throne of Delhi, the Nawab is deputed with the emperor's son to pursue Sultan Shuja. The prince accompanying Mir Jumla deserts his rank, and joins Shuja whose daughter he marries. Mir Jumla then marches against Cooch Behar and Assam without express orders from the emperor, as he thinks that the Arakan campaign could not be undertaken immediately, and his army would be better employed in the meantime in an expedition against Assam whose ruler had encroached upon Mogul territory and reoccupied Gauhati. The emperor ratifies the action of the Nawab. The general compels the Assam Raja to enter into a treaty favourable to the invaders, and returns with large treasures and a princess for the imperial harem, but he dies on his way. His son Masudami Khan, or Muhammad Amin Khan, appears before the emperor who expresses his regret at the death of such a great general. The account of Mir Jumla is vivified by human touches. As commanded by Aurangzeb he interviews the emperor's maternal uncle, Shaista Khan, governor of Bengal. In the interview Mir Jumla is discourteously treated by Shaista Khan, being given presents worthy of a *panch-hazari* Nawab. Mir Jumla comes home broken-hearted, and says to his confidants,—"The reputation which I have acquired during these seventy years of my life has all been smashed at the hands of Shaista Khan". Later on when Mir Jumla was taken to task for the desertion of the prince to the camp of Shuja, the Nawab replied to the emperor,—"I would like to inform His Majesty, that if I, Mir Jumla, only shake the sleeves of my cloak, dozens of such Padshah-zadas will come out instantly". Prominence has been given to Mir Jumla by the chronicler because he was the most outstanding figure in the Assam-Mogul relations of those days.

A chapter is devoted to the Nawabs of Dacca, Man Singha, Mushaf Khan, Burhan Khan Koka, Islam Khan, Azam Khan, Sultan Shuja, Shaista Khan, Fede Khan, and Sultan Azamtara, the son of the emperor. Azamtara neglects the duties of government, spending most of his time in sports. He loses the jewel of his head which is most ominous. The Sultan attempts to gag the waqayanavis, but fails. The Prince deputes Mansur Khan to take delivery of Gauhati from its treacherous viceroy Laluk Barphukan.

The careers of the three Rajas of Amber,—Man Singha or Mandhata, Mirza Raja Jai Singha, and Ram Singha, are described in full. Man Singha fights most of the battles of Akbar and Jahangir, which were directed against refractory Hindu rulers. He sees through the motive which goads his imperial masters to keep him always engaged in war. Jai Singha subjugates Eastern India after a long struggle. The Raja of Cooch Behar agrees to pay a tribute of one lakh of rupes to the emperor during the Naoroza celebrations, which afford an opportunity to the chronicler to paint the gaiety and splendour of the occasion. Jai Singha's ultimatums to refractory princes were worded as follows :

"Have you heard of the prowess of Emperor Shah Jahan ? Have you also heard the rattling of my invincible sword as well as that of Mandhata ? If you have, then come promptly and seek our friendship ; or otherwise be prepared for war".

After a protracted campaign where Muhammadan generals could not achieve much success, the Rajput prince Jai Singha was deputed against Kandarpa Singha, the Raja of Sewa. The royal hero attended the Mogul court, and gave the following reply to Aúrangzeb's proposal for submission : "I cannot deviate from my determination to shake off your vassalage, nor can I accept your proposal even on pain of death".[30] Ram Singha, the host of the undaunted

[30] The chronicler has evidently combined here the story of Rajah Karan Bhurtiyah of Bikaner, and Sivaji, against both of whom Aurangzeb deputed Jai Singha. Raja Karan was himself sent against Sivaji. See Irvine's *Storia do Mogor,* Vol. II, pp. 22-23.

chief, came to the latter's rescue. A son was born to Ram Singha; on that occasion he used to send out presents in big boxes of copper and brass. He released Sewa Raja, put him in a box, and sent him back to his kingdom. Ram Singha did the same with the Sikh Guru Teg Bahadur for whom the former was a surety. The emperor said to himself—"Ram Singha's actions have become intolerable. But I cannot take any drastic measure against him remembering what his forefathers have done for our empire. There is also the fear that if Ram Singha is punished he may organise a resistance movement among the Rajputs which will be disastrous to us". The emperor deputed Ram Singha to Assam to die in the midst of its poisonous waters, noxious airs and forest-covered hills. The Rajput prince is received very cordially at Dacca by Shaista Khan, an intimate friend of Mirza Raja Jai Singha.

Besides the narrative details we have specifications of distances from Delhi and Agra to important places in Mogul India; the names of the Rajput-Mahratta chiefs who formed a confederacy under Sewai Jai Singha of Amber, including Mulahar Rao Holkar, with their quota of soldiers, camels, horses and elephants; and letters that passed between Jahangir and the rebellious prince Khurram, between Shah Jahan and the Adil Shahi Sultan of Bijapur, including the famous letter on the receipt of which the Bijapur captains cried words of defiance culminating in the despatch of a haughty reply to the emperor.[31]

Writing on Muhammadan history in a remote

[31] J. N. Sarkar, Aurangzeb, Vol. I, p. 256.

corner of India our chronicler has committed mistakes here and there. Jalal Husain is mentioned as the ruler of India during whose time Timur invaded India. We all know it was Muhammad Tughlak. This mistake is due to the confusion with Jalal-ud-din Muhammad, the Keiani prince of Sistan, whose army was routed by Timur, during which engagement the conqueror received a wound in his foot which was permanently crippled, and for which he was called Timur-langa or Timur the Lame.[32] Humayun is described as having lost his throne, being ousted by Sher Khan, a slave of a Nawab. Before occupying the throne Sher Khan had to fight several battles with the emperor, but he could not succeed till an old woman taught him the proper method of attack from the analogy of a dish which must be eaten from the sides and not from the middle. We read in Manucci,—"The old woman laughed heartily, and at the same time taught him (Timur incognito) a good lesson, saying 'You are like Taimur-i-lang, who did not know how to take this country, for he came right into the middle of it, and had to go out again defeated. If he had begun by attacking the confines, he could in time have made himself master of the whole.'"[33]

I feel very strongly that if workers in the field of Muhammadan history had access to the virgin materials embodied in the Assamese *Padshah-Buranjis,* they could much appreciate them. They were written from a detached quarter with the help of materials which may now be lost. The testimony of reporters like Muhammad Ali and Gakulpuri would have been

[32] Sykes, Persia, Vol. II.
[33] Irvine's *Storia do Mogor,* Vol. I, p. 100.

recorded in the pages of historians like Minhaj-i-Siraj Jurjani, Muhammad Qasim Ferishtah and Muhammad Amin bin Abu'l Hasan Qazwini, where frequent references are made to the report of reliable witnesses.

Conclusion : But Assam suffers by being curiously reticent about her past achievements. She is not vocal and there is not that atmosphere here which leads to cultural intercourse with other countries. The antiquity of Assamese prose literature was unheard of even in Bengal till the year 1918, when Sir P. C. Roy, after returning from a tour in Assam, introduced the fact to his countrymen. Who ever heard of the martyred Princess Jaimati before it was broadcast throughout the length and breadth of India from the pavilion at Pandavanagar in December 1926? Kamarupa played an important part in the history of Northern India. The Emperor Harsavardhana fell gratified at the friendship of Kumara Bhaskaravarman. According to Hieuen-Tsang the colleges of Kamarupa attracted students from all quarters. The Kumara king was himself a man of learning. A special school of *Smritis* had developed here fostered by the penetrating genious of Kamarupa Brahmans. The *Tantras* are believed to have originated here as a result of the reconciliation between the demands of the preliterate tribes and the gentle concessions of their Brahmanical neighbours. Assam was one of the few provinces in India which could successfully stem the tide of Mogul invasions. All this is not a mere matter of chance. There was at its foundation a culture which permeated the life of the people and raised the average man to a superior level endowed with a consciousness of patriotism which would never desert him even under the severest temptations. But the glories of Kamarupa remain buried because no vigorous investigations have been launched to discover the treasures and reveal them to the rest of India which may as well be proud of them.

The fact that the Hindus of Kamarupa possess a systematic record of events, which is historical in the true sense of the word, will be of the greatest interest to Indian scholars. It may not be comparative and critical, but it states the bare truth without any embellishment or attempt at concealment. Foul deeds as well as good ones are recorded in all their particulars. Neither the king nor his nobles are spared if they perpetrated a wicked deed. A family history written under its auspices is likely to be marked by undue colouring, but contemporary chronicles written in impartial and neutral quarters will help us to test the veracity of the former.[34]

November 2, 1928.

[34] For full bibliography of Assamese historical literature *vide,* Appendix B.

ASSAMESE MANUSCRIPTS

From time immemorial the ancient kingdom of Kamarupa or Assam has been swept by a wave of Hindu civilisation which has maintained its cultural homogeneity with the rest of India.[1] Monarchs have reigned here whose exploits and achievements have been recorded in the Hindu epics and *Puranas*; the rituals and laws which regulated the spiritual and temporal lives of the inhabitants of Kashmira and Kalinga were adopted with slight variations, due to local exigencies, by those of the Brahmaputra Valley. Physically isolated, Assam was not outside the cultural hegemony of Aryyavarta.

One vast means of conserving and transmitting Hindu civilisation and culture was through *puthis* or manuscripts, elucidated by the verbal comments and explanations of the learned. The Hindus of Assam read the books which their co-religionists in the Gangetic Valley perused with solemnity and reverence. They were inspired by the same ideals of life and conduct which constituted the main-springs of action of the other Hindu inhabitants of India because those ideals were enshrined in a stereotyped form in their classics and scriptures. Mahadeva and Indra, Ramchandra and Srikrishna had the same meaning to the humble cottager of an Assamese village as they had to the farm-labourers of Malava and Bundelkhund. Learning flourished here rendering it attractive to scholars of other countries. Hieuen-Tsang, Kavir, Sankaracharyya, Guru Nanak, Guru Teg Bahadur visited Kamarupa to imbibe the culture of the country and to give the best they had to give.

King Bhaskaravarman, the ruler of Kamarupa in the seventh century and friend and ally of Harshavardhana of Kanauj, presented to the emperor "volumes of fine writing with leaves made from aloe bark and of the hue of the ripe pink cucumber." * Susuddhi, the consort of the king of Kamata, listened daily to the reading aloud of portions of the *Hara-Gauri-Samvad* by Chandrasekhar, son of the high-priest Nilambar. The modulation of the voice of the young and handsome reciter transferred unconsciously the love of the queen from the learned leaves of the manuscript to the son of the high-priest. As a consequence the three kingdoms of Cachar, Kamata and Gauda were plunged in a whirlpool of bloodshed and long-continued hostility.* Maharaja Naranarayan of Cooch-Behar employed eminent scholars and poets to translate the *Bhagavata*, the *Puranas*, and the *Mahabharata* into Assamese, and to compile treatises on arithmetic, astronomy and grammar. The laborious works of this glorious band of scholars were widely circulated among the people of the country as a result of which "women and Sudras all became learned."†

* Bana's *Harsa-carita*, tr. Cowell and Thomas, Chapter VII, p. 24. অগরু বল্কলকল্পিতসঞ্চয়ানি চ সুভাষিতভাঞ্জি পুস্তকানি পরিণতপাটল-পটোলত্বিংষি। Nirnay-sagar Text, p. 217.

* Ms. Assam quranji recovered from the family of Sukumar Mahanta by late H. C. Goswami, now forming part of the Assam Govt. collection of puthis. Since pub. by D.H.A.S.

† *Darrang-raj-vamsavali*, pub. by the Assam Govt., stanzas 604-612.

The precursors of the Vaisnava revival as well as the actual promulgators of the message of the *Bhagavata* brought about an unprecedented intellectual awakening in Assam. The Vaisnava creed, as expounded by Sankaradeva and his apostles, enjoined upon the placing of a *grantha* or religious manuscript in an altar whether for congregational worship in a *namghar*, or family adoration in a domestic chapel. In every Satra or Vaisnava religious institution of rank a Bhagavati or Bhagati was attached whose duty was to read aloud and explain to the audience chapters from the Bhagavata daily, while a Pathak or reader was an indispensable member of the usual quota of village functionaries. Assamese Hindus have a belief that an impending calamity, in the shape of the disastrous consequences of an illness and other misfortunes, can be averted by a solemn promise to arrange for the recital of a few chapters of the scriptures. To touch a copy of the *Kirtan*, the *Bhagavata* or the *Gita*, is regarded as an infallible token of the sanctity of a man's oath or promise.

Sankardeva, the great Vaisnava reformer of Assam, had to leave his ancestral home at Alipukhuri, Bardowa, under the oppression of the Kacharis. In the hurry of departure he forgot to take with him the manuscript of the *Kirtan* over which he had spent so many years of toil and pain. When the fugitives had proceeded a few miles from the village, Sankardeva returned alone to his house at the imminent risk of his life, took the manuscript and joined his friends and relatives in their flight.‡ Garib Nawaz, the king of

† *Assam-Bandhu*, edited by Gunabhiram Barua, Vol. I, pp. 300-01.

Manipur, is said to have taken the *Bhagavata* from his neighbouring state and popularised it in his own kingdom. Religious music and recital were so much in vogue in Assam, that the mother and the wife of Raja Ram Singha of Amber warned the Mogul general of the dire consequences of an invasion of Assam, saying,—"We are told that there is universal *nama-kirtan* in that country. By invading it, Oh, how long could Mir Jumla thrive? So take heed, and do as you think proper."*

To cope with the universal use of manuscripts in Assam, there were distinct communities whose subsidiary means of livelihood was the transcription of manuscripts; and their skilled and artistic penmanship was so much in demand that one scribe usually specialised in the copying of one particular book instead of becoming a free-lancer in his profession.

The manuscript leaves in Assam were made of two materials. *Sanchi-pat* or the thicker variety was made from the bark of *Sanchi* tree or aloes wood, *Aquilaria Agallocha.* The preparation entailed a laborious process of curing, seasoning and polishing the raw slices before the leaves could be made to retain the ink. The details of the process of preparing *Sanchi-pat* have been given by Sir Edward Gait in an appendix to his *History of Assam.* The sizes of the leaves were of various dimension and thickness. Big-sized leaves, measuring more or less six inches by two feet, were reserved generally for highly revered classics

* Ms. Buranji recovered from Sukumar Mahanta. *Vide* my article "Mir Jumla and Ram Singha in Assam" in *Journal of Indian History* for Dec. 1926.

and scriptures, and for manuscripts prepared specially for the king and his nobles. The leaves were numbered, the figures being inserted at the second page of a folio. The centre of each leaf was perforated for the fastening string to pass through. Leaves thicker than those used in the body of the manuscript were used for covers, and occasionally wooden pieces were also used. There were always some spare leaves or pages to record changes of ownership, or other important events in the life of the owner or his family. These additional leaves were known as *Beti-pat,* or attendant leaves. The whole manuscript was wrapped up again in a piece of cloth, or enclosed in a wooden box. These boxes, in the case of valuable manuscripts, were coloured and painted, the pictures being generally appropriate to the subject-matter of the book itself.

The manuscripts sacred to Manasa Devi, the goddess of snakes, dealing with the adventures of Behula and of the miracles of the goddess were wrapped in cobra-skins. Pocket editions were also prepared, specially of popular books. Srijut Lakshmikanta Barua sent me from Mangaldoi an Ahom pocket-book containing sixty leaves, each being of the size 1½ inches by 3 inches. This is a *mantra-puthi* containing invocatory addresses to the deities of the Ahom pantheon. There is another pocket-book of songs, known as *Gitar Bakala* in the collection of Srijut Hemchandra Goswami, now preserved in the premises of the Kamarupa Anusandhan Samiti. The commencement of a manuscript is denoted by the insertion of a benedictory symbol, and by the invariable phrase "Ganesaya namah" or "Sri Krishnaya namah." At the end of each chapter pauses are indicated by some systematic mark or symbol. The termination of a book is indicated by the word *Samapta* or finished, with the apologetic verses of the scribe in assurance of his faithful transcription of the original *puthi*, allowing at the same time some margin for inevitable mistakes not uncommon even in sages.

The printing press has done away with the noble art of penmanship, but even now, for religious purposes manuscripts written on *Sanchi* leaves are preferred to their reproductions on the machine. The introduction of machinery has thrown out of employment many people who lived upon the productions of their leisure hours and by the fruits of their cottage industries. The profession of a scribe used to feed many members of the literate classes who earned a decent competence from their trained labours, in addition to the normal yield of their arable lands. An attractively executed and finished copy of the *Kirtan* of Sankardeva used to fetch the scribe a remuneration of upto one hundred rupees or so.

Tulapat leaves were made by pressing cotton. They were used for inferior manuscripts, for letters, for private documents, and for official orders, despatches and records. It does not follow, however, that the leaves are not lasting as we have seen records in *tulapat* made three hundred or four hundred years ago. All revenue grants, records of rights and judicial trials were written on *tulapat*, a name which is still applied to all kinds of paper by the older section of the Assamese people.

The ink that was used in old Assamese manuscripts was made of very peculiar ingredients the formula of which is known to men of the older school. The chief characteristic of Assamese ink is its tenacity to glossy and slippery surfaces. Its durability has been proved by the old manuscripts whose ink has not appreciably faded though the folios have crumbled down through the destructive influence of insects and the no less destructive agency of mildew and damp. Manuscripts written with inferior ink have the letters faded in course of time, and they can be read only with considerable difficulty and perseverance. There was a regular process of reviving such faded scripts, which has now become obsolete and forgotten. The king of Cooch Behar once sent to the Ahom monarch Sukhampha Khora Raja, A.D. 1552-1603, an epistle written in invisible ink, which baffled the ingenuity of the Ahom court, till an abstruse mathematician deciphered the letter by reading it in darkness where the letters appeared in their unexpected brightness as they were written with the sap of earthworms. The courtier was no other than Durgacharan Barkaith, who had brought from Bengal the mathematical treatise *Lilavati.** He was thenceforth known as Manik-chandra for reducing the invisible letters to pearl-like brilliancy.† He became the progenitor of a long line of distinguished descendants, the last of whom was Anundoram Borooah, the first and the last Assamese to compete successfully in the Indian Civil Service Examination. He was a great Sanskritist and scholar. The Assamese ink was the

* Srijut Sonaram Choudhury's article on Lilavati, in the *Usha*, Vol. III, pp. 131-33.

† Ms. Assam Buranji recovered from Sukumar Mahonta.

product of the distillation of *silikha, terminalia citrana,* and the urine of bulls. The pen used was a goose quill or reed.

The skill of a painter was generally requisitioned to decorate the labours of penmanship. The scribe was sometimes a painter himself; and if not, a regular painter supplemented the work of the transcriber by sketching appropriate pictures on spaces left blank for the purpose. The epics were generally illustrated, specially those prepared for the entertainment of princes, nobles and the principal Gosains. When pictures could not be inserted, illuminated margins occasionally made up the deficiency. Many manuscripts contain pictures of the deadly sins, and of the incarnations according to Hindu conception. The secular pictures usually represented kings sitting on thrones or elephants, or soldiers in battlefields. The pictures are available in all combinations of colours, the most prominent of them being yellow and green. The formulas of the colours, which are so fast, have now been practically forgotten. Pictures of Sankardeva sitting in a *Siksha-mudra* posture and surrounded by his apostles are met with occasionally in his biographies.

The most notable of the illustrated *puthis,* hitherto discovered, is undoubtedly the treatise on elephants, known as *Hasti-vidyarnava.*‡ It was compiled in 1734 A.D. by one Sukumar Barkaith under the orders of King Siva Singha and his consort Queen Amvikadevi, the pictures being supplied by two court painters,

† The Govt. of Assam is contemplating to publish an English translation of the book.

Dilbar and Dosai. We have pictures of the king and the princes sitting on caparisoned elephants and sedans in all the pomp and splendour of oriental sovereigns. All classes of elephants are illustrated with great precision, and their ailments and their appropriate remedies detailed in full. At the sight of the manuscript Sir Archdale Earle, sometime Chief Commissioner of Assam, remarked that it would be an invaluable treasure in any library or museum in Europe.

The manuscript of the *Gita-Govinda,* with the Sanskrit original and its Assamese rendering is another notable specimen. It was transcribed and illustrated under the orders of King Rudra Singha, 1696-1714. The author was Kaviraj Chakravarty, who had also translated the *Brahmavaivarta Puran, Sankha-churabadh* and *Sakuntala.* The painter's name being omitted, it may be presumed that the author himself supplied the illustrations. There are five illustrations depicting the court of the poet's patron. The remaining pictures, one on each page, represent the amours of Srikrishna with Radha and other *Gopinis* in Brindaban. At the corner of each painting there is a vignette of Jayadeva, watching with his mind's eye, as in a series of motion pictures, the creations of his imagination. The Sanskrit text with the pictures, when published, will be of great interest to all lovers of Jayadeva in India.

The Assamese manuscripts afford an invaluable opportunity for the study of the evolution of the Assamese script, which is used in all *puthis* even in the Sanskrit ones. Its difference from Bengali consists in several letters ; but at present only the letters "ৰ"and"ৱ"

have maintained the distinction between the two alphabets. The letter "ঙ" is a reproduction of "ড" with a small dash projecting from the bottom of the latter. The letters "ন" and "ল" are sometimes indistinguishable, though some copyists put a dot below "ন" in order to represent "ল". In many manuscripts অ, আ, কু, হু, ত্য and ক্ষ apporach their Sanskrit prototypes more than their modern Assamese equivalents. Words written at one stretch without demarcation from each other by the necessary gap present enormous difficulties to the uninitiated reader. The habituated copyist or reader has, in these cases, to read the text by anticipation, which is possible only when he is intimately acquainted with the contents or allied subjects. Thus manuscript reading and copying were confined to a fixed trained class of people. There were several schools of Assamese script, *viz.*, Gargaiyan, Bamunia, Lahkari and Kaithali, but their distinctions have not been closely studied, and they have a tendency now to merge into one another, thus, more or less, producing a common script, which has further been accelerated by the uniformity of the printing press.

Attached to the palace of the Ahom kings there was a set of apartments for the preservation of royal manuscripts, records, letters, despatches, and maps in charge of a high official named Gandhia Barua. There was another officer named Likhakar Barua, literally, the superintendent of scribes, who supervised the work of an army of clerks and copyists.* The recovery of a manuscript was a matter of concern and importance

* Sj. Hiteswar Barbarua's historical notes in *Banhi*, Vol. XIV, p. 237..

in those days as in the present. A *Buranji* describing the vigilant steps taken by Swargadeo Lakshmi Singha, 1769-1780, to combat the growing anarchy and lawlessness in the first phase of the Moamaria rebellion, mentions a list of books found in the possession of two insurgents during the search of their houses. The names of the manuscripts are, *Bara-ghosha, Swarga-rohana-pada, Parijat-haran, Rukmini-haran, Sashtha-Khanda, Gunputhi, Siddha-tantra-pada, and Gita-muktavali.* The same *Buranji* while recording the proceedings of a criminal trial for conspiracy to subvert the lawful authority of the reigning sovereign, reproduces the following deposition of a witness,—"I am told that Baga possesses an old *puthi* with the help of which all can be subdued, including the king and his subjects. The Deka-Barua tried his utmost to get possession of the book, but he was expelled from the Satra with Baga, where also he tried for the book though without success."†

From the above pages the extent of the circulation of Assamese manuscripts can be easily inferred. Sanskrit classics and commentaries are also to be found in the libraries of Assamese families as well as in the archives of Satras or religious institutions. Sanskrit works on music, rhetoric, astrology, mathematics and rituals are found in many places. Though their counterparts are available in other localities in India, they have a value of their own, as they help in collating

† Ms. Assam Buranji of the reign of Lakshmi Singha in possession of the American Baptist Mission at Gauhati. The puthi referred to may be the famous *Dhatu-tamrakshari*, or *Kalpa-taru-sastra*, or *Dhanurveda-Tantra*, which became the gospel of the Moamaria insurgents.

the correct text of the originals, and as they illustrate the high-water mark of Sanskrit culture in this ancient land of Kamarupa. Original Sanskrit books were also compiled by Assamese scholars. Purushottam Vidyavagis compiled his *Prayoga-ratna-mala-vyakaran* which has become a classic on the subject in Eastern India. The work on Smriti compiled by his contemporary Purushottam Siddhantavagis set up in Assam a rival school to combat the influence of Raghunandan. We are told that there is in the possession of a Zamindar in Mymensing a treasise embodying the doctorines of the Kamarupa school of Smriti, known as *Kamarupa-Smriti-Gangajala.** One Vaidyanath Dwija compiled a delightful lyric named *Tulasi-duta-kavyam* describing the amours of Srikrishna and his mistresses.† Though this book figures in the list of other *Duta-kavyas* of India, still the fact that the author describes himself as a resident of Kamakhya has an additional significance.

There may be a desire in certain quarters to minimise the importance of non-historical manuscripts under the belief that they are mere reproductions or translations of Sanskrit books, and that the only books of importance are the chronicles or *Buranjis.* We have realised that the manuscripts avowedly non-historical have also great historical importance. Besides illustrating the different schools of painting or penmanship, they throw light on the evolution of the Assamese script. They were generally compiled under the orders of Assamese monarchs and nobles, and the

* I heard this from the late Srijut Hemchandra Goswami.

† This MS. is in possession of the American Baptist Mission at Gauhati.

literary protegé usually returns his obligation by scribbling panegyrical lines in praise of his patron, with the result that our Maecenas goes down to posterity, if not for his verses, at least for his liberality. These contemporary encomiums remove to a great extent the cloud of obscurity hanging round many historical personages. The autobiographical remarks inserted in the colophons throw much light on the life-history of the poets and writers, and on the localities where they took their birth or lived.

In every old Assamese family there is a Vamsavali or genealogical history which, besides enumerating the ancestors, gives also short sketches of their lives and careers. These Vamsavalis thus supply information which is not found in political chronicles or *Buranjis*. Some of these Vamsavalis have seen the light of day while the rest still lie buried in family archives. Srijut Harakanta Sarma Barua Sadar-Amin compiled a Vamsavali of the Naga-Majumdar family which is replete with historical materials.‡ It describes the part played by members of the family who held the office of Majumdar-Barua or private secretary to the Ahom kings. The duties of that office as well as of other allied functionaries are described at length, while the reforms introduced by King Rudra Singha are also touched upon. During the decadence of Ahom supremacy one of the members of this family had the hardihood to beard the lion in his den. He was appointed master of the ceremonies in connection with the celebration of Durga Puja at the Kamakhya

‡ This Vamsavali is appended to Harakanta Barua's *Assam-Buranji*, being published by the Department of Historical and Antiquarian Studies, Assam. Since published in 1930.

temple under the auspices of Badanchandra Barphukan. There was some misunderstanding between the viceroy Badanchandra and his subordinate regarding items and articles of worship. The indignant master of the ceremonies abused the Barphukan publicly to the bewilderment and consternation of all assembled. This incident is not recorded in any other *Buranji*, but is greatly valuable as illustrative of the irritation and unpopularity caused by the highhandedness of Badanchandra which subsequently led to the passing of orders for his arrest, after which he fled to Burma from where he fetched a contingent of soldiers to oust the Buragohain Purnananda from his alleged usurpation of royal power.

The Bania-Kakatis of Assam who claim descent from Chando Sadagar, the great merchant of Assamese legends and the father-in-law of Behula, have published their family history which throws additional lights on the strategy of the Moguls employed in their conflicts with the Assamese, specially during the historic struggle between Raja Ram Singha and Lachit Barphukan.

In fact the Vamsavalis of the well-known families are supplementary fragments of regular history, and the future historians of Assam will have to turn to them for information of a recondite character. The term Vamsavali was used in a wider sense with reference to the chronicles themselves. The Vamsavalis of the Dimarua Rajas, the Rani Rajas and the Jayantia Rajas are mere histories of these princely families. It is interesting to know that the *Buranjis* of the Ahom kings themselves are termed Vamsavalis in many cases, as *Swarga-narayan-rajar Vamsavali*, and *Tungkhungia-*

vamsar Vamsavali, which, to all intents and purposes, are chronicles and histories. Every religious institution, besides its usual cluster of manuscripts, possesses a history of the institution, detailing forth the circumstances under which it was founded, the lives, the teachings and the reforms of each pontiff or Gosain installed as Adhikar or head of the Satra. These chronicles or *Satria Buranjis* are brought up to date as time goes on, and contain abundant materials for the future compiler of an ecclesiastical history of Assam. Independent volumes were generally written dealing with the lives and achievements of the more prominent of the religious reformers and saints, both male and female. They are generally known as *Charitra-puthis.* It should be remembered that in Assam, as elsewhere, music, painting, literature, sculpture, wood-carving and dramaturgy prospered in the religious centres; and so the chronicles of the Satras afford materials for a history of the fine arts and literature of the Assamese people. The Satras received revenue-free grants of land and other concessions from Assamese sovereigns; they contributed to the royal coffers during emergencies; they were visited by kings and nobles which are elaborately described in political and religious chronicles. Thus the *Satria-puthis* are an invaluable mine of materials for the reconstruction of a secular history of the country.

A word must be said about the Ahom manuscripts which according to the verdict of experts abound in works on numerous subjects. They are chiefly owned by the Deodhais and Bailungs, the remnants of the priestly clans of the Ahoms, and possibly they are the only people who are capable of reading and understanding the Ahom language. Sir Edward Gait has given in his *Report on the Progress of Historical Research in Assam,* the substance of an Ahom *puthi* entitled *Malikha,* which corresponds to weird Alexandrian romances of the Mediæval Age. Another book, *Laitu* or *Laophala,* dealing with the Ahom version of the creation of the world, was published by Rai Sahib Golapchandra Barua,. I have seen two Ahom *puthis* in possession of Srijut Hiteswar Barbarua. One of them was the famous *Chaklang-puthi* describing the rituals to be observed in an Ahom marriage; and the other was a book of divination, generally known as *Kukura-theng-puthi,* describing the processes involved in the calculation of the future with the help of the legs of a fowl, having illustrations of circles, parabolas and triangles, with indications of the respective positions of the soothsayer and the victimised fowl. The Ahom priests and astrologers divined the future of the king and the country with the help of these *puthis.* The non-fulfilment of their predictions was generally followed by severe punishments being meted out to the priests. Sir Edward Gait further refers to an Ahom book, curiously named *Amar,* supposed to be a dictionary or word-book. I was told by Srijut Gauriprasad Bora of Nazira that an Ahom *puthi* containing the criminal code of the tribe which constituted the statute book of the Ahom sovereigns of Assam was lent to a European gentleman from whom it could not be recovered. A few years ago I myself acquired a voluminous Ahom *puthi* from Srijut Abhaycharan Gohain of Nowgong, a descendant of Purnananda Buragohain. It was shown to Rai Sahib Golapchandra Barua, who said it was an invaluable treatise on Ahom cosmology. Besides chronicles in the Assamese language, many more were compiled also in the Ahom language. The latter contain details which could not be recorded in those written in popular Assamese. They were compiled by Ahom priests, who naturally wanted to show the superiority of their profession in matters involving a conflict with Brahmanical priests. It is interesting to note that in the Ahom *Buranjis*, national or royal calamities are occasionally attributed to the neglect of the warnings of Ahom astrologers and the non-observance of Ahom rites and customs.

But unfortunately the treasures hidden in the Ahom *puthis* have not yet been brought to light. The number of men conversant with the Ahom language has dwindled to a great extent; even among the orthodox priests there are few who can read and interpret the Ahom language with any amount of accuracy. Rai Sahib Golapchandra Barua is the only man now living who has a scientific knowledge of the language, and there is no immediate likelihood of a successor stepping into his place.* It can be predicted that within another twenty years at the latest no man will be found who knows the Ahom language, and the manuscripts written in the language of the whilom rulers of Assam will remain as hieroglyphics beyond decipherment by any future antiquarian and linguist.

Dr. J. Van Manen has aptly issued a note of warning when he says, "The Ahoms of Upper Assam had an extensive manuscript literature of which only a few books were in public institutions. These works were written in an old form of the language no longer

* A monograph on the literature and language of the Ahoms from the pen of the Rai Sahib would be an invaluable supplement to his *Ahom Dictionary*.

understood by the people in general, so that unless they were rescued their term of future existence was problematical."†

The first attempt to collect Assamese manuscripts was made by Rev. Nathan Brown and other early workers of the American Baptist Mission stationed at Sibsagar. This was approximately between the years 1840 and 1850 when Mission activities were also directed to the improvement of Assamese literature. The collection passed through the hands of Rev. A. K. Gurney of Sibsagar and Rev. P. H. Moore of Nowgong till ultimately it was deposited in the godown of the American Baptist Mission at Gauhati. I came upon them in May 1925, and exhibited them at the anniversary of the Kamarupa Anusandhan Samiti held on October 27, 1925, under the presidency of Dr. J. H. Hutton, C.I.E., I.C.S., M.A., D.Sc. The collection comprised several *Buranjis* two of which were published in the pages of the *Arunodoi*, the organ of the Mission.

Sir Edward Gait under the auspices of the government of Sir Charles Lyall, Chief Commissioner of Assam, instituted in 1895 a regular investigation in the domain of Assamese manuscripts, specially those of a historical character. His efforts have been recorded in his *Progress of Historical Research in Assam*, published in 1897. Though Sir Edward's collection represented an infinitesimal fraction of the actual number of manuscripts existing in Assam, it roused interest in such endeavours, which was followed by individual

† Dr. Van Manen's interview with a representative of the *Statesman* on neglected ancient manuscripts, reported in its issue of October 12, 1929.

and institutional enquiries though of a sporadic character. The Assamese Language Improvement Society of Calcutta compiled a list of all Assamese publications, besides known Assamese manuscripts scattered all over the Brahmaputra Valley.

In fact, the first serious attempt to collect Assamese manuscripts was made in 1912 by Sir Archdale Earle, Chief Commissioner of Assam, when he deputed Srijut Hemchandra Goswami for this purpose. Considering the shortness of the period of deputation Mr. Goswami's effort was an amazingly successful one. The manuscripts have now been deposited in the premises of the Kamarupa Anusandhan Samiti and have been described fully in Mr. Goswami's *Descriptive Catalogue of Assamese Manuscripts*.

Though manuscript hunting has got its romance, it is still fraught with numerous difficulties. Manuscript owners are shy all over the world, except in certain European countries where transactions in manuscript constitute a regular business concern, and where the untold wealth of American plutocrats is always available for the acquisition of old manuscripts and early editions of the works of celebrated authors. There exist in those countries libraries and museums where manuscripts are carefully preserved and catalogued, and the owners have the full assurance that their family heirlooms will be more carefully looked after in those institutions than in their untrained hands. Besides, manuscripts have been divested there of their esoteric character. But the condition of things is different in India and Assam. The manuscripts owned by private families or religious institutions have a sanctity of their own and are not handled by the owners themselves at all hours and seasons. Besides, with regard to manuscripts containing recipes and remedies, there is a strong superstition that the efficacy of the antidotes mentioned will diminish by the publication or handling of the manuscripts. It is, however, curious that family misfortunes are occasionally attributed to the presence of a particular manuscript, in which case the leaves are taken out and thrown adrift on the waters of a neighbouring stream or river. The manuscript hunter must be endowed with uncommon tact and ingenuity, and must know to adjust his *modus operandi* to the mentality and position of the parties he deals with. Manuscript owners are not willing to reveal their treasures to men of all classes. Besides, there are traditions in every family of the loss of manuscripts through lending. Pressure on the part of the manuscript hunter only stiffens the hands of the owner because he is led to think that something precious must be lurking in those sibylline leaves. He dismisses the enthusiastic antiquarian with the plea that he cannot say anything final with regard to the parting of the manuscript concerned without consulting his customary advisor, who, when approached, flings in additional doubts and misgivings. The manuscript hunter will do well to remember the advice of the founder of the Khuda Buksh Oriental Library at Bankipore—"There are three kinds of blind men,—first, those who have no eye-sight; secondly, those who part with valuable books; thirdly, those who part with or return valuable books after once getting them in their hands".*

* I am quoting the passage from memory; it is to be found in V. C. Scott O'Connor's *An Eastern Library*, Part I.

Any future scheme to collect the existing manuscripts must be preceded by a preliminary survey or census of the existing materials. I venture to set forth here a scheme based primarily on the assumption that the manuscript owner will not hesitate to hand over to trusted and responsible gentlemen a *list* of the manuscripts in his possession, provided a clear assurance is given to him that no attempt will ever be made to deprive him of the *puthis* or otherwise interfere with his vested rights without his specific consent. Printed forms should be issued to all local officers of the Government, *viz.*, Gaonburhas, Mandals, Mauzadars and Sub-Deputy Collectors, and even officers in charge of Police Thanas. The forms should be prepared to elicit information on the following points :—name of the owner with address ; names of the *puthis* ; names of the authors and copyists ; language of the *puthis* ; dates of composition and transcription ; contents of the *puthis* ; and any other valuable information. It may not be possible to procure information on all the points. The owner may be illiterate in which case some trusted and literate friend of his should come to his rescue. The forms should be signed by the officer, who deals directly with the owner, and countersigned by the Mauzadar or Sub-Deputy Collector with the object of discouraging the enlistment of non-existing manuscripts and of ensuring personal examination. This is a scheme, which will entail upon the Government very little expenditure, and can be undertaken during the slack seasons of the year. Such a census will be immensely valuable as a basis for all future attempts to collect the manuscripts or to reconstruct the history of Assamese literature in all its numerous branches and divisions. We understand such a census was made by Sir Edward Gait, and by Sir Archdale Earle prior to the deputation of Srijut Hemchandra Goswami, but the scope was limited and the results are not available to the public.

With the gradual realization of the immense wealth of materials buried in the manuscripts, there has been an insistent demand all over India for the institution of organized measures to recover them from their destined loss and disappearance. Assamese manuscripts are vauable not only for scholars interested in the history of Assam but to those who are working in a wider field. The *Pudshah-Buranji* containing a history of the Delhi Sultanate has roused considerable interest among the historians of Mogul India.* Some fortunate manuscript hunter in Assam may come upon a manuscript, which will be as momentous as the *Artha-sastra* of Kautilya, the dramas of Bhasa and the *Samarangana* of King Bhoja.

The destruction of manuscripts under the peculiar conditions of India has been apprehended by distinguished orientalists. Mahamahopadhyaya Dr. Ganganath Jha issued in picturesque terms a note of warning as president of the Madras Session of the All-India Oriental Conference,—"India is subject to such ravages of fire and water that each year we are losing in the shape of manuscripts, burnt or washed or crumbled away, an amount of treasure, which could not be replaced in future even at the expenditure of millions

* *Vide* my articles "New Lights on Mogul India from Assamese Sources," published in *the Islamic Culture* from July 1928 to July 1929; and "Assamese Historical Literature" published in *the Indian Historical Quarterly* for September 1929.

of rupees; and the callousness which the public display towards this would be appalling anywhere else except in this unfortunate country."

Dr. Van Manen, another eminent orientalist, who, as Secretary of the Asiatic Society of Bengal, has played a prominent part in the acquisition and preservation of ancient Indian manuscripts, pointed out the irreparable loss to the cause of culture and civilization by the neglect in instituting organized attempts to collect the forgotten treasures :

"No tiger lures its hunters into more out-of-the-way places than say, a bundle of manuscripts written in the dialect of some insignificant hill tribe. The great fields of research are of course Sanskrit, Arabic and Persian literature. Enormous amounts of material still await discovery in various odd corners of India. It is sad, I think how not hundreds, but thousands of neglected manuscripts are in the possession of people who have perpetuated the learning and literary attainments of their ancestors. Insects, the borer, and the white-ant are the sworn enemies of all this literature and so are the monsoon and its attendant mildew and moisture. Every year they destroy a vast amount of the ancient literature of the country. Happily, within the last few decades, private, institutional and governmental agencies have started to collect the manuscripts in earnest, but funds are often insufficient, specially when it is a question of stepping in at the right moment to save important books at a comparatively small outlay. Recently I had the opportunity of buying an important set of Vedic manuscripts, but I was unable to raise the money necessary for acquiring them for some institution where they would be carefully preserved. In the Muhammadan towns of Northern India, families in straitened circumstances are often in possession of stacks of books which may not all be of great importance, but which in almost all instances contain valuable portions. Yet these books are treated as old rubbish and are rapidly deteriorating before the climate and the insects. In the south of India where palm leaf is used more than paper, I have bought thousands of Sanskrit manuscripts that were sold by weight like sacks of potatoes. ....Some ten years ago, the All-India Conference of Librarians at Lahore pressed Government to inquire into this problem and take measures and rescue such literature. The Government opened an enquiry, and the Asiatic Society of Bengal urged immediate action, but it was found that lack of funds would not allow such a step. In consequence, there remains a great bulk of this literature to be rescued, though the amount dwindles from year to year. I can promise the manuscript hunter thrills, for this bloodless form of *shikar* has its romantic side; but he must have the collector's instinct, and must also be possessed of sympathy with vernacular expression of the soul of India"*

To the agencies of the loss and destruction of manuscripts mentioned in the extracts above, may be added their growing neglect due to the decrease in their use. The neat products of the printing press have displaced the use of manuscripts where toilsome practice is necessary. With the growth of liberalism and rationality in religious matters, the performance of ancient rites and ceremonies necessitating a recital from

* *The Statesman*, Calcutta, issue of October 12, 1929.

manuscripts has diminished to a great extent. Though in orthodox ceremonies the use of the printed book is regarded as a tabu, this fact of conservatism has not been able to combat with the disuse of manuscripts in secular and semi-religious circles. All this has proceeded side by side with the practically total absence of manuscript production at the present time with the result that the demand and the supply are both undergoing concurrent diminution. The effect has been a disastrous one. The wisdom and knowledge of our ancestors enshrined in the pages of the manuscripts are being gradually forgotten, with the result that the confidence in our capacity and potentiality which would have been kindled in us by the knowledge of our past achievements, lacks the requisite foundation to rest upon. Great thought-leaders have been born in this land of Kamarupa, but where are their thoughts except in the dilapidated pages of the folios themselves ?

It is high time to collect the manuscripts and to preserve them from their inevitable destruction. Nations have become great not by their achievements in the material field but by the high-water-mark of culture they attained. If the Assamese people are destined to play once more their role as leaders of culture in Eastern India and to protect themselves from the encroaching hands of denationalization and consequent effacement, their primary duty is to rake up the outline of the structure of their past on which they will have to raise the edifice of their future.

October 29, 1929.

HEMCHANDRA GOSWAMI

The late Srijut Hemchandra Goswami's chief claim to the recollection and gratitude of posterity consists in his life-long devotion to the cause of Assamese literature and history. He pursued his labours in the midst of the heavy duties of an executive officer of the Government, and there is hardly any branch of historical investigation in which he did not actively and arduously exert himself. A born scholar and investigator he was a source of inspiration to all who came in contact with him; and wherever he went, he, by his earnestness and affability, created an atmosphere of learning and scholarship. By the art of gentle persuasiveness of which he was an adept master, he enlisted the sympathy and patronage of high Government officials in the cause of historical research. His personality was of no less consequence than his performance.

Hemchandra Goswami was born on January 8, 1872, at Gaurang Satra, near Golaghat in the district of Sibsagar, Assam. His father Srijut Dambarudhar Goswami, Mauzadar, died at Benares when Hemchandra was only eight years old. His mother Srijukta Ghanakanti Devi, now the sole guardian of the family consisting of two sons and a daughter, was reduced to the verge of despair regarding the maintenance and education of her chidren. Hemchandra had to remain at home for some time without any school education, but this was the time when he learnt from his mother a large mass of traditional history with which every Assamese lady of the older generation was naturally equipped. He further initiated himself in the reading of manuscripts, and he committed to memory a large portion of the *Amar-kosha,* the two things which marked the early education of every Brahman youth of those days. When Hemchandra was only thirteen his mother arranged to have him sent to Nowgong to live with a relative of the family for purpose of education.

Nowgong was then the centre of the literary revival which followed the due recognition of Assamese as the language of the schools and courts. The leading figure was Rai Bahadur Gunabhiram Barua, the virtual dictator of the Assamese literature of the nineteenth century. Among the members of the circle were persons whose contributions have mainly formed the nucleus of modern Assamese literature. They were Bholanath Das the poet, Ratneswar Mahanta the antiquarian, Padmahas Goswami the free-thinker, Rudram Bardaloi, Dharmeswar Goswami, Baladeva Mahanta, Bolinarayan Bora, Naranath Mahanta, Ratnadhar Barua, Chandrahas Bhuyan, Mahadananda Bhattacharyya, Mrs. Padmavati Devi Phukanani and Mrs. Bishnupriya Devi. Being thrown into the atmosphere of Nowgong an impressionable youth like Hemchandra Goswami, whose literary instincts had already been roused to some extent, could not long remain outside its dominion and away. Rai Bahadur Gunabhiram Barua was not slow in detecting the potentiality of the youth, and welcomed the latter's articles in the pages of the *Assam-Bandhu* of which he was the founder and the editor. Mr. Goswami wrote a number of poems in the pages of the same journal which were marked by simplicity of diction and ideas, as a reaction against the prevailing school of Assamese poetry with its outlandish half-Bengali jargon and structure mainly popularised by the contributions of Bholanath Das.

Having passed the Entrance Examination from the Nowgong High School in 1888, Mr. Goswami joined the Presidency College at Calcutta. He read there for four years but failed to get the B.A. Degree, which was due to his engrossment in the work of the Assamese Language Improvement Society. It was a very critical juncture in the history of Assamese language and literature. Systematic attempts were made in certain uncritical quarters to brand Assamese as a mere patois of Bengali. Assamese youngmen who lived in Calcutta as students took up arms against this humiliation and did all that lay in their power, by carrying on a regular propaganda in the press, to restore to their mother tongue its legitimate recognition as a daughter of Sanskrit, as different from Bengali as English is from Spanish or Italian. They stinted themselves of the meagre allowance remitted from home and conducted two papers, the *Bijuli* and the *Jonaki*, to champion the cause of Assamese, and to rekindle in the minds of all Assamese-speaking people a confidence and interest in their native literature. The resultant effect of this strenuous literary campaign was the failure that attended the University career of several Assamese youngmen who afterwards distinguished themselves in various spheres of activity. Among them are included men like Srijut Lakshminath Bezbarua, the premier Assamese man of letters of the present day, Rai Bahadur Anandachandra Agarwala, the poet and Superintendent of Police, and Rai Sahib Padmanath Gohain, Barua, special literary pensioner, and Chandrakumar Agarwala.

Mr. Goswami identified himself with the successful conduction of the *Jonaki* and he wrote a series of articles on the history and development of Assamese language and literature. Though he failed to get a degree he cherished a great love for Presidency College, and his face glowed with enthusiasm when he spoke of his distinguished Professors, F. J. Rowe, W. T. Webb, C. H. Tawney, J. C. Bose and H. M. Percival.

Mr. Goswami's family circumstances did not allow him to remain longer in Calcutta as he had to earn bread for himself and the other members, he being married in the meantime. He served as the Headmaster of the Sonaram High School at Gauhati after which he went to Shillong, the capital of Assam, to try his fortune there. He was in the Secretariat for some time where he came in contact with Mr. (now Sir) Edward Gait, who was then engaged in collecting materials for the purpose of compiling a critical history of ancient and modern Assam. Lt.-Col. P. R. T. Gurdon justly remarks,—"Hem Goswami was of great assistance to Sir Edward Gait in his work of historical research in which the former's knowledge of Sanskrit and acumen for digging and delving in a previously unknown field supplied a collaborator with just the equipment that Sir Edward required".[1] The services which Mr. Goswami rendered to Sir Edward have been well appreciated in the letter which the distinguished historian wrote to the present writer soon after Mr. Goswami's death, in which he said,—"It is over thirty years since I saw Hemchandra Goswami. He

[1] Col. Gurdon's letter to the present writer, dated June 19th, 1928, published in the *Cotton College Magazine* for February 1929.

was then quite a young man, but already took much interest in Assamese history and literature. He helped me a good deal in hunting up references to ancient Kamarupa in the *Puranas, Tantras,* etc. He also, as you have already noted, collaborated with Col. Gurdon in editing Hemchandra Barooah's Assamese Dictionary. His death will be a great loss to his country."

Mr. Goswami was commissioned by Mr. Gait to translate into English an Assamese chronicle recovered from the family of Yuvaraj Keshavkanta Singha, grandson of Chandrakanta Singha, the last reigning king of Assam. Mr. Goswami's masterly translation of the chronicle which bristled with untranslatable archaisms at once brought him to the notice of the Local Government, and he was appointed on the 17th Mav 1897, as Sub-Deputy Collector, though he was not a graduate. As for Sir Edward Gait, he has duly acknowledged Mr. Goswami's services in his *Report on the Progress of Historical Research in Assam,* published by the Assam Government in 1897.

As a Sub-Deputy Collector Mr. Goswami won the estimation of his administrative superiors. Col. Gurdon, who had an extensive experience of the administration of Assam, refers in glowing terms to Mr. Goswami's career as a Sub-Deputy Collector,—

"I remember how well he supervised the work of his subordinates at that time and how he met any difficulty with that determination and sangfroid which always distinguished him, for the work of a Sub-Deputy Collector Tashildar provided no bed of roses in those days, and revenue and settlement duties were full of difficulty more specially at a time when the whole settlement system was reorganised by Sir Bampfylde Fuller. It was about this time that the first resettlement operations on scientific principles were undertaken in the Assam Valley, when Hemchandra Goswami was easily marked out by the authorities as just the man for settlement work under the new conditions; and I remember how highly the settlement officer, Mr. Barnes, spoke of Hemchandra Goswami's keenness and driving power."

On May 2nd, 1905, Mr. Goswami was promoted to the Assam Executive Service and appointed Extra Assistant Commissioner or Deputy Magistrate at Gauhati. He was then transferred to Tezpur, where with his old friend Rai Sahib Padmanath Gohain-Barua he evolved many schemes for the improvement of Assamese literature. Mr. Gohain-Barua founded the *Usha*, a monthly Assamese periodical, which established a reputation for chaste and lucid diction, no less for the classical character of the subjects dealt with in its pages. Mr. Goswami contributed a series of articles on several ancient Assamese manuscripts, but the most momentous contribution from Mr. Goswami was his account of the battle of Saraighat, in which the Mogul hordes under Raja Ram Singha were completely defeated by the Ahom forces under the general Lachit Barphukan. The unparalleled heroism of Lachit Phukan, revealed for the first time through the glowing narrative of Mr. Goswami, was portrayed in numerous dramas and poems written subsequently. Lachit became a national hero of the Assamese people who found in him a new source of inspiration. Mr. Goswami had the gratification of seeing annual celebrations on the occasion of the hero's anniversary and the dedication of several dramas to himself for having brought home to his countrymen a new ideal and a new message. In collaboration with Mr. Gohain-Barua he compiled a note on Assamese language and literature for the use of Mr. F. W. Sudmersen, who was commissioned by the Government to compile a monograph on the origin and development of the Assamese language. Mr. Goswami was mainly responsible for the award of a special literary pension to Mr. Gohain-Barua, the first distinction conferred by the Government upon an Assamese man of letters. The difficulties were many, and when Mr. Goswami broached the subject to Col. Gurdon the latter simply remarked,—"You have given me a very tall order to execute".

One of the recommendations of Mr. Sudmersen was the appointment of a responsible Government officer for the collection of the Assamese *puthis* lying forgotten in Assamese families. Mr. Goswami in an interview with the Chief Commissioner of Assam showed him several valuable Assamese manuscripts partially destroyed, and pointed out the necessity of taking immediate steps to collect all *puthis* that might be recovered. Sir Archdale Earle, who several years previous to his connexion with Assam, had guided the educational destiny of Bengal as its I.C.S. Director of Public Instruction, acknowledged the urgency of the matter, and Mr. Goswami was, as a matter of course, placed on special duty from October 1912 to March 1913. He was to act under the guidance of Col. Gurdon, the Honorary Provincial Director of Ethnography. The appointment met with a chorus of approval from all quarters, and Mr. Goswami put himself in earnestness about his new work, for which he was more naturally equipped than for sifting the complications of Civil and Criminal litigation. As a preliminary step, the Sub-Deputy Collectors of the Assam Valley Division were requested to prepare censuses of *puthis* in their respective jurisdictions. Mr. Goswami visited the districts of Goalpara, Kamrup, Nowgong, Sibsagar and Lakhimpur; he also paid a visit to Cooch Behar, where in the State Library a large number of Assamese manuscripts have been deposited since the days of Maharaja Naranarayan, who like his great contemporary Akbar, commissioned a number of Assamese scholars to translate into Assamese the *Mahabharata* and treatises on mathematics and astronomy. Mr. Goswami's visit to the Satras, or Vaishnava monasteries of Assam and to different centres was rewarded by the recovery of a large number of manuscripts in Assamese and Sanskrit, the most remarkable of them being the treatise on elephants entitled *Hastividyarnava* compiled by a scholar of the court of King Siva Singha, 1714-44. Mr. Goswami's collections included Assamese chronicles, song books, dramas, aphorisms, books on medicine and arithmetic, commentaries on the *Bhagavata* and *Raghuvamsa*, a treatise on the artistic manipulation of the fingers known as *Hastamuktavali*, an Ahom dictionary, besides the usual cluster of manuscripts found in old Assamese families. The deputation lasted till March 1913. The manuscripts acquired as gifts or loans were deposited at the office of the Commissioner of the Assam Valley Division, from where they have been since removed to the premises of the Kamarupa Anusandhana Samiti. The next task which occupied Mr. Goswami was the compilation of a descriptive catalogue of the manuscripts collected, for which he was placed on special deputation in August 1914. He had to write an account of each *puthi* under the following heads,—name, subject, author, date, description, opening lines, closing lines, colophon, contents, owner, place of deposit, and remarks. The compilation of this volume entailed great labour upon Mr. Goswami, and it will not be far from the truth that it aggravated the symptoms of his failing health; but as Lt.-Col. Gurdon has said,— "The descriptive catalogue of Assamese literature was the work of Hem Gosain's alone, and it is on this great achievement that his fame will probably rest and go down to posterity".

Mr. Goswami played a leading part in the establishment of the Kamarupa Anusandhana Samiti, or the Assam Research Society, at Gauhati in the year 1912. The growing desire of all the scholars interested in the history and antiquities of Assam to co-ordinate their individual efforts was felt for several years. Mr. Goswami in concert with Mahamahopadhyaya Padmanath Bhattacharyya, Mahamahopadhyaya Dhireswar Bhattacharyya, and Rai Bahadur Kalicharan Sen represented to the Government the extreme desirability of extending its patronage to an institution of that type. Sir Archdale Earle again came up to meet this cultural demand of the province under his administration. Mr. Goswami was seen romping about the antiquarian sites in the neighbourhood of Gauhati in the company of his ardent fellow-workers. Many were the schemes which they took up for execution by the new-born society. A critical edition of the *Yoginitantra* and a collection of the diplomatic letters of the Ahom court was undertaken by Mr. Goswami himself. He edited for the Samiti the chronicle of the Ahom Rajas recovered from Keshavkanta Yuvaraj. He was in fact the permanent President of the Samiti except at intervals when he was away from Gauhati. His interest in the advancement of the Samiti remained undiminished till the last moment of his life. His ready counsel was a source of inspiration to the younger generation of workers. The translation of the Samiti into a full-fledged museum with a permanent staff and systematic arrangements for collecting relics and finds from all parts of the Province, was the dream of Mr. Goswami's life, and his attempt to enter the provincial Legislative Council in 1926, was mainly inspired by this ambition.

The next phase in the life of Mr. Goswami was his association with Sir Asutosh Mookerjee. Being the foremost antiquarian of Assam his name was already known in literary circles in Bengal. He was one of the chief promoters of the Bangiya Anusilan Sabha of Gauhati, established with the avowed object of disseminating knowledge of the history and literature of Assam. One chief achievement of the Sabha was the popularisation in Bengal of the story of the martyred Assamese princess Jaimati. This Sabha is still existing in the shape of the Gauhati branch of the Bangiya Sahitya Parishad. Mr. Goswami read papers in Bengali on Chaitanya's visit to Assam and on the antiquities of Kamakhya. His home was the resort of all Bengali scholars who came to Gauhati on flying visits. Mr. Goswami had seen Sir Asutosh on several occasions at Bhowanipur, Calcutta. When the latter came to visit the colleges of Gauhati in March 1918, as a member of the Calcutta University Commission, he found an opportunity of further extending his scheme of publishing typical selections from Indian literatures, and selected Mr. Goswami to undertake the Assamese section of the work. The whole scheme was discussed by the Senate of the Calcutta University in August 1918, and Mr. Goswami obtained formal appointment for the work on an honorarium of Rs. 2,000. The University subsequently sanctioned a grant of Rs. 400 for copying the selections from original manuscripts, books and periodicals. After some correspondence with Sir Asutosh Mookerjee, Mr. Goswami settled upon a definite plan of work dividing Assamese literature into six periods. He was fully occupied with this work for more than three years. This gigantic work was carried on in addition to his heavy duties as Extra Assistant Commissioner. The manuscript of the Typical Selections was handed over to the University towards the end of 1921. It was approved by the University, but difficulties arose regarding the expenses of its publication. The University was passing through a financial crisis and the newly organised Vernacular Department had naturally to suffer in spite of the best endeavours of Sir Asutosh. In January 1922 Mr. Goswami stayed as a guest at the Howrah residence of Mr. Bholanath Barua, an Assamese gentleman who had risen to wealth and eminence by extensive business concerns in India and England. Mr. Goswami persuaded Mr. Barua to come to the rescue of Sir Asutosh in the matter of publishing the Assamese selections. This possibility was pointed out to Sir Asutosh, who motored down to Mr. Barua's house one fine afternoon and obtained from the merchant and philanthropist a promise to finance the publication of the Assamese selections. The next day a cheque for Rs. 10,000 reached the hands of Sir Asutosh. The printing of the book was undertaken at the Calcutta University Press, but some difficulty arose owing to the absence of types of some Assamese letters. Sir Asutosh got them cast in a leading Calcutta foundry. The printing of the book went on apace though some inconvenience arose for the distance at which the compiler lived. The printing of the first volume was postponed till the last for obvious reasons, chiefly because it had to contain the introductory matter relating to the entire compilation. Only six parts were published during the lifetime of Mr. Goswami, four parts of the second volume and two parts of the third.

The Assam Sahitya-Sabha was established in December 1917, with the object of promoting the cause of Assamese language and literature, on the lines of the Bangiya Sahitya Parishad. After some change of fortune its headquarters were permanently established at Jorhat. The momentous task which the Sabha has undertaken is the compilation of an exhaustive dictionary of the Assamese language to be known as *Chandrakanta Abhidhan,* to the memory of the late Srijut Chandrakanta Handique, B.A., son of Rai Bahadur Radhakanta Handique, the munificent patron of the compilation. Hemchandra who had presided over one of its annual sittings, was transferred to Jorhat in October 1922, and he at once became the friend, philosopher and guide of the Sahitya-Sabha, which was then running through a financial crisis. The cause of Assamese literature has always suffered for the absence of a wealthy leisured class; men who have to follow other vocations in life have to work in the field of literature; and every financial project has to be executed by Government support or by contribution from individual donors. Hemchandra approached His Holiness Naradeva Goswami, the Adhikar of Dakshinpat Satra, and obtained from him a donation of Rs. 8,000; another Satradhikar, Srijut Radha Nath Deva Goswami of Mahara Satra, made an endowment to perpetuate the name of the donor's mother. The object of the latter endowment was the publication of juvenile books. Hemchandra's personality and persuasiveness were mainly responsible for the second gift as well. Mr. Goswami approached His Holiness Kamaldeva Goswami of Auniati Satra and obtained from him a promise for a donation of Rs. 5,000, but the unexpected death of that cultured and philanthropic Satradhikar Gosain could not then materialise the gift.

Mr. Goswami had in the meantime collected the old Vaisnava dramas of Assam, known as *Ankiya Nats* and sent them to the press. He also edited the voluminous prose translation of the *Bhagavata* by Bhattadeva known as *Katha-Bhagavat.*

Incessant literary labours coupled with the sedentary work of a judicial officer had in the meantime produced symptoms of a disease which was responsible for Hemchandra's premature death. He retired from Government service in February 1925. He proposed to utilise this long-sought leisure in undertaking more arduous tasks. He convinced Mr. H. C. Barnes, Commissioner of the Assam Valley Division, of the desirability of publishing old classics with English translations, representing different phases of Assamese culture. Mr. Barnes accordingly moved the Government for sanction and financial assistance which were readily obtained. The editing and the translation of the classics were entrusted to responsible scholars, under the general direction of Mr. Goswami, and the books selected were,—*Hasti-vidyarnava*, *Kamaratna-tantra*, *Vaidya-kalpa-taru*, *Dak-bhanita*, *Kitabat-manjari*, historical letters, *Ghora-Nidan* and two Assamese chronicles. But during Mr. Goswami's life-time only one book, *Kamaratna-tantra*, could be sent to the press. The book has now been published.

Mr. Goswami's well-deserved retirement and rest were converted into a period of strenuous labour. He became the Director of one or two local banks at Gauhati, and proposed the publication of a periodical from Nalbari. In November 1926, he stood as a candidate for election to the Assam Legislative Council from the Golaghat constituency, but was defeated by his Swarajist rival.

While a student of the Presidency College, Mr. Goswami had married Srijukta Bamasundari Devi, the daughter of Kesavchandra Sarma Barua of the Rasendra-Barua family, who were hereditary physicians of the Ahom monarchs. The children of the marriage were Kiranchandra Goswami now deceased, Sarat-Chandra Goswami, Prafullachandra Goswami, Tarunchandra Goswami and three daughters Muktabala Devi, Hiraprava Devi and Kamalakumari Devi.

On the 13th of December 1927, Mr. Goswami's eldest son Kiranchandra who was opening a tea-garden in the Golaghat Sub-division died of pneumonia leaving a young and childless widow. Hemchandra's mother long confined to bed, followed her grandson in February 1928. Towards the end of April 1928, a diabetic carbuncle appeared on the face of Hemchandra, and after two weeks of suffering he breathed his last on the morning on May 2, 1928. His remains were cremated at the foot of the Kamakhya Hill, facing the vast expanse of the Brahmaputra river.

The death of Hemchandra Goswami has created a void which it is very difficult to fill. His earnestness and infinite capacity for work are best revealed in the books or articles he edited or compiled. The keynote of his life was his intense patriotism which manifested itself in an indomitable desire to dig up the past glories of Assam and place them before his countrymen as a stimulus and inspiration. His Gauhati house was the rendezvous of scholars who happened to visit Assam. We had seen there Sir Prafullachandra Roy, Mr. Kasinath Dikshit, Dr. D. R. Bhandarkar, Prof. G. Tucci and Sir Devaprasad Sarvadhikary, all listening rapturously to the antiquities and civilisation of ancient Kamarupa from the lips of the Assamese savant. The gorgeously illustrated manuscript of *Hasti-vidyarnava* was shown by Mr. Goswami to Dr. Rabindranath Tagore and Mahatma Gandhi. Lord Reading, to whom this manuscript was shown by Mr. Barnes, expressed great delight on seeing this marvellous specimen of Assamese painting and scholarship. Mr. Goswami's object in exhibiting these rare tokens of Assamese civilisation to distinguished visitors to Assam was to raise their estimation of his much abused and misrepresented countrymen.

Literary Works. The literary career of Hemchandra Goswami spread over a period of forty-five years commencing from his school days at Nowgong under the irresistible association of Rai Bahadur Gunabhiram Barua. Mr. Goswami's literary performance is in the main critical and editorial, though in his earlier years he wrote verses with considerable ease and spontaneity.

He was chiefly engaged in suppyling the raw materials with the help of which constructive and scientific criticism may be undertaken in future when more materials will be forthcoming. He was bewildered at the sight of the immense mine of sources and data for a history of Assam and of Assamese language and literature. Large numbers of manuscripts representing the culture and civilisation of Assam are lying untraced and forgotten in the archives of Assamese families, besides numerous inscriptions and archaeological relics scattered throughout this hoary land of Kamarupa. The first task of the historical pioneer in Assam is to collect the data now readily available, but which will be effaced during the course of a few decades.

Hemchandra's performance has the risk of being superseded by the more critical, scientific and academic attempts of future workers; but their value will lie chiefly in the fact that they have been able to rouse and maintain a sustained interest in historical investigations in Assam. The achievement of the pioneer or spade-worker is as laudable as that of the constructive historian, the latter being impossible without the former. The pioneer is a martyr to his cause while the fortunate reconstructor reaps the fruit of his earlier pathfinder's labours. While the majority of his countrymen remained deeply engrossed in worldly pursuits, Hemchandra's life was dominated by an overwhelming, if not fanatical, zeal for research. He had to create his own facilities. The arduous duties of a judicial officer could not hold him back from the performance of what, he thought, was his life's mission. He will live in the grateful remembrance of posterity, not as an efficient revenue officer or magistrate, but as an earnest and zealous Assamese worker whose patriotism was primarily directed towards the revivification of the glorious past of his motherland. The regrettable spectacle of Hemchandra poring over official files or over the contending versions of deponents,—Hemchandra who by his natural equipment and taste could perform tasks of more enduring and permanent importance—was nothing short of a national calamity.

The first appearance of Hemchandra before the public was with an article on agriculture contributed to Rai Bahadur Gunabhiram Barua's *Assam-Bandhu* for February-March 1885, of which Mr. Goswami himself wrote on the copy of his own volume,—"This was my first Assamese composition when my age was thirteen years and I was reading in the fifth class of Nowgong Government High School." In this piece the young author deplored the abandonment of agricultural pursuits by the educated middle classes of Assam. The style is direct and earnest in tone. This was followed by a number of poems published in the same magazine. These poems have been incorporated in his collection of juvenile verses published in 1907 under the title *Phular Chaki,* literally a nosegay of flowers. The pieces do some credit to a young lad in his early teens.

Mr. Goswami's historical contributions are mainly embodied in the books he edited, and in the occasional papers he wrote to Assamese periodicals. We give below short notices of his more important works with the belief that they will afford us glimpses into certain phases of the history of Assamese literature.

Hema-kosha.—Hemchandra Barua, one of the founders of modern Assamese literature, died in 1896 leaving unpublished his dictionary of the Assamese language, known as *Hema-kosha* after the name of the distinguished author. The manuscript of his voluminous compilation was handed over to Lt.-Col. P. R. T. Gurdon by the late Dulalchandra Chaudhury. Mr. Gait, realising the importance of the work, moved the Government for having it published at their expense. Sir Henry Cotton, the then Chief Commissioner of Assam, granted a sum for the purpose. During the earthquake of June 1897, the buildings of the Government Press at Shillong were completely destroyed, and Mr. Gait had to rescue the manuscript of *Hema-kosha* from below a heap of debris. Col. Gurdon and Mr. Goswami jointly undertook the editorial responsibility. The coadjutors were engaged in this work for many months in addition to their ordinary official duties. 'This important work', writes Col. Gurdon, 'occupied us for many months and gave us plenty to do, the revision and editing being undertaken by both of us in addition to our ordinary duties. While engaged, Hem Gosain and I were naturally much thrown together, and many were the talks we had over the antiquity and beauty of the Assamese language and Assam historical research'. Hemchandra was entrusted with the editing of the vernacular portion of the work, and the fact that *Hema-kosha* has served as the only authority for the spelling and meaning of Assamese words during the space of nearly thirty years since its publication in 1900 pays a glowing tribute to the careful compilation and editing respectively of the earlier and the later Hemchandra.

Darrang-raj-vamsavali.—This is a metrical chronicle of the descendants of Biswa Singha, the founder of the Koch dynasty, who established themselves as rulers in Cooch Behar, Bijni, Darrang and Beltola. The book was composed by Suryyakhari Daivajna during the latter part of the eighteenth century under the patronage of Samudranarayan, Raja of Darrang. The original manuscript embelished with copious illustrations was examined by Mr. Gait who wrote an account in the Journal of the Asiatic Society of Bengal for 1893. Mr. Goswami recovered the book in 1912 from Kumar Khagendranarayan of the now faineant Darrang Raj family. The book was edited by Mr. Goswami and published by the Assam Government in 1917. The language of the book is refined and artistic, and the handling of the materials systematic and picturesque. Apart from the general history of the Koch rulers down to Balinarayan, *alias* Dharmanarayan, brother of Parikshit, grandson of Chilarai, the interest of the book centers round the vigorous description of the victorious expeditions of Sukladhwaja or Chilarai, and the construction of the Kamakhya temple at Gauhati by an architect named Megha Mukdum under the orders of King Naranarayan of Cooch Behar. The king was a reputed patron of scholars, poets and saints; and his commissioning of the erudite Pundits of the land to translate Sanskrit masterpieces into Assamese for 'the edification of Sudras and females, and of Brahmans at a later age' has its counterpart in a similar attempt made by his great contemporary Akbar. King Naranarayan summoned all the scholars of Gauda and Kamarupa and commanded them to compile new treatises or translate specific classics. Purushottam Vidyavagis was entrusted with the compilation of a grammar entitled *Ratnamala-vyakaran*; Rama Saraswati was to translate the entire *Mahabharata*, the *Ramayan* and the eighteen *Puranas;* Sankardeva was asked to translate the twelve cantos of the *Bhagavata;* Sridhara compiled a popular treatise on astronomy; and Bakul Kayastha was to render *Lilavati* into Assamese. The description of the above attempt of the king for the cultural regeneration of his countrymen was not an artistic device to bring in all the poets and scholars of Naranarayan's time together on one canvas. It is a historical fact and has been corroborated by the independent testimony of the writers themselves who have all acknowledged their gratitude to the royal patron in the colophons of their respective works. This measure of King Naranarayan places him on the same line with Alfred, Akbar and Sir Asutosh Mookerjee. The *Darrang-raj-vamsavali* has been an invaluable source-book for all studies connected with the early history of the Koch rulers.

Katha-Gita.—This is a prose rendering of the Gita by Baikunthanath Kaviratna Bhagavata-Bhattacharyya, commonly known as Bhattadeva, a contemporary of Sankardeva and a learned exponent of the Vaisnava cult. His descendants are still holding charge of two notable monasteries of Kamrup, Patbausi Satra and Biahkuchi Satra. Bhattadeva was also the author of the Assamese prose translation of the *Bhagavata* known as *Katha-Bhagavata*, the word *Katha* being prefixed to titles of books written in prose as distinguished from verse. *Katha-Gita* is a monument of religious Assamese prose which has a conventional Sanskritic ring and a marked affinity to the artificial diction of old Assamese poetry. The style though not racy has a majestic simplicity of its own. At the end of every chapter the author has inserted a brief peroration pointing to the glory of Srikrishna and urging all men and women to attain salvation through the adoration of Srikrishna. Mr. Goswami published this book with his introduction in 1918. Sir Praphullachandra Roy who presided over the Tezpur session of the Assam Students Conference, marvelled at the antiquity of Assamese prose literature and recorded his impressions in a language worthy of the scientist and patriot,—"Indeed the prose Gita of Bhattadeva composed in the sixteenth century is unique of its kind. I had an opportunity of coming across an excellent edition of this book which we owe to the patriotism and scholarship of Pundit Hemchandra Goswami. It is a priceless treasure. Assamese prose literature developed to a stage in the far distant sixteenth century which no other literature of the world reached except the writings of Hooker and Latimer in England. There has been a controversy for long about the independence and identity of the Assamese language. This is extremely foolish. This is due, to the provincial patriotism and the national conceit of the Bengalees living in Assam. The *Katha-Gita* shows clearly that the Assamese literature developed to a standard in the sixteenth century which the Bengalee literature had reached only in the time of Iswar Chandra and Bankim Chandra. In fact, if some Assamese scholars now get up and say that it is the Bengali who has borrowed his prose from Assamese literature and enriched his own, it will be very difficult to dislodge him. I think the question may now be considered as solved and settled for good. I say this not as a representative Bengalee but as the ex-president of the Bengal Literary Conference".

Sir Asutosh Mookerjee's opinion was equally gratifying,—"The people who could write *Gita* in such prose in the sixteenth century was not a small people".

Purani Asam Buranji.—In 1922 was published *Purani Asam Buranji* under the auspices of the Kamarupa Anusandhan Samiti. Mr. Goswami supplied the introduction and the editorial paraphernalia. The manuscript of the chronicle was recovered from the family of Yuvaraj Keshavkanta Singha, grandson of Chandrakanta Singha, the last reigning king of Assam. This particular volume dealing with the history of the Ahoms from King Sukapha to King Gadadhar, A.D. 1228-1696, is one of the many Buranjis which are a distinctive feature of Assamese literature.

The editor points to some of the characteristic aspects of Assamese Buranjis. He refers to the regrettable loss of an Assamese chronicle of Bardhaman which he proposed to publish and which was exhibited in the Gauripur session of the Uttar Banga Sahitya Sammilan. It may be mentioned that *Purani Asam Buranji,* published by the Kamarupa Anusandhan Samiti, is the first Assamese Buranji or chronicle to see the light of day.

Typical Selections from Assamese Literature.—This voluminous compilation was undertaken at the instance of the late Sir Asutosh Mookerjee in execution of his extensive scheme for promotion of the study of the Indian Vernaculars in the Calcutta University. The work was commenced in 1918 soon after Sir Asutosh's visit to Gauhati as a member of the Sadler Commission. The whole range of Assamese literature has been divided, for the purpose of this compilation, into six distinctive periods, *viz.,* the lyrical period or

Giti-yuga; the period of *mantras* and aphorisms or *Mantra-aru-bhanita-yuga;* the pre-Vaisnavite period or *Prak-Vaisnava-yuga; Vaisnava-yuga,* or the period of Sankardeva and his immediate successors; the period of extension or *Vistar-yuga;* and the modern age or the *Vartaman-yuga.* The original plan adopted in consultation with Sir Asutosh included the insertion of a historical introduction, a glossary of archaic terms and short notices of the authors selected; but the death of the editor when only the second and the third volumes had been published and the first volume was in the press made the insertion of the proposed editorial matter an impossible task. As a pioneer work undertaken by a man of Mr. Goswami's limited leisure, it does credit to the editor and will serve as the necessary basis for the comparative study of the history of Assamese language and literature, though a future work of the same type may benefit by the unavoidable deficiencies of Mr. Goswami's performance. It may be mentioned that Mr. Goswami's own contributions have been inserted in the third volume of the *Typical Selections,* Part 2, pages 527 to 564. The original plan was to bring down the selections to the date of compilation, but it was modified with a view to include writers up to the end of the nineteenth century.

Kama-ratna-tantra.—The publication of this book was undertaken in execution of the Assam Government scheme to translate representative Assamese classics into English. Assam, the reputed home of the *Tantras,* has a large assortment of manuscript specimens of old Tantric literature, and Hemchandra could not do better than select this *Kama-ratna-tantra,* the prescriptions of which are still adopted by some sections of the Assamese for purposes laid down. According to the editor, 'the book describes how by incantations and other methods a man as well as a woman can be subdued and attracted, made hostile, paralysed, killed, freed from evils, excited and so on. It gives the methods to be adopted for the performance of the above facts in the forms of medicines, *mantras* and *jantras*'. The *Tantra* prescribes the remedies necessary, among others, for the following objects,—subduing of wives, subduing of husbands, prevention of sleep, causing quarrels, protection of crops, success of one's speech, besides other objects verging on the side of obscenity, which made the editor write,—'To an ordinary eye the book will appear full of indecencies, but in the light of science everything will appear instructive and illuminating'. Mr. Goswami used to repeat the story how Mr. Barnes at once welcomed the idea of printing the book saying,—'This book must be published', when Mr. Goswami pointed out to him the recipes for taming refractory wives and shrews. It is not surprising that Assam where the magical potents prescribed in this *Tantra* were practised, should be known to the rest of India as a land of witchcraft and black arts.

In accordance with the general plan of this series the English translation is inserted on the page facing the corresponding Assamese text, thereby rendering the book highly helpful to foreign scholars who want to master the peculiarities of the Assamese language as employed in technical purposes.

The manuscript of *Kama-ratna-tantra* was recovered from the Na-Gosain family of North Gauhati, who were *gurus* of some of the later Assam Rajas. Mr.

Goswami supplied the preface and the foreword which are dated April 17, 1926. The book has been printed at the Assam Secretariat Press, and published posthumously in May 1929.

A Descriptive Catalogue of Assamese Manuscripts.—This book contains a descriptive account of the *puthis* collected by Mr. Goswami during his deputation in 1912-13; and it is being published from the Calcutta University Press at the expense of the Assam Government. The first part, pages 1 to 184, deals with Assamese manuscripts, and the second, pages 187 to 256, with Sanskrit *puthis.* This catalogue was compiled during a short period of deputation commencing from August 1914. Every manuscript is described under the following heads,—name, subject, author, date, description, the opening lines, the closing lines, colophon, contents, owner, place of deposit and remarks. The compilation of the details under the above heads was a work of unceasing labour, and the words of Lt.-Col. P. R. T. Gurdon who was associated with the collection of the manuscripts and the preparation of the catalogue may be quoted,—"The descriptive catalogue of Assamese literature which is, I believe, still in the press, was the work of Hem Gosain's alone, and it is on this great achievement that his fame will probably rest and go down to posterity". Though Mr. Goswami did not live long enough to write a constructive history, the mass of valuable information supplied in this catalogue will serve as the foundation for all such endeavours in future. The book records the result of Mr. Goswami's life-long acquaintance with old Assamese literature. It also affords scattered glimpses into the political history of Assam which had always a close relationship with the progress and development of its language and literature.

Ankiya Bara-nat.—The antiquity of Assamese dramas as well as its historical literature is a feature conspicuous by its absence in Bengal. The early Vaisnava poets, in imitation of their Maithili fore-runners and compatriots, adopted numerous devices for the popularisation of their creed. Sankardeva translated the Bhagavata and other classics glorifying Srikrishna, while his chief apostle Madhabdeva busied himself in interpreting and expounding the cardinal principles of his master's creed. Sankardeva introduced the custom of singing religious hymns to the accompaniment of musical instruments and of reading aloud to a devoted audience portions of religious and semi-religious classics. One of his most momentous innovations was the propagation of his faith by the spectacular appeal of dramatic performances, an idea which he might have seized during his extensive travels in Bihar and Orissa, having seen the enactment of Vidyapati's dramas, the Assamese poet being much junior in age to his Maithili contemporary. Thus in Assam as in Europe motives of religion led to the birth of the drama. Sankardeva was himself a master of music and of the histrionic art, and like the great Shakespeare, took part in the acting of his own dramas.

The volume *Ankiya Bara-nat* is a collection of twelve dramas written by Sankardeva and Madhab-deva, viz., *Kalia-daman*, *Patni-prasad*, *Rasa-krida*, *Rukmini-haran*, *Sriram-vijay*, *Parijat-haran*, *Arjun-bhanjan*, *Chordhara Jhumura*, *Bhumi-lutiwa*, *Pimpara-guchua*, *Bhojan-vyavahara* and *Srikrishna-janma*. The language of these dramas presents a curious mixture of

Maithili and Assamese. Songs are closely interspersed, and the original Sanskrit texts on which a particular scene is based are inserted in apposite places with simple rendering in Maithili-Assamese. The Sutradhar introduces the main theme of the drama, as well as the scenes and characters as they come along. The illusion is maintained by the preponderance of music, the archaic ring of the diction and the sacred character of the subjects treated.

The popularity of the Vaisnava dramas has continued till this day. Their performances are generally known as *Bhawanas*. They are acted in the *nam-ghars*, or houses of public gathering, attached to every Assamese Hindu village. The anniversaries of the saints and the major *tithis* of the year are occasions when these plays are enacted in the public halls without the aid of a stage or scenes. They are also performed on secular occasions which necessitate a large congregation of individuals, such as marriages and *sraddhas*, in temporary sheds erected for the purpose close to the residences of the families who perform the ceremonies. The Ahom monarchs honoured distinguished visitors to their courts by inviting them to the performance of *Bhawanas* arranged for that sole purpose. A stranger paying even a flying visit to any Assamese village will hear the music of drums indicating that rehearsals are going on for some dramatic entertainment. It has been customary with the Vaisnava Satradhikars of the Assamese monasteries to give tokens of their learning and religious zeal by first composing a drama before they are formally ordained as pontiffs.

Mr. Goswami sent his collection of dramas to the press several years before his death, but they have not seen the light of day as yet on account of the dilatoriness of the Calcutta press of which almost every Assamese publisher of books is an invariable victim.

Katha-Bhagavata.—Mr. Goswami sent this second work of Bhattadeva to the press several years ago, but the voluminous character of the book will necessarily take many more years before it sees the light of day. Sankardeva translated the *Bhagavata* into Assamese verse jointly with Ananta Kandali, while Bhattadeva rendered the same into simple and majestic Assamese prose thus laying the foundation of the *Bhagavati Dharma,* another name of the Vaisnava creed as it obtained in Assam through its principal sponsors. The diction of the *Katha-Bhagavata* is no doubt artificial and far removed from the actual language spoken by the people. It has great affinity to the artistic diction of Assamese Vaisnava poetry which is familiar to every Assamese Hindu, the reading aloud of Vaisnava classics to a devoted audience being universal in Assam. Even the uninitiated and illiterate Assamese peasant can follow the stories of the *Katha-Bhagavata* and draw morals from them. The *Bhagavata* had thus a great influence in humanising the Assamese people and educating them in the cardinal principles of religion and morality as propounded through the life and teachings of Srikrishna. The *Katha-Bhagavata* when published will be of interest to all scholars of Eastern India on account of its linguistic catholicity, inasmuch as it can be followed by any man of Orissa and Bihar, not to speak of Bengal and Assam.

Publications in periodicals.—Among the most important of the contributions of Hemchandra to the vernacular periodicals mention may be made of the following :

1. Presidential speech delivered at the fourth session of the Asam Literary Conference, published in *Chetana*, Volume II, No. 5, pp. 231 sqq. The author describes the inter-relationship between literature and national advancement, and the wealth and variety of ancient Assamese literature, with suggestions for the recovery and publication of ancient Assamese classics.

2. Presidential speech delivered at the seventh session of the Assam Students' Conference, published in *Milan*, Volume I, No. 1, pp. 9-27. The address dealt with the educational ideals of the East and the West, and the pursuit of literature by students.

3. Essays on old Assamese manuscripts, published mainly in the first and second volumes of *Usha*. The books described were,—*Santa-akhyan* or the story of the saints, by Viswanath, detailing the various sects of Vaisnavism, their founders, and the principal Satras or monasteries representative of the sects ; *Chaitanya-patal* in Assamese prose by Srikrishna Bharati, describing the excellence of Chaitanya's creed, and the reformer's alleged visit to Kamarupa ; *Govinda-charit* by Bhavanath Misra, a metrical biography of Govinda Thakur, a disciple of Madhava Deva, and a propagator of the Vaisnava creed in Darrang ; *Chandi* written by Ruchinath Kandali during the reign of Rudra Singha, A.D. 1696-1714 ; *Sial Gosair Puthi*, written by Kaviraj Daivajna during the reign of Madranarayan, Raja of Darrang, describing the life of Dharmadeva whose son was brought up in the den of a jackal in the first year of his infancy. Two more papers were contributed to

the third volume of the *Usha*, one on *Kavyasastra*, an Assamese translation of the *Hitopadesa*, and the other on *Santa-muktavali* dealing with the lives of several Vaisnava saints. Mr. Goswami also wrote two more illuminating papers on Madhava Kandali, in *Chetana*, Volume IV, and the other on Hema Saraswati, in *Milan*, Volume II, the two poets being predecessors of Sankar Deva, who acknowledged his obligations to the first in lines which have been immortal like Dunbar's tribute to Chaucer and Shakespeare's more famous one to Marlowe.

4. A short history of Assamese language and literature was compiled by Mr. Goswami when he was a student of the under-graduate classes of the Presidency College. This was read at the second anniversary of the Assamese Language Improvement Society, Calcutta, held under the presidency of Rai Bahadur Gunabhiram Barua, and was published as a serial in the *Jonaki*, Vol. III. The author pointed out the three distinctive stages in the history of Assamese literature, which have been elaborated for the purpose of the *Typical Selections* into six periods. According to the earlier division the first period ranged from the earliest times to Sankardeva; the second from Sankardeva to the British occupation of Assam; and the third is the modern period characterised by the influence of the western contact. The author describes the salient features of each age and concludes with an appreciation of the two leading litterateurs of the day, Rai Bahadur Gunabhiram Barua and Hemchandra Barua. This portion has been incorporated in *Assamiya Sahityar Chaneki*, Voume III, Part 2, pages 527-542. This series of articles represented the first systematic attempt to

trace historically the growth of Assamese language and literature, and gave early promises that its author was a competent person to undertake investigations on the subject, and they have been justified by the subsequent achievements of Mr. Goswami.

5. Another valuable contribution of Mr. Goswami was the publication of the texts of some old Assamese copper-plate and rock inscriptions with historical prefaces. The bulk of these articles was contributed to the seventh and eighth volumes of *Alochani*, and included the texts of the inscriptions at Vasisthasram, Chilaparvat, the Barphukan's Dopdar or Durbar Hall, the Barphukan's Victory Pillar, Sukreswar Temple, Samdhara Fort, Siddheswar Temple, Rudreswar Temple, Phatasil Duar or the western entrance of Gauhati, Kanai-barasi-boa Rock, Durga Temple, Janardan-Phalgutsav Temple. In 1925 Mr. Goswami recovered a second copper-plate of King Indrapala from a village in Kamrup, the first one being published in the Journal of the Asiatic Society of Bengal by Dr. Hoernle in 1897. It is now in the worthy hands of Mr. K. N. Dikshit who is engaged in its decipherment.

6. Another contribution of great importance was the publication of the texts of some historical epistles exchanged between the Ahom court and the courts of Cachar and Jaintia. They were published as a serial in the seventh and eighth volumes of *Banhi*. They embody specimens of the diplomatic diction and court language of the time, whereas the letters addressed by the Cachari and Jaintia Rajas have an additional importance as they are written in Bengali prose, though somewhat quaint and adulterated. Before his death Mr. Goswami was engaged in the translation of the

historical letters in execution of the scheme inaugurated by Mr. Barnes and himself.

7. Besides the above, Mr. Goswami also contributed a number of historical articles to periodicals. He wrote on Chaitanya in Assam and on the construction of the Kamakhya temple in the twenty-second volume of the Bangiya Sahitya Parishad Patrika. His description of the battle of Saraighat where the Assamese troops under Lachit Phukan routed the Mogul army under Aurangzeb's general Ram Singha, Raja of Amber, was published in the first volume of the *Usha*. It was an epoch-making contribution reminding the Assamese of the heroism and chivalry of which their ancestors were capable. Mr. Goswami also translated into Assamese Mr. (afterwards Sir) Bampfyilde Fuller's *Land Revenue Policy of the Government of India*, and it was published by the Assam Government. He translated with Col. Gurdon the story of the Prodigal Son in standard Assamese for Dr. Grierson's *Linguistic Survey of India*. Mr. Goswami also wrote an illuminating introduction to the present writer's *Life of Anundoram Borooah*, published in 1920. He gave there a short account of the biographical literature of ancient Assam, and referred particularly to the biography of a female saint named Ai-Lakshmi.

Conclusion.—Thus lived and worked Hemchandra Goswami, affable and inspiring in personality, versatile and catholic in scholarship, undaunted and unflinching in the service of his country's history and literature, an ardent patriot, a true Indian and a truer Assamese. Diverse are the ways of serving one's motherland; and Hemchandra's mission was to make his countrymen realise their past greatness specially in their cultural aspects; and this he regarded as the stepping stone to the revival of his country's consciousness and all endeavours for its regeneration. Inspired by this noble ideal Hemchandra worked unceasingly for its realisation, devoted all his leisure which his heavy official duties could permit, sacrificed his health and comfort, worked when others slept, and died before his time and before his life's goal was finally reached. But he wakened his countrymen to a phase of patriotism which posterity will not let willingly die. He has sown the seeds of possibility which in time will yield a rich harvest to the delight and amazement of all beholders. When Assam will be culturally discovered by Bengal and the rest of India, Hemchandra's contributions will serve as guide-posts suggesting lines of research and investigation. To repeat the words of Lt.-Col. P. R. T. Gurdon, "truly a great and good man has passed away and one whose place it will be extremely difficult to fill."

September 3, 1929.

MODERN KHASI LITERATURE

Khasi literature and history have not as yet elicited from the enlightened community the amount of attention and nourishment which they deserve. Of all the preliterate tribes of Assam the Khasis are believed to have most rapidly adapted themselves to western methods of life and manners. This has been made possible chiefly by the establishment of the headquarters of the Province in their midst, which has brought in a large concourse of cosmopolitan population. But the two factors which distinguish all advanced societies, love of literature and love of the past, are not to be generally found among the educated section of the Khasi community. They have been greatly influenced by the culture with which they have come in contact, and they hardly perceive that there is good in their own. They have desisted from building a new structure upon the old, nor have they made any organised attempt to lay the foundation of their cultural progress which will serve as a link between the past and the present.

It is a well-known fact that Khasi literature is of very recent origin, there having been no alphabet or any systematic method of recording facts and impressions before it was introduced through the enterprising zeal of Welsh Missionaries. Under these circumstances, the literary activities of the educated class can be directed towards establishing the nucleus of a national literature which will conserve their fast disappearing traditions and customs, and which will eventually supply the raw material, and even the inspiration to future generations of original and artistic workers. For this purpose the work that should be taken up immediately can be stated as follows :

The folktales that are now and then repeated by men and women of the older type should be collected and preserved. The Khasis are now passing through a period of transition from the old order to the new, and persons who represent the former are gradually dying out, and in the course of a few decades, the Khasis will fall victims to that level uniformity which has been rather a dreadful sequence of the processes of civilisation. The folktales will perpetuate the customs and manners of days gone by, and will serve as a cement between the past and the present. The value of folktales for purposes of sociological and anthropological investigations is immense. Some Khasi folktales with English renderings have been incorporated in Lt.-Col. P. R. T. Gurdon's monograph on the tribe, and some are available in English form in Mrs. Raffey's delightful little book. But one will admit that they represent only an infinitesimal proportion of the total mass of folktales actually in circulation.

Besides the folktales, the legends and traditions of the people should be collected in their unadulterated and unsophisticated form. The Khasis unfortunately do not possess any recorded history, and these traditions afford the only materials which will help the future historian to reconstruct the past of the country, where warriors have fought, and where the mighty hordes of the Kashmirian invader Lalitaditya are said to have been vanquished by the charms rather than by the valour of the women of the *Stri-rajya*, the kingdom of females, to which the contiguous territories of the Khasi and Jaintia Hills are supposed to have the closest identity.* A history of the Khasi states jointly, and of each of the states separately, has become a desideratum. The traditional information will be greatly helpful in compiling such a history.

As in other countries, the Khasis also possess their own repertory of national songs and ballads recounting tribal feuds and the exploits of their tribal chieftains. These, if collected in their native garb, will make up to a great extent the deficiency arising from the total absence of written chronicles. We are told there was one ballad-singer named Haridhan Singha, who, with his harp, brought down tears from the eyes of his hearers in the neighbourhood of Mawphlang. Such a minstrel or gleeman would have been welcomed in the halls of lords and ladies in days gone by. But alas, the age of chivalry is gone !

However illiterate or 'preliterate' a tribe may be, it has in circulation a number of apt sayings, precepts and proverbs which represent the accumulated wisdom of the people, treasured down from father to son. In moments of hesitation, dilemma, indecision or excitement, the recollection or recital of such a saying or proverb has proved to be of the highest value amongst all peoples of the world. The Khasi proverbs represent the indigenous methods of solving or interpreting critical problems in life, and hence they are imbued with all the elements of a national literature, though they are not without some flavour of universal interest.

* Calcutta Review, Volume XLV, May, 1867, *Ancient Assam.*

In the paucity of materials regarding the history of the Khasi Hills, the enterprising historian is compelled to transcend the limits of the Khasi region, and seek for information in the literature and records of neighbouring territories. The chronicles and inscriptions of Jaintia Hills will afford glimpses into the history of the Khasi Hills as well. The systematic chronicles of the Ahom kings of the Brahmaputra Valley and the records of the Koch kings contain numerous references to the Assam-Khasi relations of olden times.* These invaluable sources of information should be collected and preserved, and a vigorous search should be made for revelations of a similar character.

Most of the items in the above list represent the traditional folklore of the Khasi people, which, if preserved in a written form, will establish the requisite background and even the foundation of all future literary activities. But in the short space of half-a-century or so the Khasis have built up the nucleus of a literature however meagre and scanty it may be. Of the workers, mention may be made of Rahdhon Singh Berry, Rabon Sing, Jeebon Roy, Nissor Sing, Sibcharan Roy, Chandranath Roy, Hajom Kishore Sing, Homiwell Lyngdoh and Mondon Bareh.

We should not leave out the selfless workers of the Welsh Mission, whose translation of the Holy Bible and other treatises have helped to lay the foundation of Khasi literature. Of them the names of John and Hugh Roberts, the compilers of a number of popular

* See *U Lurshat* for July to November, 1926, for Professor S. K. Bhuyan's series of articles on the Assam-Khasi relations compiled from old Assamese records.

books ; W. Williams, editor of the first Khasi periodical, and of John Ceredig Evans who has been editing with untiring devotion one of the oldest Khasi periodicals, *U Nongialam Khristan,* stand pre-eminent,. The journalistic enterprises of James Joy Mohan Nichols-Roy, Wilson Reade, Rai Sahib Hormurai Diengdoh, Idon Kha, Siang Blah, Sibcharan Roy, Monmotho Nath, Lowell Gatphoh and Shai Rabooh have served to create a reading public among the Khasis.

It should be noted that literary pursuits in the Khasi Hills have certain encouraging factors which are absent in those of the Brahmaputra Valley. As an off-shoot of the peculiar matriarchal system obtaining in the Khasi Hills, female emancipation here is a long-established fact, whereby women are not excluded from any programme of national regeneration. The beneficent activities of the various Missions, especially the one connected with the Welsh Presbyterian Church, have led to the establishment of schools in several parts of the Khasi Hills, where a larger percentage of girls are receiving their education than is possible in the plains where the reformer or educationist has to fight an uphill battle before he can override obstructive time-honoured customs. These educated girls form a large proportion of the reading public in the Khasi Hills.

The Siems or semi-independent native chiefs with their extensive resources can be regarded as potential patrons of literature and of historical investigations. When we remember that in the East as well as in the West, literature and poetry have flourished under the patronage of lords and princes, the munificent co-operation of the Siems in this useful channel of national activity has yet remained an untapped avenue of encouragement. There is also the spirit of patriotism inherent in the Khasi blood, in however latent a form it may be, which can be evoked and brought to bear upon the creation and growth of their national literature.

Of the present workers in the strictly literary field the name of U Soso Tham stands pre-eminently distinguished. His poems are imbued with the native simplicity of the Khasi Hills and their people. The magic charm of the Khasi surroundings are meet nurse for a poetic child, and they should have produced a Scott or a Robert Burns long long ago. Dr. J. D. Anderson, who served Assam for such a length of time, referred to the poetic potentiality of the hills of Assam when he wrote,—"Yet here the blue hills that frame the Brahmaputra Valley are clad with noble forest, filled in spring with odorous bloom, above which soar flashing and nameless snowy peaks, which anywhere else in the world would be the subject of legend and poetry".*

U Soso Tham was born in 1873 at Cherrapunjee, which has a world-wide reputation for its heaviest rainfall. He comes from the old Khasi clan of Tham. The picturesque sights and sounds, and the roaring cataracts in the neighbourhood of Cherrapunjee early imbibed the young Tham with the riotous revelry and mystic splendour natural to such surroundings, and these he has brought out in his poems of maturer years. The early necessity of earning his bread led Mr. Tham

* *The Assam Borderland* published in the *Indian World* for December, 1910, Volume XII.

to move from place to place in the Khasi Hills, and after fourteen years of a wandering life as a village schoolmaster, he came finally to Shillong, the capital of Assam, where he has been serving as a teacher for the last twenty-three years. In his personality Mr. Tham embodies a combination of the spirit of western culture and the stolid simplicity and straightforwardness of a Khasi clansman : and though he has accepted the light emanating from the Cross at Calvary, his patriotism has led him to an overwhelming bias for the manners and traditions of his nativeland.

The manifold duties of a school teacher and a father of a large family have not allowed Mr. Tham to devote himself entirely to the worship of the Muses. What we have lost in opulence and variety is made up, as in the case of Gray, by the chiselled polish of his verses. Besides, the atmosphere is not yet ripe for a continuous outpouring of poetic effusions. In Hellenic conception the poet and the prophet were one in their inspiration and performance, the same word *Vates* indicating both. But in one respect the two classes of mortals or immortals are not placed in the same category. The prophet's message becomes more vehement and trenchant when he confronts opposition, callousness or indifference; while the poet's fire dies out when the atmosphere is not responsive, and his contemporaries are not in a position to correctly gauge the depth of his message. U Soso Tham has been born an age too early. His countrymen have not as yet been trained to appreciate the inner beauty of his poetry. In such an atmosphere even the most poetically-minded genius will languish for want of inspiration and stimulus for self-expression.

But what little he has done in the field of Khasi poetry has been of the nature of a pioneer work, for before him no other person had taken to the pursuit of Khasi poetry in a serious manner. As time goes on, a history of Khasi poetry will have to be written, and there the name of U Soso Tham will figure as the harbinger of a new age in the cultural life of his countrymen. His poems have the *naivette* of ballads, and hence they have been sung by the educated and the uneducated alike. They have a catchiness which the reader or hearer can scarcely resist. They represent Khasi life and manners and depict their sorrows and sufferings, with all the pathos of the short and simple annals of the poor. The environs of Shillong and Cherrapunjee which have been an attraction to visitors of all nationalities and countries have yielded forth their inherent charm and beauty in the magic lines of this unassuming Robby Burns of the Khasi Highlands. He has translated a number of popular English poems, where he has been able to retain intact their original charm and beauty.

It is a well-known fact that there has been no regular Khasi poetry before Mr. Tham. His services in its foundation have been a far more difficult task than one can conceive. There was no prosody in Khasi; and Mr. Tham, after studying the metrical laws of English poetry, had to evolve a law for himself. The necessity for putting the symbol *u* or *ka* before almost every noun, and *jing* and *nong* before an abstract noun, and a noun of agent respectively, leads to the multiplication of words of the same sound, producing a monotony which the Khasi versifier has assiduously to avoid. Besides, the preponderance of monosyllabic words in the Khasi language makes it practically impossible to adopt any metrical law based on accentuation. The only possible recourse is the syllabic system which must be punctuated by rhythm and variety. The last eleven years which cover the poetical period of Mr. Tham's life have been devoted to the formulation of the laws of Khasi prosody; and his poems, necessarily few, embody the results of his long-pursued pioneer efforts. Mr. Tham's non-poetical works include his translation of Aesop's fables which has served as a model of Khasi prose style, and his initiation of the Khasi monthly *U Lurshai* of which he was the editor for the first three years, after which he retired leaving its management to the able hands of Mr. Wilson Reade.

Mr. Tham's poems are all of a lyrical nature. In fact, at this pioneer stage there is greater room for a lyrical poet like Mr. Tham, than for an ambitious and sustained epical genius whose appreciation involves the necessity of some amount of presupposed knowledge, coupled with some training on the part of the readers. Mr. Tham has sown the seed which will grow into a gigantic tree, whose branching foliage will shelter hordes of kindred spirits in ages to come.

June 4, 1928.

MANIPURI SAHITYA PARISHAD

Ladies and gentlemen, I am thankful to the organisers for having asked me to inaugurate the present general session of the Manipuri Sahitya Parishad thereby giving me an opportunity to see for myself your great and beautiful country and to meet my old friends and acquaintances. Manipur has formed part of my dreams since my early childhood, and I have been greatly charmed by your history and culture. As a Professor at the Cotton College, Gauhati, I came in contact with a large number of Manipuri young men whose refined manners, affability and courtesy, and patriotic love of their country made a deep impression upon my mind. I had the good fortune of personally meeting the late ruler of Manipur, His Highness Shri-Shri Panchayukta Chura Chand Singha Maharaja Bahadur. I have also come in contact with several of your reputed scholars whose keen desire to unravel their country's glorious past was visible at every utterance they made. I have also witnessed the exquisite performances of Manipuri artists, singers and dancers, and have been amazed at the fine textures woven by your sisters and mothers. I have therefore been longing in my heart of hearts to visit your picturesque and ancient valley. And so when I received the kind invitation from Professor Hawaibam Ranbir Singh, Secretary of the Manipuri Sahitya Parishad, that I should inaugurate the present session I readily accepted the offer. I therefore thank you again for the honour and opportunity which you have been so generously pleased to bestow upon me.

I must congratulate you at the outset on the establishment of a literary and cultural organisation in the shape of the Manipuri Sahitya Parishad. It is brimful of possibilities not only for Manipur and Assam, but for the whole of India. The genius of the Manipuris has unfolded itself in diverse ways, both in the arts of war and of peace; and it should be the foremost duty of the Sahitya Parishad to acquaint the world with the salient features of your culture and civilisation in order that their vitalising elements may lead to revivification and reorientation in matters where the soil is suitable for improvement and progress.

The civilisation of Manipur has been moulded by the fertility and green verdure of your valley surrounded on all sides by high hills and mountains; it has been invigorated by the life of the sturdy races living on your borders. Vaisnavism, introduced into your valley more than two hundred years ago, has added a new element of enlightenment and edification to your receptive progressive mind. it has besides served as the bridge of religious fellowship between India and Manipur—thanks to the farsighted policy of your great king Gharib Newaz.

The beauty of Manipur did not fail to attract the attention of the inhabitants of India in olden times. It finds a place in the great Indian epic Mahabharata, according to which the Pandava prince Arjuna passed some time in Manipur where he fell in love with Chitrangada, daughter of King Chitrabhanu of Manipur. According to ancient Indian traditions Babrubahan, son of Arjuna and Chitrangada, was the founder of the ruling dynasty of the Manipuris.

The political history of Manipur bears ample evidence of its vitality and capacity for recoupment. Your fertile valley and its attendant charms had excited the cupidity of your neighbours who invaded your territories and brought misery and desolation upon the hapless inhabitants. Manipur has also served as a gateway to India, and invading hordes have crossed your borders in order to reach the Indian mainland.

It must be admitted that the Manipuris had stood their ordeals well. Temporary reverses had failed to unnerve them, and they soon established themselves in their old prestige and power. As you all know Manipur has acquired a distinct individuality to-day as a part and parcel of the sovereign republic of India.

The doings of your monarchs and the exploits of your warriors have been recorded in your chronicles known as Ningthaurols. You will be gratified to know that the two sister states of India, Assam and Manipur, alone possess written accounts of their past, the former in their Buranjis and the latter in their Ningthaurols. One of the first duties of the Parishad should be to collect the chronicles, and to edit and publish them in their original form, and with their English translations if possible. It will be seen that besides throwing light on wars and embassies the Ningthaurols reveal many aspects of the social life and eocnomic condition of the people of Manipur. Several Ningthaurols were translated by Shri Nithor Nath Banerji for the use of Mr. T. C. Hodson, author of *The Meitheis;* and some have seen the light of day through the enterprise of Manipur scholars. But the richness of the prospective harvest requires a larger number of reapers and gleaners.

Captain R. B. Pemberton, author of the *Report on the Eastern Frontier of India*, during his residence in Manipur about the year 1832, had a Shan chronicle translated into Manipuri. The book contains a detailed narrative of the history of the Shans before their invasion of Assam under Sukapha. The members of the American Baptist Mission reported some years ago that they had come across several indigenous chronicles in Manipuri dealing with the Assam-Manipur relations of ancient times. A vigorous search should be made for all these manuscripts, and they should be collected and deposited in the library of the Sahitya Parishad.

The study of the chronicles will have to be supplemented by that of your traditions, folk-songs and folktales. There must be numerous stories of your heroes and heroines circulated amongst the people, some being in verse forms or ballads. Traditions should not be discarded on the ground that they are not authentic materials. They reveal the light in which certain events of the past have been viewed by your unsophisticated people. Your folktales also posses an enormous value in interpreting the mind and the sufferings of your people. The romantic story of Khamba and Thoibi has inspired many a work of painting and drama. Your proverbs or wise sayings deserve similar treatment as they enshrine the wisdom of your people based on their age-long experiences. The heart of a nation beats through its folk literature; and a philosopher has wisely said,—"Give me the folktales and ballads of a people and I shall tell you what the people are".

You shall also have to think of establishing a

museum as an annexe to your Parishad, where you can deposit your ancient treasures,—manuscripts, inscriptions, old articles used in domestic life and religious ceremonies, articles belonging to your eminent men and women of the past, ancient relics and other specimens of your art and industry, so that by looking at the collections a visitor may form a picture of the achievements of the Manipuris in different spheres of human activity. A study of your ancient monuments and ruins should also engage the serious attention of the Parishad.

A very rich mine of information is embodied in the records of the East India Company, specially with regard to the history and resources of Manipur, and its relations with the British. Manipur first came in contact with the E.I.C. about the year 1762 when Mr. Verelst led a British contingent to give succour to its ruler Maharaja Jai Singha. The late Mr. A. F. M. Abdul Ali compiled a short account of Manipur's early relations with the British with the help of the materials obtained from the old records as had been done by several authors preceding him. These documents are preserved in the Record Room of the Assam Secretariat at Shillong, the Bengal Record Room at Calcutta, the National Archives of India at New Delhi and the India Office Library at London. I would suggest that some scholar should be deputed to study the Manipur records at the above depositories; he should be given facilities to prepare transcripts, abstracts and press-lists with a view to their publication later. Two volumes of these records have already been published, the first one in 1859 and the second in 1870. I have dealt with the subject of Manipur records in my book *Early British Relations with Assam*, published by the Government of Assam.

It is gratifying to note that Manipur has been well represented in printed books and articles written by English, Manipuri, Assamese and Bengali authors; and Sir Charles James Lyall, sometime Chief Commissioner of Assam, had claimed 'that the Manipuris have received no small share of attention in the past, and that the interest shown in them by investigators compares favourably with that roused by the inhabitants of many other more accessible parts of India.'—Introduction to Hodson's *Meitheis*. The Sahitya Parishad should take up the work of compiling a complete list of the books and articles about Manipur so that an investigator may know what has already been done and what still remains to be done. The nucleus of such a list or bibliography is to be found in Hodson's *Meitheis* and *Naga Tribes of Manipur*, and in my two books *Early British Relations with Assam* and *Anglo-Assamese Relations*. There are also some valuable bibliographies in the several monographs by Mills, Hutton and Smith.

The programme of work to be accomplished by the Sahitya Parishad can preferably be drawn up on the lines of the desiderata set forth in the second bulletin of the Assam Government Department of Historical and Antiquarian Studies, and modifications can be made where necessary. I would even suggest that some energetic scholars from Manipur should visit that Department, the Assam Provincial Museum and the Kamarupa Anusandhan Samiti at Gauhati, and the Asam Sahitya Sabha at Jorhat, and also the Asiatic Society of Bengal and the Bangiya Sahitya Parishad at Calcutta, in order to form some idea of the work normally carried on in an institution established for the furtherance of historical and literary studies.

I must however point out that the execution of the programme suggested above will require a steady and continuous supply of scholars who must be prepared to devote themselves wholeheartedly to the work without any consideration of personal profit or advantage. The work is an uphill one, and patience, industry and disinterestedness will be very much in demand. The main-spring of action on the part of your workers should be a spiritual one : they should remember that a common heritage is the cementing bond of the different members of a race, and no factor is so very powerful in preserving the solidarity of a people than their acquaintance and realisation of the redeeming features of this common heritage.

Manipur is a small country with an area of about 9,000 square miles and a population of about six lakhs. This smallness should not dishearten you in the least. A small country has the supreme advantage of intensively looking after its individual members, or organising them on an effective footing and of bringing the message of progress to every home and person. In the ultimate evaluation of a nation's greatness what weighs most prominently is the height of the mind and the depth of the soul, and not necessarily glamorous achievements in the material sphere. The words of the late Mr. David Lloyd George, Prime Minister of England, can be reproduced in this connection,—"The world owes much to little nations and to little men....The greatest art of the world was the work of little nations. The most enduring literature of the world came from little nations. The greatest literature of England came from her when she was a nation of the size of Belgium fighting a great Empire. The heroic deeds that thrill humanity through generations were the deeds of little nations fighting for their freedom. Ah, yes, the salvation of mankind came from a little nation. God has chosen little nations as the vessels by which He carries the choicest wines to the lips of humanity, to rejoice their hearts, to exalt their vision, to stimulate and to strengthen their faith". I hope to be excused for giving this quotation at length.

It will not be out of place to mention here what the little Manipuri nation has achieved. It has attained a great deal of fame in India, and to some extent in the world, by the beautiful performances of its dancers who are adding a new feature to the form and pattern of Bharata-nrittyam or classical Indian dancing. But the music and dancing of the Manipuris constitute only one single—though a very unique item of their culture. There are other important features which will excite similar amazement if their significance is properly brought home to the people of the world. As we have already said the Manipuris have cultivated the arts of war side by side with those of peace. The manly game of polo is believed to have originated in Manipur, and it is still being practised with zest by Manipuri stalwarts. Wrestling with tigers and buffaloes, and manly scuffles, known as *malla-yuddhas,* have continued to be a favourite pastime of the Manipuris. They are also deft masters in the handling of the spear. Dramaturgy is the special hobby of the Manipuris; and spectators of their dramatic performances have told me that they have not seen the like in any other place. The paintings of Manipuri artists have a delicacy and sweetness which are beyond the expression of words. Manipuri women have been enjoying a freedom which their sisters in India have failed to attain even up to the present day. Their activities are not confined to the four walls of their domestic life, they go out freely for purposes of petty trades mainly in the sale of the products of their own hands. They weave fine and durable textures where colours are assembled in the most attractive manner. At the same time Manipuri women have shown their gallantry and valour in desperate and critical situations. The combination of love of art and martial ardour which is so characteristic of the Manipuris reminds us of what Pericles, the great Athenian statesman and orator, had said of his fellow-citizens,—"We are lovers of beauty without extravagance, and lovers of wisdom without unmanliness."

But Assam and Manipur have both suffered because the great and singular traits of our life and civilisation are not generally known to the outside world. In Assam, on the banks of the Brahmaputra and in the territories lying on its fringes, we have produced a civilisation which is unique in its character owing to the peculiar georgraphy of the area and the character of its inhabitants who are of different origins, and who follow different customs and speak different languages. In living together for ages we have been subjected to reciprocal influences. This indispensable assimilation has led to the evolution of a culture which is dominated by exreme liberalism, a realistic outlook, an emphasis on essentials, and versatility and vigour. Though we have been living in a hinterland, cut off from the main tide of life in Northern and Southern India, still we have been able to receive and imbibe the best that India has to give. While we have received freely we have not been able to give freely, with the result that the impact of our civilisation has not been felt so perceptibly by the rest of India.

It was the great Chinese philosopher Confucius who said that the superior man blames himself while the inferior man blames others. We have therefore to blame ourselves if we have not been able to communicate the message of our civilisation to our countrymen in India. I am confident that India will be stronger, both socially and politically, if there flows into its life the light emanating from Eastern India.

An incessant output of books and articles will be able to place our history and culture in the proper perspective. But a more potent instrument will be the establishment of an instituion somewhere in Assam for the specific purpose of giving facilities to outside students and scholars to study our life, manners and customs ; and to home students to know their compatriots from the west. The visitor alumni of the institution will go to the villages and see first-hand the life lived by the masses. Concentration in towns may be useful for detached studies, but the real heart of Assam beats in the villages, far from the madding crowd's ignoble strife. Is it possible for a fashionable from Lucknow to conceive of the Buddhist Phakials near Jaipur and Margherita, of the Buddhist Khamptis near Sadiya, of the Nagas near Mokokchang, or of the Garos near Tura ? Similarly, visits to Barpeta, Kaliabar, Sotia, Majuli and Dhakuakhana, Sualkuchi and Imphal will reveal pictures which inhabitants of Delhi could hardly ever dream. These first-hand studies should be supplemented by lectures in the class-rooms of the institution. This institution may be called Purba-bharati as its primary object will be the diffusion of knowledge about Eastern India. May I request the Manipuri Sahitya Parishad to bear the dream of Purba-bharati in their mind? Assam has always looked towards India for guidance and inspiration; it should now be the turn for India to cast its eyes towards the east, to our Pragjyotish, the land of early enlightenment.

It would be a glaring omission if a man hailing from Tekhau-Laipak and speaking before an audience at Imphal, the capital of Meithei-Laipak, fails to say a few words about the relations of the two countries Assam and Manipur, specially on an occasion like the present. Manipur first emerges in the written accounts of Assam in connection with the conquering expeditions of King Naranarayana of Cooch Behar and his brother Prince Sukladhwaja. They overran the territories to the south of Assam. The Raja of Manipur is reported to have established friendship with Cooch Behar by promising to pay a handsome tribute in money and elephants. The accounts become fuller from the latter part of the eighteenth century both in the Assamese Buranjis and the Manipuri Ningthaurols, and they centre round the two visits paid to Assam by Jai Singha Karta-Maharaja of Manipur, first, about the year 1767, and again in 1790.

During his first visit to the capital of Assam, which was then situated at Rangpur, near Sibsagar, Jai Singha sought military aid from Swargadeo Rajeswar Singha, king of Assam, to expel the Burmese who had taken possession of Manipur. This request was supported by the offer of the princess Kuranganayani—the Takhao-Leima of the Ningthaurols, whom the Assam king married and raised to the status of his principal consort. A large army was despatched to Manipur, but it had to return having lost its way in the jungles. A second expedition sent under more favourable auspices succeeded in reinstating Jai Singha on his ancestral throne.

King Rajeswar Singha died in 1769, and was succeeded by his brother Lakshmi Singha, during whose reign the Morans first raised the standard of revolt. The king was imprisoned, and the government passed into the hands of the insurgents. The royalists now instituted measures for the recovery of the throne for Lakshmi Singha, and the services of the widowed queen Kuranganayani were harnessed to promote their plans. She initiated the campaign by inflicting a deadly blow upon the person of the rebel leader Ragha Moran, and it was soon followed by the massacre of his principal associates. Lakshmi Singha was restored to the throne, and honours and gifts were heaped on Kuranganayani in recognition of her intrepidity and valour.

The Morans continued their hostilities during the reign of Lakshmi Singha's successor Gaurinath Singha. The king fled from the capital and lived as a fugitive in Nowgong and Gauhati. He despatched messengers to Manipur to request Jai Singha to come to Assam with a detachment to render help in the suppression of the rebels. The grateful king of Manipur revisited Assam accordingly, and took an active part in the attempt to expel the Morans from the neighbourhood of the capital.

Jai Singha's visits to Assam exercised a far-reaching influence in promoting friendly relations between the two states. A section of his camp-followers settled in the villages near Sibsagar where they are to be found even till this day. Kuranganayani occupies an honoured place in the pantheon of Assam's heroic women. A tank was excavated in her name near Gaurisagar which is still known as Magalu-jiyekar Pukhuri. The Manipuri chronicles refer to Jai Singha's successful passage through the elephant ordeal instituted by the Assam monarch Rajeswar Singha to ascertain whether the fugitive was a real Raja or an imposter. On the night before the ordeal Jai Singha saw a dream in which he was told that he would come out unscathed provided he promised to introduce the worship of Radha and Govinda after his restoration to the Manipuri throne. After the systems prevailing in Assam, Jai Singha introduced land surveys in Manipur, excavated large-size tanks, and established smithies for making muskets and cannon. Gharib Newaz had already popularised the Bhagavata in Manipur by taking the original manuscripts from Assam; and this fact is recorded in the Manipuri chronicle *Ahanba*.

The sentiments of esteem and friendship which the Assamese entertained towards the Manipuris come out in the utterences of King Rajeswar Singha's minister. "The Manipuri Raja," said the ministers, "is descended of old from Babrubahana. He is a Kshattriya, and there is no doubt about it. Your Majesty should marry the princess Kuranganayani.........If Your Majesty can restore the Manipuri Raja to his kingdom, your fame, virtue and glory will be resounded in your own land as well as in other regions." During the second visit, Assam's prime minister Purnananda Buragohain alluded to the existing friendship between the two states,— "The predecessors of our present sovereign had been enjoying the friendship of the former chiefs of Manipur.........If the Raja succeeds in extirpating the enemy then his triumph, virtue and renown will increase and our old friendship will be further strengthened." The prime minister then recited two verses, which can be translated as follows,—

> "The pious are ever the agents
> to relieve the virtuous of their calamities;
> Of elephants that are stuck fast in the mud
> an elephant is the only extricator."

A detailed account of Maharaja Jai Singha and princess Kuranganayani was compiled by me from materials derived from Assamese and Manipuri sources several years ago, and it has been inserted as Chapters 7, 8, 9 and 10 of my history of the reign of Rajeswar Singha which is awaiting publication. The Manipuri chronicles, mostly printed, were placed at my disposal by the Manipuri students of Cotton College. The Assamese chronicle *Tungkhungia Buranji* contains a detailed account of Assam-Manipur relations of the eighteenth century; the original Assamese version and its English translation have both been published by the Department of Historical and Antiquarian Studies; and glimpses of Assam-Manipur relations are also available in my book *Anglo-Assamese Relations*.

It is a truism to say that as long as the present disposition of the earth remains and as long as the primordial hills and flowering valleys shine as before,

Assam and Manipur will have to play their role as eternal neighbours. There will be occasions of joy as well as of sorrow, and the two states will have to remain by the side of each other in remembrance of the mutual aid offered in the days of Karta-Maharaja Jai Singha. Tekhao-laipak and Meithei-laipak are one and indivisible ; we rise and fall together. Let the realisation of the indispensable necessity of mutual co-operation govern the progressive relations of the two states. The object of the Manipuri Sahitya Parishad should be to explore the details of Assam-Manipur relations to strengthen the foundations of our enduring friendship and good-will.

The Manipuri Sahitya Parishad will be engaged in the most laborious task of collecting facts relating to the history and culture of Manipur with the ultimate purpose of making a better Manipur, in point of enlightenment, solidarity and moral grandeur. In interpreting the facts you should be absolutely fair and impartial, and there should be no touch of propaganda whatsoever. The blunders which Manipur had committed in the past—and there is no country which has not committed mistakes—will have to be scrutinized in order to avoid their repetition in future. In the same way the strong points and redeeming features must also be brought out fully to serve as an inspiration to the rising generations of Manipuris. In short your motto should be,—"We should weaken our weaknessess and strengthen our strong points".

The propagation of moral principles and noble ideas should also be the objective of the Manipuri Sahitya Parishad. No country can stand on its feet for long if its people are bereft of the idea of what is ethically right and what is ethically wrong, and if they are not prepared to practise this great idea. Society will soon turn chaotic if its members do not try to act on moral principles both in their private and public life, if virtue and merit remain unrecognised, and if wickedness and villainy be tolerated and hoodwinked. Speaking of decadent Rome the poet Juvenal had said,—"In Rome, it is money and not character that counts". The Manipuri Sahitya Parishad will justify its existence and its labours only if it succeeds in generating a love for righteousness, disinterestedness, helpfulness and charity, for the end of all human institutions is the establishment of amity, social harmony, and spiritual uplift; and it has been the aim of all philosophers and saints, and it has been emphasized forcibly in the Vaisnava scriptures which are the special subjects of study by your countrymen.

Speaking at Imphal on the eve of the visit to this land of the Prime Minister of India Shri Jawaharlal Nehru, I can not but allude to the warmth of affection which that great patriot and statesman entertains for Assam and her neighbours. Only a few days ago, he has sent a substantial amount for the relief of the distressed in Manipur; and his visit, planned in spite of his multifarious preoccupations, shows the love he bears to us in Eastern India.

With these few words I inaugurate the 1952 session of the Manipuri Sahitya Parishad hoping that this tiny sapling will grow into a colossal tree with its leaves and foliages covered with blossoms and flowers emitting their sweet fragrance to the surrounding regions.

October 1952.

BANIKANTA KAKATI

The sudden demise of the distinguished savant of Assam Dr. Banikanta Kakati has cast a gloom over the hearts of all people. The lamentable event took place this morning, Saturday, the 15th November 1952, at his home at Rehabari, Gauhati. He was alright till this morning, and had taken his usual early morning stroll. Having returned home at about six he felt giddy, a convulsion followed, and he breathed his last when he was carried to his bed, before any kind of medical help could be given. As usual, he had gone out last evening and had returned home hale and hearty. His end has been so unexpected that his numerous friends and acquaintances have been deeplv mortified and taken aback by the melancholy event.

Dr. Kakati had not been keeping good health for some months past, and the death of his wife two months ago, just at the time when he needed her most by his side, made him extremely disconsolate and he was not able to long withstand the sorrow of this bereavement.

I had been an intimate associate of Dr. Kakati for the last forty years, and in his demise I have lost a dear and esteemed friend, Assam an eminent scholar and an able interpreter of her culture and civilization, India a great philologist, and the world a devoted student of literature and learning. Men of Dr. Kakati's genius and personality are not easily repeated, and Assam will have to wait for many long years before a scholar of his eminence appears in the field again.

Dr. Kakati first emerged into limelight by his unique result in the I.A. Examination of 1913. He stood first in Calcutta University, a distinction never before attained by any Assamese student. This achievement at once proved that brilliant academic distinctions were not outside the possibilities of our country's youths. Dr. Kakati's performance created a sensation, and I still remember how widespread was the satisfaction all over Assam. We were together at the Presidency College, Calcutta. I was in the Fifth Year Class when he joined the Third Year in 1913. We lived for two years together at the Eden Hindu Hostel, and I remember how books afforded him the only pleasure, and how assiduously he kept himself aloof from other diversions and pastimes. He was of a shy and retiring disposition, but those who came in intimate contact with him were stuck by his extensive knowledge. He passed the B.A. with Honours in English in 1915, and the M.A. in English, Group A, in 1918.

About that time there was a demand sponsored by the people of the Assam Valley for the appointment of Assamese Professors in the Cotton College, Gauhati. A vacancy was created, and I was taken in to fill it in July 1918. Dr. Kakati was appointed in November 1918 in a vacancy caused by the transfer of Mr. Narendranath Chatterjee to Bengal. As we were then the only two Assamese members of the Cotton College teaching staff it was our constant endeavour to give a good account of ourselves so that the entrance of other Assamese Professors might be an easy one. We had naturally to work hard, and both of us put in more than what was ordinarily required of us.

Dr .Kakati took the M.A. Examination in English

in 1923 again, this time in Group B, which was mainly concerned with old English. He stood First Class First. His philological talents were greatly appreciated by Dr. Suniti Kumar Chatterjee, one of the examiners, and from that time on Dr. Kakati's scholarly labours drifted gradually towards linguistics and phonetics, the culmination of which was reached in his monumental work *Assamese, Its Formation and Development.*

Dr. Kakati made his first *debut* as a critic by his article on the element of pathos in literature which was published in a collection of essays read before the Assam Students Association. About the year 1919, Srijut Ambikagiri Rai Chowdhury brought out a monthly paper *Chetana*; and we decided that Dr. Kakati should deal with old Assamese literature and myself with modern Assamese literature. Dr. Kakati's essays on a number of old Assamese classics at once created a new field of approach, critical and appreciative; and persons who had looked upon ancient Assamese books as materials for the entertainment of old-fashioned people now began to think that they could be brought within the ambit of high literary criticism not incomparable with the standard appreciations of classical English masters like Shakespeare, Milton and Wordsworth.

Dr. Kakati's essays at once convinced the Assamese reading public that a new genius had entered into the field of Assamese literature. It was Dr. Kakati who redeemed the nature-poet Srijut Raghunath Choudhury from comparative obscurity; and criticisms of books, both ancient and modern, came out of his pen incessantly. His older essays have been published in book form, and the new ones are still to be collected. His pioneering work in the sphere of scientific literary criticism in Assam will be one of the factors that will keep his name ever-memorable.

About the year 1920, Dr. Kakati was drawn towards the study of Assamese Vaisnavism, and the booklet written by him on the great Assamese reformer Sankardeva was published by Messrs Natesan in the Saints of India series. A few years later Dr. Kakati appeared as a dialectical contestant in a number of papers on Assamese Vaisnavism under the *non-de-plume* of Bhavananda. These articles at once proved his extensive study of the religious classics of India, and his ability to bring to bay his opponents by his depth of learning, witticisms and invectives.

Perhaps the most significant performance of Dr. Kakati was his book *Assamese, Its Formation and Development*, and I was instrumental in its publication by the Department of Historical and Antiquarian Studies of which I have been the Director. It has been favourably received not only in India and England but also in the Continent and America. This book set at rest the old stand taken by some uncritical writers that the Assamese language is a mere patois of Bengali. Dr. Kakati has amply proved that the origin, development, morphology and vocabulary of the two languages are distinct and separate. This book has remained the only authority on the subject till this day. The book obtained for Dr. Kakati the Ph.D. Degree of Calcutta University in 1935, which itself was a signal achievement as he was the first Assamese scholar to receive this degree from Calcutta. The sensation created by this success was equal only to Dr. Kakati's earlier achievement in the I.A. Examination of 1913.

As a Professor at the Cotton College Dr. Kakati became an object of veneration owing to his profound learning and his unassuming manners. He was noted for his witty remarks both among his colleagues and his students. He was a deep observer, and he refused to put up with anything which in his opinion smacked of charlatanism or intellectual frivolity.

Towards the end of 1947, Dr. Kakati became the Principal of the Cotton College. A year afterwards he could have become the D. P. I., Assam but he preferred to serve as Professor of Assamese at Gauhati University. He was in harness till this morning. As the Head of the Department of Assamese and as Dean of the Faculty of Arts of the young University of Gauhati, Dr. Kakati's guidance and direction have been of immense help in its growth and development.

In recent years Dr. Kakati published two small treatises, one on the Kalitas, and the second on the Mother Goddess Kamakhya, both of which bear evidence of his profound erudition and deep knowledge of the social and religious background of the civilisation of Eastern India. Dr. Kakati has also contributed a large number of articles and notes on different aspects of Assamese language and culture; they have been published in Oriental Journals and commemoration volumes, and also in the periodicals of Assam.

The life of such a man as Dr. Kakati will be a source of inspiration to our rising generations. He was not born with a silver spoon; and he had to struggle against enormous odds; in fact, he had to pursue his higher education with the aid of charity. But he has left behind an indelible fame, by achieving the highest distinctions that a University can offer, and by devoting himself wholeheartedly to the cause of education and learning. He has given his best to his motherland. All this has meant very hard and strenuous labour the grim character of which can be realised only by those who have worked on similar lines. But throughout the entire tenure of his life "books were his dukedom", and he has given an illustration to his countrymen of the singleminded Prospero spirit in learning and scholarship ; and as these ideals are fast disappearing owing to the impact of new forces, the example of Dr. Kakati will be enshrined and adored in the annals of his country's history. May his soul rest in peace !

November 15, 1952.
Talk broadcast from All India Radio, Gauhati.

INDIAN HISTORY CONGRESS

Ladies and gentlemen, I am grateful to you for the honour you have bestowed on me by asking me to preside over the Modern History Section at this fifteenth session of the Indian History Congress. I have been a lonely worker trying to unfold the history of an obscure corner of India. Publicity was outside the orbit of my activities as I considered work to be its own publicity; nor had limelight entered into the sphere of my achievements. But I have been animated throughout my life by a religious zeal to let the world know the great and good things of Assam which forms an integral part of Mother India. I am sure, it is in the way of recognition of my humble labours in the field of history that you have honoured me with the privilege of presiding over your deliberations.

But in taking my stand before you I am seized with a feeling which amounts almost to diffidence. I am not a professed student or a trained teacher of history like many of you assembled here. I had to earn my bread by teaching Shakespeare and Milton. But history has been my beloved pursuit to which I have consecrated all my thoughts and my energy.

Since the Indian History Congress met last at Jaipur we have lost some distinguished workers in the field of Indology. Sri Brajendranath Bandopadhyaya of Calcutta died a few months ago. His was a life of ceaseless devotion to the cause of historical learning as will be known from his numerous papers read at the different sessions of the Indian Historical Records Commission, and his contributions to *Bengal: Past and Present,* and the vernacular journals of Bengal, and his history of the Begums of Bengal published in English.

Assam has also her own share of bereavement. Only six weeks ago we lost Dr. Banikanta Kakati, a brilliant product of Calcutta University, a literary critic and philologist of rare acumen, and an interpreter of the social and religious history of Eastern India.

In January 1952, died Srijut Radhakanta Handiqui at the ripe old age of 95. He made liberal donations for promoting the cause of education and learning, and it was through his munificence that the Department of Historical and Antiquarian Studies in Assam obtained a permanent building for the location of its office and library of manuscripts and printed books.

Amongst the notable achievements, mention may be made of Colonel R. H. Phillimore's two volumes of the Historical Records of the Survey of India, packed with valuable information and citations of sources which can be explored by generations of scholars interested in the early phase of British administration in India. Dr. N. K. Singhà has brought out the long-awaited volume of records containing the correspondence between Fort William and India House. Though it is the story of the administration of Governor Verelst, 1767-68, the records, in the words of the reviewer Prof. P. C. Gupta, are indispensable for writing an adequate history of the Company's early rule in Bengal. The Ministry of Defence are bringing out two volumes of the history of the Indian Armed Forces in World War II. Though there have been several publications relating to the history of the Indian Army the present series represents a laudable attempt to write a part of that history in a systematic manner under the direct auspices of our countrymen. India is awaiting the result of the project initiated by the Government of India for compiling a history of the Freedom Movement.

The history of the period with which the section is mainly concerned has been dealt with by many distinguished historians both British and Indian. The materials at our disposal are voluminous and almost endless. Correspondence played an important part in the Government of the East India Company on account of the distance between the administrators in India and the authorities at home. It is a good sign that steps have been taken to publish some of these materials which can be used for scientific reconstruction of Indian History by future investigators.

The main trends of the history of this period have been examined by scholars undoubtedly more qualified than myself, and I cannot add a word to them. But I feel that one aspect has not been brought out in a pronounced manner. Now that we are independent we can afford to engage ourselves in self-scrutiny in order that this self-scrutiny may produce a beneficent result in future. We have to answer the question, how was it that a handful of foreign traders could establish their political supremacy in India so rich in resources and man-power? Some will attribute their success to a superior navy and a superior strategy. Though the foreigners could draw upon their naval strength the conflicts were not coastal or maritime; and foreign strategy was effective because the soil was fertile for its successful implantation. How was it that the Marathas, the Rajputs and the Sikhs, Hyderabad and Mysore could not pool their resources together for counteracting the designs of the foreigners, and for establishing a strong power to replace that of the tottering Timurids ?

The answer leads me to a story in the old history of Assam. King Rajeswar Singha, 1751-69, was sitting in his amusement pavilion watching games, contests and dances in a vast field in front of him. There was a great concourse of people, and the king was seized with the apprehension as to what the assembled crowd could not do if they aimed at any mischief. He expressed his fears to his chief executive Kirti Chandra Barbarua. The shrewd official pointed out that the king's fears were baseless as two men could never be united into one. It was India's incapacity to unite and adopt concerted measures that led to its servitude for nearly 200 years. The effect was marvellous when India offered a united resistance to its foreign masters under the inspiration and guidance of Mahatma Gandhi, culminating in the recovery of our long-lost independence in 1947. I will implore historians, scholars, poets, journalists, artists, and all and sundry, who form a part of the great Indian nation, to do all that is in their power in order to foster the spirit of unity so that India may never undergo again the consequences of disintegration and divided political ambitions. In the reconstruction of history there should be no mincing of matters and no attempt to wash out our faults ; our blunders and pitfalls should be thoroughly analysed so that their repetition may be averted. I would request them to remember the saying of Confucius : "The inferior man blames others, the superior man blames himself." Periodic introspection is good for the spiritual health of an individual as well as of a nation.

I am one of those who believe in the existence of a divine programme in all human relations and endeavours. India suffered the humiliation of enslavement, and it is a common question as to why a spiritual-minded and civilised nation like the Indians should be subjected to this humiliation. India's heritage is glorious and magnetic. It has enriched the blood of China and of South-East Asia; its message of peace and good-will has even in this age of conflicting ideologies elicited the admiration of the great countries of the world. The ocean that had girdled the Indian sub-continent had offered a barrier for its free intercourse with the western world. The West now came to India and saw for itself what India stands for; and it should be admitted that western scholars were amongst the pioneers to interpret India's culture and civilisation to the rest of mankind. India in her own way has seen for itself what the West has to give. The intense realism of western thought and practice has not failed to influence the Indian mind, and India which has been over-spiritual in the past has imbibed from the West many elements of a practical code of life. The West has not very much assimilated India's ideology till now, though there is a feeling that it is drawing their attention more pointedly as an instrument of peace and international amity. India has thus become complete, its spiritual nature being reinforced by the science and realism of the West. With this over-all completeness India is bound to emerge triumphant in its future undertakings in all spheres. It may be said that the price we paid for this contact was exorbitant. India became impoverished, but it has got a wonderful capacity for recoupment, and its eternal wealth lies in the Himalayas and the monsoons of which it can never be deprived. Besides, during this period of our western contact India has become politically unified by virtue of a common administration and a common language, and independent India has been able to march ahead with the advantages appertaining to a united territory. Let us look into the future and shape it on the basis of what we possess both in strength and in weakness.

The old conception of history has become entirely changed. History was for long a record of the transactions of the rulers; and in fact, an Assamese monarch, King Siva Singha, 1714-44, distinctly instructed his historiographer that "the histories of his predecessors should be compiled, the succession of the Ahom monarchs mentioned in detail, and that history should only contain the names and transactions of the Swargadeos or kings". Rulers are now regarded as representatives and symbols of the nation, and therefore new elements like the condition of the masses and the progress of art and literature have entered into the texture of historical reconstruction.

I for myself will not be satisfied by merely giving a picture of the externals of a nation; and I would ask historians to explore how moral superiority has led to the peace, prosperity and solidarity of a nation, and how moral degradation has been the cause of its downfall and decay. It will be seen that a country has gone to the depth of political ruination because its morals are too low, because selfishness plays an important part in the day-to-day actions of its rulers and nobles, because they can not subordinate themselves to the interests of their country. A nation may be well-equipped with all the paraphernalia of success in arms, but defeat is sure if its commanders are corrupted at the sight of an ass laden with gold coming from the opposite quarters, if its officials justify iniquities by sophistries and subterfuges, if the people lose confidence in their security, and if their expectations of justice are blurred by apprehensions to the contrary. History will show that the well-being of a nation has been dependent on an all-pervasive moral force, on rigid elimination of unjustness and selfishness in the minutest details of administration.

Of all the countries of the world, India has the greatest opportunities for the enforcement of this moral order. It has been enjoined in its scriptures and classics, in its religious code and the daily worship of the people. The great emperor Asoka engraved moral teachings in his edicts on rocks and pillars. Moral degradation on the part of India will doubtless be a nullification of our glorious heritage and culture. I will therefore ask my brother historians to emphasise on this aspect of things so that India may tread on careful grounds in order to avert the tragedies which befell us in the past.

The saints of India have not as yet received the attention they deserve at the hands of our academic historians though their lives and teachings are a very powerful instrument for the strengthening of our moral fervour and for the propagation of the message of peace and brotherhood. Their influence on the life and society of the masses has been deep, enduring and extensive; and its study will give us a genuine picture of the evolution of Indian rationalism. Monographs on each one of our saints can be compiled on scientific lines for which there are plenty of materials in the shape of contemporary literature, traditions, relics and monuments. What can be more inspiring than the fact that both Hindus and Muslims quarrelled over the possession of the mortal remains of their master Kabir for performing the funeral obsequies according to their respective customs? Similarly, men and women of different faiths, from the highest to the lowest, sought the blessings of the great Muslim saint Nizamuddin Aulia. Each of our saints, living on the droppings into his begging bowl and clad in the scantiest habiliments, was a monarch in the spiritual sphere, and his life has shed a more beneficent and far-reaching influence upon his age and posterity than that of many an anointed head of the temporal order.

In our own field of historical activities a lessening of sustained efforts has been clearly perceptible in recent years. As my predecessors have often remarked, and as we have all experienced, historical research is a matter of expense. The results are unremunerative from the economic point of view. Living is becoming gradually harder on account of the rise in the price of essential commodities. The historical worker, however earnest he may be, is tempted to abandon his unprofitable chase and take to labours where the needed money may be obtained. The great personalities who are with us till now belong practically to the past; and there is a marked paucity of devoted workers among the new generation. The Indian History Congress representing the interests of historical research should, in my opinion, take up the question of evolving practical measures which will attract talented young men to the field. Preferments in the hierarchy of academic appointments may come sometimes as a reward for original work; but this is not always the case. Preferments depend on many factors, and approved capacity for sustained work and scientific reconstruction may not always carry weight in selection to higher positions. Of course, love of learning has its own merit; but, in Shakespeare's words, we must have "our cakes and ale". The Government can come to our rescue directly, or through the numerous Universities, educational institutions and research organisations. Unless something tangible is done in this direction the genuine worker will be tempted to seek fresh woods and pastures new.

The object of the Indian History Congress is to produce an atmosphere in which historical investigations may thrive properly and steadily. Continued application to historical pursuits may appear repelling to people who have neither the time nor the equipment to engage themselves in it. The real historian's work must be supplemented by ancillary workers. They can pave the way for future historians by collecting materials and compiling works which are not purely historical. India has been very earnest and active in the domain of political warfare during the last thirty years ; many great deeds have been done, and many great patriots have worked and died in the cause of India's liberation. The accounts of these events and these patriots have not come out as profusely as they ought to have come. There are still amongst us the stalwart participants and eyewitnessess, and narratives compiled by them will be of immense value to the future historian inspite of the possibility that the narratives will be tinged with sentiments and emotions inseparable from proximity.

We may refer particularly to the history of the greatest period of the national movement, that under Mahatma Gandhi. Several biographies and some reminiscences have come out; but we wish that some academic historian will compile a history of Mahatma Gandhi and his times so that it may be a distinct work of scientific reconstruction. Amongst the co-workers and disciples of the Mahatma there is a galaxy of talents still living; and the Indian History Congress should approach them to write out their personal reminiscences in order that the spirit of the great movement with all its attendant details may be preserved and transmitted to posterity.

The great Mahatma himself is believed to be abundantly represented in his writings and in contemporary literature. But his utterances made on different occasions to different individuals and groups and the little incidents of his life occurring in different corners of India have still to be recorded. His contemporaries are not immortal, and it will be regrettable if they have to leave the world before they have handed down the story of their contacts with Mahatmaji. As you all know, soon after the Mahaparinirvana of Lord Buddha his eminent disciples gathered together at Rajagriha and recorded the Master's sayings and instructions and constituted them into the Tripitakas. I have always been wondering as to why the disciples and co-workers of Bapuji could not meet in different places and record all that they had seen and heard in their contacts with the Mahatma. Time is flitting, and there should be no delay. The resources of the sovereign republic of India are certainly more extensive than those of Ajatasatru, king of Magadha, under whose patronage the First Buddhist Council was held. The work undertaken by the Gandhi National Memorial Trust to perpetuate the living presence of Bapuji is epical, historic and unprecedented.

The greatest landmark in the history of modern India is undoubtedly the attainment of our long-lost independence preceded by a non-violent struggle in which India's moral strength was brought to full play under the leadership of the Father of the Nation. The moral outlook thus invigorated has become visible in the idealistic trends of the administration both in its domestic affairs and its foreign relations. It has synchronised with the growing popularity of Buddhism as an easily comprehensible code of correct conduct in thought, speech and action. Buddhism has come back to the land of its nativity after centuries of sojourn in neighbouring lands. The installation of the relics of the two Chief Disciples of Lord Buddha—Arahans Sariputta and Moggallano—at Sanchi Vihara last month bespeaks the fervency of India's love and respect for the message of the Tathagata. We only regret that Buddhism did not stay all the time in India. Just imagine the lessons of peace and brotherhood, of forbearance and love which generations of our countrymen would have learnt and practised, and the sorrows which would have been assuaged if the Indian mind had passed through the simple and matter-of-fact teachings enshrined in the literature of Buddhism. Signs are not wanting to show that the coming centuries will witness the rallying of the progressive mind of the world round the banner of *Ahimsa* and *Metta*—non-violence and love—which the study of Buddhism kindles in the heart of humanity.

Brother historians, I would venture to draw your attention to the inadequate representation of the subject of Indian History in the curriculum of our University studies. It does not generally find a place in the Intermediate stage; it is taken up by a limited number of students going up for the B.A. and M.A. Examinations. A large majority of our Indian students can thus obtain the highest degrees of a University with only a smattering of the knowledge of Indian History acquired during their school days. Now the Government of the country is in the hands of our own people, and every citizen must take an intelligent interest in its affairs to ensure its welfare and prosperity. But how can one do so if he does not possess a critical knowledge of the country's past on which the present is based? In this audience their are many scholars associated with different Universities, and I would request them to consider whether Indian History could not be made a compulsory subject for the Intermediate and Degree Examinations in Arts as well as in Science.

I must refer to a regrettable experience which must have fallen to the lot of us all in one shape or other. A historian, after strenuous labour on his part, unearths a fact and writes an account thereof. Another man repeats that fact in a compilation of his own without acknowledging his indebtedness. The second writer sometimes quotes the authorities, cited by the first, without having seen or consulted them for himself. I am told that an eminent Indian scholar gave up the habit of citing references lest a subsequent writer mentions them without first-hand examination. This hesitation to acknowledge one's indebtedness amounts certainly to intellectual dishonesty; and no credit should ever be given to a performance which bears evidence of this unscholarly and discourteous practice. An author is naturally reluctant to seek the protection of law for remedies against infringement of copyright; this does not mean that one should take advantage of another man's labours and appropriate the credit to himself.

As a worker in the field of Assam History I cannot resist the temptation of saying a few words about it. Assam has been an organic part of India from time immemorial. It is mentioned in the Ramayana, the Mahabharata and the Puranas, and in the classics and inscriptions of Northern India.

No Asoka pillar has yet been discovered in Assam. There are however traces to show that it had once been swayed by the influence of Buddhism. Remote from the main currents of thought in Aryyavarta, Assam has evolved a code of life in a sort of semi-isolation. The non-Aryan tribes, both inside the state and on its frontiers, have contributed towards the growth of a unique culture and civilisation. Recorded materials are plentiful, specially from the thirteenth century when the Ahoms first conquered the province. The Assamese chronicles, known as Buranjis, throw light not only on the history of Assam but on the history of India as well. There were distinct monographs on the Muslim conquerors of India compiled so early as the seventeenth century. Many phases of Indian History come out in the diplomatic letters exchanged between Assam and the Mogul courts. Some of these sources have been published; but a voluminous mass of materials is still to be published for which workers and money are urgently needed.

The story of Assam of the modern period is mostly of the same tenor as that of other parts of India. The disintegration of the Mogul empire after the death of Emperor Aurangazeb had its repercussions in Assam. King Rudra Singha, 1696-1714, after having brought the neighbouring states within his hegemony wrote letters to the Rajas of Hindusthan seeking their co-operation in his plan to invade Mogul India. In one such letter the Assam king wrote—"Reports have been received that owing to the hostile conduct of the Moguls the religion of the Vedas is not receiving any protection. If you are interested in the counteraction of this situation then you should consult your nobles and supporters and inform me of your resources and the extent to which you can help me". The Hindu Rajas wrote back that they would support the patriotic enterprise of the king of Assam as they had become tired of saluting the Moguls. Rudra Singha collected an army of four lacs, and halted for sometime at Gauhati to perfect his preparations; but he died there in August 1714, just on the eve of marching into Bengal.

His successor Siva Singha was not able to push forward the unfulfilled scheme of his ambitious father. About the year 1756, the French merchant and soldier J. B. Chevalier who had gone to Assam on a trading excursion was prevented from leaving his boat, and was made to return to Bengal without setting his foot on the soil of Assam.

Peace reigned in Assam up to the year 1769, and no European, not even the great geographer Major James Rennell was allowed to enter the kingdom.

Assam's relations with the East India Company commenced from the year 1771 when the Court of Directors first admitted the desirability of establishing a commercial intercourse and instructed the Government of Fort William to adopt the necessary measures. The relations continued till the year 1826 when Assam passed into the hands of the Company by the treaty of Yandabo, concluded on the termination of the war with the Burmese who had acquired possession of the country four years earlier.

The people of Assam were grateful to the British for having relieved them of the oppressions and ravages of the preceding period. But when they found that the British had firmly entrenched themselves in Assam having first entered it for the purpose of expelling the Burmese, they took steps, though abortively, to get rid of their new masters. "The inhabitants of Upper Assam", wrote David Scott, the first Commissioner, "are far from being reconciled to our rule, and it may be expected that the higher classes will continue to cherish hopes and engage in schemes for the re-establishment of the ancient form of Government under a native prince". Things happened as expected. There were several uprisings which were however suppressed and the principal leaders executed or sentenced to banishment. In May 1831, Scott urged that "by establishing a native prince an end will be put to the plots and intrigues, and we shall without loss of revenue avoid the odium necessarily attached to the exclusion of the royal family, the depression of the nobles, the neglect of the national religion and the disgust occasioned by frequent executions for criminal offences of a popular character". Raja Purandar Singha was in consequence installed as a tributary ruler of Upper Assam, but he was deposed in 1838 for his inability to fully pay up the stipulated amount.

During the Sepoy Mutiny, the dispossessed princes and nobles again raised their head and rallied round Purandar Singha's grandson Kandarpeswar Singha, whom they now planned to set up on the throne. The plot was soon detected ; the prince was put under detention and sent down to Bengal as an externee. Maniram Dewan who had encouraged the plot by despatching emissaries and epistles from Calcutta was arrested and hanged together with the prince's local adviser and friend Mahes Chandra Sarma Barua. Other accomplices were sentenced to transportation or imprisonment.

From the transfer of the Company's territories to the Crown in 1858, Assam enjoyed the fruits of peaceful administration though there were sporadic manifestations of discontent here and there. The Assamese put their heart and soul into the national movement under the leadership of Mahatma Gandhi. The movement permeated the masses, and women also gallantly participated in the common effort for gaining the independence of the country.

The most notable feature in the history of Assam is the fact that it had enjoyed sovereignity while the rest of India was subjected to foreign domination, and Assam was one of the last provinces to be occupied by the British. Assam was therefore able to develop itself on its own national lines. The nobles patronised literature, art and religion, and the political leaders evolved and perfected measures for the successful resistance of foreign invaders. Assam's cultural life and its social and political outlook were based on intense realism; and the manner in which its people devised methods of utilising their resources to the full advantage was an achievement of great significance. It is desirable that the versatility and vigour of the Assamese people which came into being in consequence of their long-continued independence, and which is so extensively represented in their literature and their economic and social systems should be the subject of special investigation at the hands of our historians, and it will be soon realised that the way in which Assam solved its political problems will be a source of inspiration and guidance to the rest of India.

Assam has also got its own quota of historians. Dr. John Peter Wade and Dr. Francis Buchanan-Hamilton were interested in Assam when it was still independent. After British occupation, Assam's principal historians were Capt. Pemberton, Robinson, Johnstone, Mackenzie, Col. Shakespeare, and Gait, besides a number of writers whose contributions are mostly buried in the pages of Oriental journals. Amongst the Assamese historians hention may be made of Kasinath Tamuli Phukan, Maniram Dewan, Harakanta Barua and Gunabhiram Barua, and a number of workers who are still on the stage, the most outstanding compilations in recent years being Srijut Benudhar Sharma's *Life of Maniram Dewan* and Dr. Birinchi Kumar Barua's *Cultural History of Assam*. Srijut Krishna Kanta Handiqui's book on the Jaina classic *Jasastilaka* is a remarkable contribution on the history of medieval India.

There are several institutions in Assam for the avowed purpose of promoting historical studies. The Assam Government Department of Historical and Antiquarian Studies has collected a large number of manuscripts, transcripts and rare books on Assam, and has brought out several old chronicles or Buranjis as well as constructive historical compilations. The Kamarupa Anusandhan Samiti, or the Assam Research Society, possesses a valuable collection of old Assamese manuscripts ; it also publishes a journal which is appreciated in learned circles in India. The old relics of Assam are permanently housed in the spacious halls and corridors of the Assam Provincial Museum. A number of teachers and students are engaged in historical research under the auspices of the new University of Gauhati. These four institutions are situated at Gauhati. At Shillong, the capital of the State, good work is being done by the Shillong Historical Society which holds occasional discourses on historical subjects.

I hope to be excused for the length of my reference to Assám, but I crave your indulgence because I feel that Assam has so many good things and they are so little known.

In conclusion, I would request all historians to realise the part they can effectively play in the rehabilitation of India. The destiny of our country should not be left to the hands of politicians alone. Historians are trained in estimating the unrefutable logic of geography, and the operation of the law of cause and effect. They can take a detached view of situations, and can predict the shape of things to come. This training and this detachment should be harnessed for the correct evaluation of problems the real character of which cannot always be gauged by politicians who are absorbed too deeply in the discovery of immediate solutions and remedies.

Let the aim and purpose of historians be extended towards a wider horizon; and instead of merely providing materials for teaching and discussion in classrooms, let them also plant milestones to record our achievements, guide-posts to direct us on the road to our destination, and signs of caution to warn us against impending catastrophes.

Gwalior, December 1952.

ASAM SAHITYA SABHA

Ladies and gentlemen, I thank you from the bottom of my heart for the honour you have bestowed upon me by asking me to preside over the twenty-second session of the Asam Sahitya Sabha. It is an institution unaffected by any evanescent element, or differences of race and community, or of wealth and poverty. It is primarily meant for the efflorescence and unfolding of the eternal ideals and aspirations of the people of Assam and for the dissemination of the vitalising elements of their culture and civilisation to the rest of mankind. The life of the Assamese people depends on the well-being of the Sabha, and they will not thrust it away from their bosom even on the pain of death. I thank you once again for enabling me to serve it as best I can within the scope of my limited opportunities.

On an occasion like this, we owe a tribute to the memory of the devotees and promoters of Assamese literature who have left this world during recent years: Lokapriya Shri Gopinath Bardoloi, Shri Radhakanta Handiqui, Dr. Banikanta Kakati, Sir Edward Gait and Shri Upendranath Barua.

Shillong, the venue of a session of the Asam Sahitya Sabha for the first time, is chiefly an administrative centre where the Government and the Legislative Assembly of the State are situated. But there is no impediment in the fostering of literary pursuits in a metropolitan town. In olden days, Gargaon was the centre of Assamese culture and political life, and many authors who have made valuable contributions to Assamese literature flourished there under the patronage of princes and nobles. The age of patronage is no more; and in its place Government aid has become indispensable for the advancement of a nation's culture and literature. It will lead to the well-being of the country if politicians follow the paths and ideals embodied in our literary remains. The recent award of the Nobel Prize for literature to Britain's Prime Minister Sir Winston Churchill should be an object of inspiration to our own politicians and leaders. The literature produced by them as men of action and affairs will have a more realistic flavour than that produced by cloistered scholars. They can at least compile their own reminiscences and autobiographies describing thier activities in different spheres. The *Reflections* of the Roman Emperor Marcus Aurelius is a noble example of such an effort, and its freshness has not lost its lustre even after the passage of eighteen hundred years. I ask my countrymen to imagine the happiness they would have derived by a perusal of the autobiographies of Kumar Bhaskaravarman, Momai-tamuli Barbarua, Purnananda Buragohain and Maniram Dewan if these luminaries had condescended to bequeath such records to posterity. The autobiographer must have a definite and steadfast purpose linking all his activities in life, and he must leave behind him sufficient achievements, whether in thought or in action, for emulation in ages to come.

Speaking at Shillong, I must refer to the age-long intercourse between the Assamese and the Khasis and the Jayantias who live in the neighbourhood of the town and the interior, necessitated by the contiguous character of their territories and the requirements of trade and commerce. The wearing apparel of the hillmen has always been supplied by the Assamese and also their other essential necessaries. The warm reception accorded to envoys of Khasi and Jayantia rulers has been graphically described in the old Assamese chronicles or Buranjis. Their sentiments of brotherhood came out forcibly in a letter written by the Rajas of Jayantia and Nartiang to the king of Assam after the invasion of Nawab Mir Jumla. "It pains us to remember", wrote the two Rajas, "that we were living in peace and happiness when your country was overrun by the Moguls. Jayantia and Gargaon are not divisible and separate. You have referred to the loss of two men on our side: why two, we would not have been sorry even if ten or twenty thousand men had perished in the furtherance of your interests. Our friendship is not of yesterday's growth: it has subsisted from ages past". These sentiments so heroically expressed should dominate our relations with the Khasis and the Jayantias ever afterwards.

History bears testimony to the eternal friendship of the Assamese people with the other original inhabitants living in Assam and its immediate borders. The wealth of Assamese vocabulary, the liberal principles of the Assamese social code, and several salient features of Assamese music and dance owe their origin and growth to this contact. The military potentialities of the tribesmen were frequently utilised in the wars waged by the Assamese since the period of the epics. The word invariably used by the Assamese in accosting a hillman is 'Mita', or a friend. Most of our tribesmen had been in Assam long before the Aryans came to this land. King Sukapha, the first Ahom conqueror of Assam, referred to the Barahis and the Morans, who constitute a branch of the great Bodo race, as 'Sthana-giris', or original settlers. Thus ran the message of Sukapha,—"We have come from the east and they are the Sthana-giris, and we are their guests. They should therefore come forward to meet us, and acquaint us with the villages and the inhabitants." Our relations with the tribes should therefore be governed by amity and helpfulness in recollection of the fact that we have been living side by side from ages past.

Our tribal brothers and sisters may not be ripe in the art of argumentation and speech-making, but their instincts are very correct and quick which enable them to detect at once whether one's behaviour is sincere or artificial, and whether it is motivated by selfish ends. We have therefore to approach them with a fund of good-will and affection and a genuine desire to help them in the right way. They are like infants in the scale of civilisation as it is understood in the context of literary progress and scientific advancement. An infant will come to your lap only if you address it with a hearty smile, sweet words and affectionate gestures. The task of winning the hearts of our tribal friends rests entirely with us, and our dealings with them must be governed by sincerity and love.

It is an astonishing fact as to how a handful of Aryans could spread their culture and their language in this land where the dominant population was non-Aryan. There were powerful chiefs among the tribes who being attracted to Hinduism gradually became earnest patrons of that religion. Hinduism itself was modified to accommodate the tribes, and the Tantrik forms are believed by many to have originated in Assam. There should be extensive investigations into the history of the fusion of Aryan and non-Aryan cultures in Assam. The Asam Sahitya Sabha has done well by declaring a prize for the best book on the tribes living in Assam and its frontiers. It will be seen that the fusion was made possible by the liberal doctrines preached by the great Vaisnava reformer Mahapurush Sankardeva and his followers.

It is customary to trace the history of Assamese literature in several epochs with Sankardeva as the pivotal figure. But from another angle this history may be divided into two main periods,—the literature of the age of independence, and the literature of the period of foreign domination. The first period extended up to the beginning of the nineteenth century, and the second represented the 120 years of British rule in Assam. This land was a renowned centre of learning in ancient times, as we know from the testimony of the Chinese pilgrim Hiuen-Tsang which is supported by inscriptional evidence and the literary remains of the subsequent times.

But it is surprising that in spite of the wide prevalence of learning in old Assam no book written in the common language of the people of those days has yet come to our hands. Learning was generally confined to the Brahmans who, according to the prevailing practice, would not write in anything but Sanskrit. It was the Vaisnava revival which first gave an impetus to the use of the popular language as the medium of literary expression; it is borne out by the injunction issued by King Naranarayan of Cooch Behar at the time of asking the scholars to translate the noted Sanskrit classics into Assamese which, he said, would be useful "for the edification and study of women and Sudras at the present time, and of the Brahmans at a later stage". As a result of the growing use of the popular medium, the epics and the Puranas, and other allied classics were all translated into Assamese by poets and scholars who as a rule enjoyed the patronage of princes and nobles, or were associated with the various Vaisnava monasteries or Satras. Present-day authors are often asked by their friends to write books on particular subjects; but nobody enquires as to how the authors are going to make the two ends meet, or what facilities are available to the authors to accomplish the task. The case was different in olden times. King Naranarayan, while commissioning the poet Rama Saraswati to translate the Mahabharata, furnished him with the necessary lands and servitors and sent to the poet's residence cartloads of manuscripts.

The output of literature in Assam was carried on on a prodigious scale during the period of independence. Portions of the scriptures were read out in religious and semi-religious functions; songs were sung and plays were performed in the Nam-ghars erected in every village and monastery. Several kings were writers of songs themselves, and one of them wrote a drama. The contents of the epics and the Puranas were thus brought home to the masses, just as during the Renaissance in Europe, even a common soldier could enter into a discussion of the Macedonian conqueror Alexander the Great. Nama-kirtan or religious recital and music was so universal in Assam that its fame spread to the remotest corners of Hindusthan; and Raja Ram Singha of Amber, the redoubtable antagonist of Lachit Barphukan, received a warning from his mother and his wife that he should not disturb the independence and peace of a hallowed land like Assam where there was universal Nama-kirtan and where Brahmanas and Vaisnavas lived in security and peace.

I shall now illustrate the high ideals of Vaisnava literature by citing a few examples from the unpublished manuscript "Santasamprada", or the spiritual gift of Vaisnava saints, written by a devotee named Govinda Das during the reign of King Rudra Singha. The author, like a modern scholiast, tries to prove that a Sudra or a Chandala is a superior being if he is endowed with virtue and true faith. "A man of faith is a man of virtue", writes Govinda Das and he supports his arguments by references to Pauranic texts. This conclusion of Govinda Das is a lesson to us moderns most of whom are led by the craze of materialism to the neglect of spiritual principles. What he says about the saint Bangshigopal Deva is equally edifying : "Bangshigopal Deva practised the rigours of a celibate with relentless self-control. He slept on the bare earth by spreading a sheet of cloth. He did not look at a woman, nor did he talk with a wicked man, and never uttered a vain word. He did not regard his possessions as dear to him, as saints look upon them as a source of trouble and fools as a source of joy. There was never a saint like Devagopal nor will there be one in future". I can assure the gathering that the learned world will be astonished when they see the unbounded wealth and variety of Assamese Vaisnava literature.

A word must be said about the historical literature of Assam consisting mainly of the Buranjis, which throw light on the history of other parts of India as well.

These chronicles reflect the condition of the masses, as there can be no courtly annals without reference to the people of the land. In addition to the description of wars and embassies these Buranjis give us an insight into the lofty ideals of the Assamese of yore; and we may cite a few instances in support :—

An old Assamese chronicle of the rulers of Delhi describes an interview between the king of Persia and the fugitive Mogul emperor Humayun. The latter is admonished for his self-engrossment in pleasure to the utter neglect of his kingly responsibilities and for having failed to mobilise his faithful officers and subjects in the work of protecting his throne. A number of female hawkers similarly rebuked the Assam king Jayadhwaj Singha when he fled from Gargaon, the capital, on the approach of the Mogul army. "O lord", said the hawkers, "you have paid your attention only to pleasure and dalliance. If you had only put during these fifteen years of your reign fifteen piles of earth at proper places your fate would not have been like this. Where are you fleeing leaving us in the lurch ?"

King Jayadhwaj Singha had previously been admonished by his principal consort for having carried on secret amours with her elder sister who had a lawfully wedded husband. "You have become the lord of this earth", said the queen, "and my elder sister is your sister-in-law, and she deserves respect from you. Still you dare to commit such misdeeds ! Where have you resigned your virtue and your prestige ?"

Several princes of Assam lived as hostages in the court of the king of Cooch Behar. They were handsome and young, and in the fitness of things they should be living in the company of their wives and chidren. The consorts of Sukladhwaj, brother of the king of Cooch Behar, took pity on the Assam princes and asked for their release, saying,—"You have kept in confinement four princes of the king of Assam for which their parents and their wives have been afflicted with great sorrow. They are all young, and they are handsome both in respect of their looks and their attainments. So please allow them leave to return to their homes." The intercession of the wives of Sukladhwaj bore fruit, and the Assam princes were released on some pretext.

On the eve of the ever-memorable battle of Saraighat, a section of the northern division of the Assamese forces were preparing to leave the field having lost their heart owing to the sudden illness of their commander Lachit Barphukan. A captain named Nara Hazarika confronted the intending deserters, and shouted,—"O my countrymen, if you want to pour poison on a platter of gold then do please flee !" This warning should be remembered by all if they ever intend to sacrifice the interests of their motherland.

Besides the Buranjis, we possess a varied and voluminous mass of court literature in Assam, compiled mainly for purposes of day-to-day administration, on such subjects as the duties of officers and regulations relating to their precedence; directions for the construction of forts and ramparts, of royal camps and tanks; royal pastimes and recreations; the several species of elephants, horses and hawks, their different uses, and medicines for their ailments; records of royal marriages; the composition of the different Ahom families including the admission of new members to their respective folds; and landgrants to religious institutions and individuals, and to eminent persons for their service to the State. This courtly literature in the popular medium was possible in Assam only because the country was independent where the rulers felt the necessity of all-round enlightenment. I have recently come across a Khampti manuscript which is a regular criminal code of the tribe dealing as it does with offences and their punishments.

The loss of Assam's independence was followed by a terrible setback to the progress of its language and literature. The personnel of the new administration were mostly non-Assamese who regarded the Assamese language to be a mere patois and a dialect of Bengali, and its use was consequently interdicted in the schools and courts. The Assamese people will remain ever grateful to the American Baptist Mission who supported the cause of Assamese and laid the foundation of modern Assamese literature by publishing a number of books and a monthly magazine all couched in a very simple and idiomatic style. As a result of the joint efforts of the American Missionaries and some patriotic Assamese scholars the language regained its lost position towards the seventies of the nineteenth century.

But in the system of education introduced in India by its foreign masters the vernacular languages and literatures played a nominal role in the curriculum of school and college studies. They were relegated to such an inferior position that the word 'vernacular' became sometimes a synonym for slipshodness and inferiority. But a great educational leader appeared on the scene in the person of Sir Asutosh Mookherji who introduced measures for the detailed study and teaching of the vernacular literatures in the highest stages of the University; and our Assamese literature enjoyed the fruits of his patriotic plan.

There has been a vigorous resurgence of interest in the vernacular literatures of India since the attainment of independence in the year 1947. Scholars all over the country are now anxious to know about the literary treasures of the different peoples of India. Till now, they had heard about the antiquity of Assamese prose literature and the wealth of its historical records : they are just beginning to hear about the great reformer Mahapurush Sankardeva, and a few achievements of the Assamese people in different fields; and there is a keen desire all over India to know more fully about Assamese literature and history. It has been progressively realised that the wealth of one individual literature belongs to the general stock of India's culture.

It is gratifying to see that the Government of the Indian Union and the States Governments have not been slow in moving with the spirit of the time. The Centre has initiated measures to help authors and artists who may be in indigent circumstances; and 54 authors of Assam have applied for financial aid under this scheme. The Government of Bihar and of Uttar Pradesh have taken steps to give material encouragement to local authors; and the West Bengal Government is awarding annual prizes to the writers of the best books in Bengali. The Asam Sahitya Sabha hopes that measures on this line will soon be adopted by the enlightened Government of our own State.

The advancement of literature is the first burden of the state, specially in a democratic set-up where the people are empowered to participate in the administration directly or indirectly. This partcipation will be effective and beneficent only if the citizens are endowed with a knowledge of their rights and obligations, and if they are trained to act with poise and disinterestedness. The voters select the legislators from whom again the ruling personnel are chosen. The incapacity of the voters to select proper and good representatives will lead to the utter ruination of the country. The Government should therefore attempt to place before the citizens the idals of correct conduct and action which can be gleaned only by a study of the literature and history of a country; otherwise citizens will not be able to exercise their franchise and their other democratic functions with judgement and foresight. I would even suggest the compilation of a treatise in Assamese on the lines of Plato's *Republic* with the object of educating our citizens and leaders in the art of good government.

Literature also serves as a bond of national unity. The binding factors are a common heritage, and the mass of events and facts in which all the people of a country are equally concerned. Assam's agricultural and domestic life has been greatly influenced by the teachings of the natural philosopher Dak; the people have been subjected to common sufferings at the hands of invaders; they feel equally proud in recollecting the martyrdom of Princess Jaimati and the gallantry of Lachit Barphukan. The hearts of the people become unified by pondering over their common joys and sorrows, and it is one of the main functions of literature to bring out these common features in an attractive and appealing garb. Indian social structure is seen to work in a manner as to encourage disunity rather than unity, and signs of disintegration come to the surface in other spheres as well; and one is afraid that India which has been dominated throughout the ages by the Vedas is going to be swayed by the corroding forces of *Bheda* or disintegration. Literature with its magic wand of cementing differences and establishing harmony and peace is the only instrument to cry a halt to all fissiparous tendencies which eat into the vitals of national solidarity.

The Assamese people have been thrown into greater contact and intimacy with their countrymen in the rest of India since the inauguration of the independence movement under the leadership of the Father of the Nation. Their representatives have visited different parts of India in connection with meetings and conferences; and Indian leaders who have come to Assam have been charmed at its natural beauty and human achievements. Besides, by following the events of the last two World Wars the Assamese have acquired a knowledge of many countries which had been to them mere geographical names. As a base for military operations during World War II, there had been a large influx of foreigners to Assam. Indians are now closely studying the march of international events impelled by the necessity to evolve a foreign policy of their own. All this has raised the once Cinderalla province of Assam into greater limelight, accompanied also by a desire on the part of its people to know more about diverse topics of national and international interest. In consequence, journalists, authors and publishers are trying their best to keep their countrymen abreast of the times. Perfection in writing prose had formerly been the attainment of a limited number of scholars, but at the present time, one cannot but marvel at the ease with which our journalists are handing out news and views in effective and forceful Assamese prose. The ground is thus well prepared for the inauguration of a vigorous epoch of Assamese literary development.

But the chief handicap in the progress of literature in Assam is the numerical inferiority of its reading public. Light books may command some sale, but serious books have to lie in unsold bundles in the godowns of authors and publishers. Publication is thus a precarious venture in Assam and publishers are unwilling to enter into it so very readily and enthusiastically. There is also a large number of valuable books written by ancient and modern authors still lying in manuscript form. One of the first measures to be adopted by the Asam Sahitya Sabha should be the constitution of a strong fund for the publication of books which, in the opinion of an expert committee to be set up by the Sabha, should see the light of day.

The president of a literary conference is expected to suggest a programme of work to be undertaken by the organisation concerned. Plans can be formulated in any number, but credit does not lie in their plenitude, it lies in the successful execution of a limited number of plans rightly conceived and properly chosen for implementation. The first requisite is the existence of workers ready to devote their time and energy in the service of the Sabha. Selfishness is soon detected, and persons dominated by selfish motives should never be allowed to associate themselves with an organisation like the Asam Sahitya Sabha which is the life and soul of the Assamese people. I would implore all workers to cast off their travel-tainted habiliments and to put on clean apparel when they enter into the sacred precincts of the institution.

I would however suggest that the following items should be taken up by the Sabha : the collection of the copies of all the issues of the magazines and newspapers published in the Assamese language, for our literary genius has found a channel of expression mainly in the pages of our periodical literature; the compilation of a list of all Assamese books writen by ancient and modern authors; the compilation of the autobiographical sketches and references, known as Bhanitas, inserted by almost every ancient author in his books, for they throw reliable glimpses into the history of Assamese literature; and the compilation of a "Who's Who" containing short accounts of all living Assamese authors. It is not a heavy list, and the work can be completed within a comparatively short time.

One word more and I will take my leave. I am fortunate to have the opportunity of taking my stand before this assembly of literary-minded Assamese ladies and gentlemen and their kind friends and neighbours. I request you to answer one question.—What is the ultimate goal of Assamese literature? What is the mission which the Assamese people are destined to fulfil in the world? What are they going to give in return for the bounties which they are receiving at the hands of the Creator in the shape of light, air, water and earth? India, Greece, Rome, Arabia, France, England and America have made significant contributions to the progress of mankind : is the life of the

Assamese people purposeless and vain ?—And I pause for an answer.

I feel that the Assamese people will have to begem the necklace of their gift to world's civilisation with pearls and diamonds representing the quintessence of their achievements in the fields of devotion, knowledge and action.

They have received into their bosom men of diverse origins and beliefs. Assamese life has been swept by an uninterrupted stream of love and religious ardour. They have proclaimed the superiority of spiritual existence over the attractions and glories of this mundane world.

Assamese scholarship has elicited the admiration of many a learned man from abroad. Their intellectuals have kept their country-men constantly equipped with knowledge of timely and permanent importance.

The systematic organisation of Assamese village life, and the universal refinement and versatility of Assamese men and women are without a parallel in any part of the world. The Assamese successfully thwarted the repeated invasions of foreigners, and they constructed impregnable forts and ramparts to guard the hallowed frontiers of their motherland.

Such a harmonious blending of the three elements of Bhakti, Jnana and Karma is nowhere to be found.

Let the message of this triple combination be spread far and wide, and let the Sabha be the herald of a new era. This is my earnest appeal to you all at this auspicious hour.

November 8, 1953.

AN ASSAMESE CHRONICLE OF TRIPURA[1]

A most outstanding example of Assamese historical literature is the chronicle of Tripura, originally called *Tripura desar kathar lekha,* and now generally known as *Tripura Buranji.* It was written by two Assamese scholars, Ratna Kandali Sarma and Arjundas Bairagi, who had visited Tripura, as envoys of the Assam government, on three diplomatic missions between the years 1710 and 1715 A.D. The compilation of the book was completed in 1724, during the reign of King Siva Singha which was marked by a great revival of literary and artistic activities under the patronage and encouragement of that enlightened sovereign and his three successive queen-regnants Phuleswari Devi, Amvika Devi, and Sarveswari Devi. The explanatory subtitle of the book, as recorded in the manuscript, runs as,—"Sri-Sri Rudra Singh Maharaja-dewe Tripura desar Ratna Manikya sahit pritipurbak Kataki gatayat kara katha, saka 1646."

Apart from the value of the narratives, the book is noted for its dignified style in keeping with the seri-ousness and solemnity of the subject, and the scholarship and circumspection of the collaborating authors. The basic structure is Assamese no doubt, but it is distinguished from the other types of prose diction in vogue in Assam, namely, the Sanskritic ring of the prose of Bhattadeva's *Katha-Gita* and *Katha-Bhagavata,* the cosmopolitan flavour of the Assamese chronicles dealing with the relations with the Mogul Court, and the racy and popular style of the chronicles describing the local affairs of Assam. The prose of *Tripura Buranji* preserves the style of conversation adopted by Assamese grandees and nobles on ceremonious occasions where an attempt was made to give an honorific twist to the vocabulary by the use of the easily comprehensible Sanskrit forms of Assamese words. There is also a conscious and deliberate avoidance of glib talking, and every sentence has a definite purpose in view, either in the way of recording an information, or a comment or a comparison. As a delineation of events by two learned and eminent diplomats of Assam in pure and unadulterated prose, *Tripura Buranji* occupies a pre-eminent position in the old vernacular literature not only of Assam but of the whole of India.

A noticeable characteristic of the narratives is their intense realism. They describe the objects and events which the authors saw with their own eyes, or about which they heard from the lips of reliable eye-witnesses. The collection of information was planned with deliberation and foresight, and no detail has escaped the attention of the two vigilant scholars. The fact that they spent nine long years in weaving out a connected account from their carefully preserved notes bears evidence of the arduous pains they took in the compilation of the chronicle.

The primary object of the two authors was to give an account of the diplomatic missions with which they were entrusted. As Tripura was comparatively inaccessible in those days, and as very little was known about it in Assam, the authors embodied in their book as much information as possible which would serve as an itinerary for visitors to Tripura, and as a helpful record for conducting Assam's relations with that state in future. They have therefore described their route which lay through hills and forests, special features of the places through which they passed, the products and resources of Tripura, its early history, the functions and equipments of its dignitaries, its festivals and amusements, and the intrigues and revolutions which took place before their very eye.

The importance of the book is derived also from the detached outlook with which it was written. The chronicle of a particular state compiled under the orders of its rulers is bound to suffer from limitations of treatment; and that compiled by a noble breathes his sense of personal or family importance. Hence arose in India a number of Khafi Khans, or "Sir Secrets," who handed down to posterity what they did not dare to publish in their life-time. But our historians Ratna Kandali and Arjundas wrote under favourable circumstances. They were immune from vengeance at the hands of the persons whose misdeeds they had to depict, for they were safe in Assam under the protection of their royal masters, and the misdeeds themselves had not failed to draw upon their perpetrators due condemnation and retribution. The unfettered exercise of this objective outlook has enabled the authors to leave behind a faithful picture of Tripura in the early years of the eighteenth century.

The authors were fully competent for compiling a work of this nature. The envoys of Assam, known as Katakis, were invariably well-informed and learned scholars, endowed with a ready wit and presence of mind, with which alone the purpose of diplomatic missions could be achieved. Failure on the part of ambassadors to present their case faithfully and effectively was bound to place their government in embarrassing situations. Assamese envoys were given regular training for which they received high praise in foreign courts. A historical monograph written by such envoys is bound to be a literary treasure and a mine of accurate information. Besides throwing light on the happenings at Tripura, the book enables us to form an idea about Assam in the heyday of its prosperity and power.

The diplomatic missions described in this book are of momentous importance to Assam and India. Emperor Auranzeb had died in 1707, leaving a legacy of discontent and disaffection, and Bengal was on the vortex of oppression at the hands of its virtual ruler Murshid Kuli Khan and his unscrupulous myrmidons. The Zemindars were subjected to inexplicable tortures if they failed to pay their rents in time. Murshid Kuli Khan was at the head of affairs in Bengal, first as Diwan from 1700 to 1713, then as deputy governor from 1713 to 1717, and finally as full governor from 1717 to his death in 1727. The real governor Prince Muhammad Azimuddin, later Azim-ushshan, 1697-1712, was lazy and covetous, and was overshadowed by his powerful and efficient Diwan and deputy. The prince and Murshid Kuli Khan were always at variance in the matter of revenue collection. The former wanted to amass money to conduct the inevitable war of succession to push forward his own claim to the Delhi throne; the latter had "to save every rupee and creat a surplus for remittance to the starving imperial court and army in the Deccan".[1] This double sucking drained the re-

1. Jadunath Sarkar, editor. *History of Bengal*, Vol. II, pp. 402-3.

sources of Bengal, and exorbitant exactions, attended by tortures, became the order of the day.

About the year 1706, Murshid Kuli Khan had been confirmed in his appointment as Deputy Nazim. "He now commenced to put in practice a system of the greatest oppression upon the zemindars, or Hindoo landholders; which, although it much augmented the revenue of the state, rendered his name dreaded and detested throughout the province......A principal instrument of the Nawab's severity was Nazir Ahmed, to whom, when a district was in arrear, he used to deliver over the captive zemindars, to be tormented by every species of cruelty; as hanging up by feet; bastinadoing; setting them in the sun in summer; and by stripping them naked, sprinkling them frequently with cold water in winter".[2]

Salimullah, author of *Tarikh-i-Bangala*, thus writes in his description of the practice of "draconic severity and bestial torture on the defaulters" resorted to by Murshid Kuli Khan for enhancing the revenue collection of Bengal,—"When Murshid Kuli Khan discovered that an amil or zemindar had dissipated the revenue and was unable to make good the deficiency, he compelled the offender, his wife and children to turn Muhammadans".[3]

When Hindu India, specially Bengal, was groaning under the burden of Mogul harassment and oppres-

2. Charles Stewart. *History of Bengal*, Bangabasi edition, 1910, pp. 403, 411.

3. Jadunath Sarkar, editor. *History of Bengal*, II, p. 411, where the relevant passage of Salimullah's description is reproduced.

sion, there appeared on the scene a great ruler, a born leader of man, and dreamer whose ancestors, down to his father, had inflicted repeated blows on the Moguls and thwarted their designs in Eastern India. He was Swargadeo Rudra Singha Maharaj, king of Assam, 1696-1714, son of the martyred princess Jaimati and Swargadeo Gadhadhar Singha. His agents, disguised as itinerant hermits, had visited different parts of India and collected information about the affairs of the Moguls, their successes and set-backs, and popular movements and feelings. The king thus kept himself fully informed of the plight to which the Hindus had been reduced. He had himself suffered humiliation at the hands of Murshid Kuli Khan who sent to him robes ordinarily meant for presents to vassal chiefs. It is recorded in the Persian chronicle of Bengal, *Riyazu-s-Salatin*,— "The Rajahs of Tipra, Kuch Behar, and Assam called themselves *chatar dhari* and ruling chiefs, and did not bend their heads in submission to the Emperor of Hindustan, and minted coins after their own names. On hearing, however, of the vigorous administration of the Khan, the Rajah of Assam presented to the Khan chairs and palkis of ivory, musk, musical instruments, feathers, fans of peacock feathers, etc., and offered his submission".[4] The above assertions which are not in conformity with the logic of events, and which are not to be found in contemporory Assamese records, indicate at least the way in which Murshid Kuli Khan wanted the Assamese to behave.

Assamese pilgrims received obstructions from Mogul officers in their visits to Hindu shrines in India,

4. Gulam Husain Salim, *Riyazu-s-Salatin*, translated by A. Salam, Asiatic Society of Bengal, 1904, p. 257.

specially in connection with their pilgrimages to the Ganges for bathing in that holy river and fetching its holy water. The humiliating overtures of Murshid Kuli Khan urged King Rudra Singha to check the tide of Mogul affronts, received not only by himself but also by his co-religionists.

He therefore planned to attack Bengal and then march to Delhi if circumstances proved favourable. Leaving aside the victorious achievements of Kumar Bhaskaravarman and King Harshadeva of Hindu Kamarupa, the Assamese had, during the regime of the Ahoms, conquered Bengal, wholly or partly, first in the reign of Dihingia Raja, 1497-1539, and then in the reign of Jayadhwaj Singha, 1648-63. There were repeated instances of Assam's victory over the Mogul arms. Animated by the recollection of these military achievements, King Rudra Singha took active measures to organise a Hindu confederacy to ensure his success by virtue of the support and co-operation of his allies. The recovery of the territory up to the river Karatoya, which was the age-old western limit of Assam, was declared as the first objective of his expedition. King Rudra Singha's message to the Rajas and Zemindars of Bengal ran as follows,—"We formerly possessed the provinces on this side of the Karatoya river, and we are now desirous to resume them. Do not prove inimical to us. If we remain friendly everything will succeed. Be yours the country, the government and the revenue; mine the name. Act in a manner to preserve peace. Fear not our approach; send friendly answer respecting your welfare without delay".[5]

5. Benudhar Sharma, editor. Dr. John Peter Wade's *Account of Assam*, Sibsagar, 1927, p. 131.

Amongst the rulers to whom requests for co-operation were sent by King Rudra Singha the following names are on record,—Raja of Morung, Raja of Bana-bishnupur, Raja of Nadiya, Raja of Cooch Behar, Kirtichandra Zemindar of Bardhaman, Udaynarayan Zemindar of Barnagar, Raja of Krishna-sundar in Rungpore, Raja of Pangia, Raja of Delhi, Raja of Amber and Raja of Jodhpur. He received encouraging replies from the Rajas, and some of them said they felt humiliated at having to salute the Moguls, and that they would be glad to pay their allegiance to the king of Assam with whose prowess and fame they were well acquainted.

Preparations for expedition had been going on meanwhile under the direct supervision of the monarch, though the real motive was assiduously concealed from the masses. The good-will of the people of Bengal was a necessary preliminary for the success of the Assamese forces when they entered that country. King Rudra Singha invited to Assam the Brahmans, physicians, musicians, artizans and merchants of Bengal, and sent them back with rich presents. Home-staying Brahmans and Pundits had gifts sent to them in Bengal. There was thus an incessant flow of men from Bengal to Assam. Amongst the Bengali visitors was a Vaisnava devotee and musician named Anandiram, designated as a Medhi in Assamese records in view of his likeness to a principal functionary of a Satra or monastery in Assam. The mediation of this Anandiram Medhi proved invaluable in initiating negotiations with Tripura for co-operation in the great enterprise of King Rudra Singha.

The State of Tripura had been in enjoyment of complete autonomy in its internal affairs, and its allegiance to the Moguls which was but nominal, was signified by an annual tribute of elephants and the necessity of confirmation by the Mogul government of a change of Rajas. The territory extended over hills and plains, and was situated between Sylhet, Chittagong, Noakhali and the Lushai country; on the west its boundary was the Meghna river which separated it from Faridpur, Dacca and Mymensing. The old Tripura State is now divided into two parts, Hill Tippera and Tippera District, with head-quarters at Agartala and Comilla respectively. Udaypur, the old capital of Tripura, is now in ruins, the only living symbol of its past splendour being the Tripureswari temple which is visited by pilgrims till this day.

There were no diplomatic relations between Assam and Tripura during Ahom rule prior to the reign of King Rudra Singha, though in earlier times there appears to have been some contact between the two kingdoms. It is even said in *Rajmala*, the old metrical chronicle of Tripura, that its earliest monarch Trilochan had married the daughter of the Kamarupa king. In the sixteenth century Tripura was overrun by the armies of Naranarayan, king of Cooch Behar.[6]

The initiation of measures for establishing friendship with Tripura was due to an accidental circums-

6. Hill Tipperah, described in the Imperial Gazetteer of India, Provincial Series, Eastern Bengal and Assam, Calcutta, 1909, pp. 605-612; and in the I.G.I., Oxford, 1908, Vol. XIII, pp. 116-122; and also in Sir William Hunter's *Statistical Account of Bengal*, Vol. VI. Dr. Pratap Chandra Chaudhury has traced the Assam-Tripuar contacts of the pre-Ahom period in his History of Civilisation of Assam. See also *Darrang-raj-vamsavali*, edited by Hemchandra Goswami, Shillong, 1917, pp. 82-84.

tance, and was inspired by King Rudra Singh's plan to extend his sphere of influence throughout Bengal and Eastern India. An Assamese priest named Tarkavagish Bhattacharyya had met Subangsa Roy, a potentate of Dacca. At the instance of King Rudra Singha, Ratna Kandali Kataki met Tarkavagish Bhattacharyya at Rangamati, the Mogul outpost near Dhubri. The priest instructed Ratna Kandali to proceed to Dacca and meet Subangsa Roy, and bring from there musicians and artists. It was Subangsa Roy of Dacca who suggested to Ratna Kandali the advisability of establishing friendly relations between Assam and Tripura, saying, "I have heard that Maharaja Rudra Singha has subjugated Jayanta and Cachar. The Raja of Tripura is a great ruler, and he will be of manifold service if he can be brought over to the Swargadeo's side by ties of friendship". King Rudra Singha had kept Subangsa Roy's suggestion in his mind.

Anandiram Medhi gave a musical performance before King Rudra Singha and his nobles. Thus says the chronicle,—"There in the presence of the Maharaja, Anandiram's men sang songs in the style of Samkirtan, and played on flutes. They also danced with flutes in their hands. A number of our musicians were asked to learn Samkirtan songs".[7]

On enquiry it was learnt that Anandiram was acquainted with Ratna Manikya Raja of Tripura. He promised to induce the Raja to enter into friendly terms

7. Dr. S. K. Bhuyan, editor. *Tripura Buranji*, published by the Department of Historical an Antiquarian Studies in Assam, 1938, whereupon this article is based, and wherefrom the relevant passages are reproduced.

with King Rudra Singha provided accredited representatives from Assam were sent along with him.

The Ahoms who were adepts in statecraft realised fully that a plausible request for friendship with Tripura would not be a politic step as it would give an appearance of anxiety and solicitude on their part. King Rudra Singha therefore thought it advisable to create in the mind of the Tripura Raja a desire for friendship with Assam. Ratna Kandali and Arjundas were sent in the company of Anandiram, not as envoys of the monarch, but as representatives of his principal executive officer Surath Singha Barbarua, with the outward object of fetching Ganges water from Bengal. The party reached Tripura sometime in June 1710.

In the audience with the Tripura Raja, the two envoys Ratna Kandali and Arjundas explained the object of their visit as the fetching of Ganges water. As prearranged, Anandiram expatiated on the achievements and qualities of King Rudra Singha, and suggested the advisability of establishing friendly relations between Tripura and Assam. The Raja having heard of the fame of King Rudra Singha declared his intention to act as suggested by Anandiram. But he enquired,—"Our men have never gone to Assam. How will they go now?" Anandiram informed Ratna Manikya Raja of the presence of the Assam envoys at Tripura who, if the Raja desired, might be induced to take with them Tripura Ukils to Assam. The two Assam envoys were then presented before the Tripura Raja ; and seizing this longed-for opportunity they said that many Rajas had sought the friendship of the Swarga-Maharaja of Assam, and that they were willing to promote the desire of the Tripura Raja by communicating his request to the Barbarua, who in his turn would place the matter before the Swargadeo.

The two envoys were then led to the presence of Ghanasyam Barthakur, brother of Ratna Manikya Raja. The Barthakur said,—"Ratna Kandali and Arjundas, you should tell your Barbarua Nawab that previously to this there was no friendship or otherwise with the Swarga-Maharaja. Our Maharaja is now desirous of entering into friendly relations with your king. He therefore proposes to send ambassadors from here with epistles and presents. The Barbarua should see that friendship between the two Maharajas may be established on a firm footing." Ratna Kandali and Arjundas promised to see to the fulfilment of the wishes of the Tripura Raja. The latter despatched Rameswar Nyayalankar Bhattacharyya and Udaynarayan Biswas as his envoys to Assam in the company of the Katakis Ratna Kandali and Arjundas.

The party left Tripura in Ashar 1632 *saka*, July 1710. Eight days later they reached Kaulas pargana where they were detained for four months during the rains on account of illnesses in their camp. From there they proceeded to Khaspur, the capital of Cachar, and then to Raha and Kaliabar. They first went to Gajpur where King Rudra Singha was encamping at the time, and then in Jaistha 1633 *saka*, they went to Rangpur along with the monarch.

The Tripura envoys were first received by Surath Singha Barbarua who informed them that in consultation with the three ministers Buragohain, Bargohain and Barpatra Gohain, he would convey the Tripura

Raja's wishes to the king, and if fortunate they might be favoured with an audience with His Majesty.

The interview with King Rudra Singha was fixed on Sravan 10, 1633 *saka*, and the venue was the *Barchora*, or audience hall in the palace of the Swargadeo at the new capital Rangpur where all the houses were made of brick. The hall was gaily decorated for the occasion, and the pillars, beams and rafters were draped with costly textures. The royal throne was placed on an elevated and carpeted plinth, with seven canopies hanging overhead. Definite positions were allotted to the archers, shieldsmen, musketers and gunners, and also for horses and elephants. The nobles and officers came to the function with due pomp and ceremony. The chroniclers concluded their description of the ceremony held at the *Barchora* by comparing it with the assembly of the gods in the audience hall of Indra.

The two envoys of Tripura were brought from their retiring place to the hall after the king had occupied his seat. Rameswar Nyayalankar approached His Majesty's presence with Ratna Manikya Raja's letter on his head. He uttered his blessings at seven stages, and Udaynarayan similarly repeated his obeisance seven times. The envoys were introduced by the Barbarua, and the Rajmantri Barpatra Gohain Dangaria made the usual enquiries about the Tripura Raja's health and happiness. The Kath Bhandari Barua then read out Raja Ratna Manikya's letter which was in Sanskrit. In the letter the Raja conveyed his desire for friendship, pointing out that distance is no impediment to such friendship as it subsisted between Yudhisthir and Virata and Drupada. The interview was a short one, at the end of which the envoys were allowed leave to retire to their camp. The meaning of the Sanskrit epistle of the Tripura Raja was then explained by the Pundits of the court.

There was another meeting on Aswin 15, where the envoys of Tripura were given final leave to return to their country in the company of Ratna Kandali and Arjundas. King Rudra Singha said in reply,—"Unending friendship is now established between us and Ratna Manikya Raja. It is our wish that the Raja should maintain this friendship in an uninterrupted manner". A letter in Sanskrit, together with costly presents, was made over to the envoys as presents to Ratna Manikya Raja; this letter contained a mere exchange of formal greetings. But the real intention of King Rudra Singha was communicated in another epistle of a secret and confidential nature, a *rahasya-patra,* which was encased in a cylinder. Both the letters were dated Kartik 5, 1633 *saka.*

The Tripura envoys were invited to witness the festivities of the season connected with the worship of Durga. A dialectical contest was arranged between the Assamese Pundit Jaigopal and the Tripura envoy Rameswar Nyayalankar. After sometime, King Rudra Singha closed the animated discussions by saying,—"Rameswar Nyayalankar Bhattacharyya has come here in the role of an ambassadar : the contest would have been proper if he had come here as a Pundit. We just had a diversion for a moment". The Tripura envoys arranged to leave Rangpur a few days later.

The four envoys Ratna Kandali, Arjundas, Rameswar Bhattacharyya and Udaynarayan, accompanied by their respective attendants then boarded their boats at Namdang, from where they proceeded to Raha, then to Demera, then to Khaspur, and then to Udarban. They continued their boat journey along the Barak river and reached Lakhipur four days later. Sailing for another five days they arrived at the mouth of the Rupini river which divided the territories of Cachar and Tripura. Three days later they reached Rangrung inhabited by, in the words of the chroniclers, "a tribe called the Kukis who are like the Nagas and Dafalas of our country." Rangrung which was within the dominion of the Tripura Raja was a place of considerable importance. The inhabitants numbered about three hundred men, and their weapons were bows, shields and Naga spears. The Tripura Raja appointed an officer called Halamsa as the governor of the village, "something like our Naga Khunbao over here in our country". The products of Rangrung are then enumerated, —methons, musks, black pepper, betel-nut and vine, paddy, and vegetables of all varieties. Traders from Tripura, Cachar and Manipur visited the Rangrung market with the products of their respective places.

From Rangrung the party proceeded to Aimul Parvat at a distance of two hours journey from the boundary of Manipur. Four days later they reached Rupinipara which was inhabited by the Kukis. They then passed through Taijalpara, Charthang, Kumjang, Chairangchuk, and then Kerpa. The inhabitants of the villages from Kerpa to the vicinity of the capital were called Tripuras. Their priests were known as Somtayas, "who are like the Deodhais of our country".

On the arrival of the party at Chota-marichai and

Bar-marichai Para, Rameswar Nyayalankar proceeded in advance to inform the Tripura Raja of the arrival of the Assamese envoys. On Chaitra 15, 1633 *saka*, the envoys arrived at the capital of Tripura, more than five months after their departure from Assam. The Katakis were given sumptuous supplies of their necessaries, and also the services of barbers, washerman and scavengers.

The authors then describe the capital of Tripura, its palace, temples and markets. The Juvaraj was the principal dignitary of the state, being in charge of revenue, elephants and soldiers. He had to take the field in person when occasion demanded. The next functionary was the Barthakur. Then there were the Uzir, Dewan, Nemuzir, Karkon and Kotwal-musib, "who are like the Barbarua and Phukans of our country; they are all Tripuras, and others are not appointed to these offices."

The next chapter deals with the early history of the Tripura Rajas. In olden days the Rajas were called Phas. One Kanchaupha, a Tripura, had a daughter, who became the mother of a son through Mahadeva. This son became in course of time a very powerful man, and was selected to be the head of the Tripuras. While going out a-hunting one day he saw in a mountain cave a brilliant light emanating from a gem on the hood of a serpent, which was in the process of being swallowed by a frog. The Tripura leader killed the frog, and extracted the gem from the hood of the serpent. That very night, Mahadeva, his divine progenitor, advised him in a dream to present the gem to the Padshah of Gaur. The advice was carried out accordingly. Being pleased with the Tripura leader, the Padshah installed him as the ruler of the Tripuras, and gave him the royal scepture and umbrella, and the title of Ratna Manikya. The Padshah enjoined that his successors on the throne of Tripura should also bear the title of Manikya. Ratna Manikya then returned to Tripura, and founded the capital named Udaypur. This account of the origin of the Tripura Rajas is supported by *Rajmala*, where it is said,—"Ratnafah, the hundred and first Rajah, was a younger brother who obtained the throne by the aid of 4,000 Mahomodan troops lent him from Gaur. This was probably about 1279 A.D. Ratnafah received from the king of Gaur the title of Manik, by which all succeeding Rajahs have been known".[8]

The first Ratna Manikya was succeeded by Amar Manikya, Jaso Manikya, Bijoy Manikya and Kalyan Manikya. The last had two sons, Govinda Manikya and Chattra Manikya. Govinda Manikya was overthrown by his brother Chattra Manikya whose administration of Tripura was notorious for injustice and oppression. It was he who entered into a stipulation with the Moguls to give them an annual tribute of elephants. The people appealed to the deposed ruler Govinda Manikya to resume the reins of government. Chattra Manikya was killed, and Govinda Manikya ascended the throne of Tripura a second time. He stopped delivering the tribute to the Moguls. He

8. Sir Alexander Mackenzie. *History of the Relations of Government with the Hill Tribes of the North-East Frontier of Bengal*, Calcutta, 1884, pp. 269-271, where the substance of *Rajmala* is given, based on the full analysis by Reverend J. Long in the J.A.S.B., Volume XIX, 1850, p. 533.

died after a long reign, and was succeeded by his son Ram Manikya.

Ram Manikya Raja looked after his brother Narendra Manikya with affectionate care. One Champakrai, a distant brother of Ram Manikya, and a man of varied qualities, was appointed Juvaraj. Ram Manikya was the father of four sons, Ratna Manikya, by his principal wife; and Durjai Singha, Ghanasyam and Chandramani, by his three unmarried consorts. When Ratna Manikya was only seven years old, his father Ram Manikya died, leaving the boy-prince together with the kingdom to the care and custody of Champakrai Juvaraj. The latter was faithful to his departed master and cousin. He placed Ratna Manikya on the throne, and himself acted as regent. This state of affairs was not countenanced by Narendra Manikya, brother of Ram Manikya. He brought a powerful force from Dacca promising to the Moguls an increase in the annual tribute of elephants. Champakrai fled from the capital, and Narendra Manikya ascended the throne. He however kept the young prince Ratna Manikya with him and looked after him affectionately. Narendra Manikya proved to be an unjust and inefficient ruler. Champakrai was invited by the people to take charge of the administration, and he came to Tripura with a considerable force from Dacca. The soldiers of Narendra Manikya and Champakrai met at Chandigarh. Narendra Manikya's followers went over to the side of Champakrai. He was deposed, and Champakrai placed Ratna Manikya on the throne once again.

Champakrai governed the country with justice and moderation. But men were not wanting to poison the ears of Ratna Manikya Raja with stories of Champakrai's nepotism and high-handedness. The Raja entertained great faith in Champakrai, but he was too weak and gullible to resist the machinations of the unscrupulous nobles. Champakrai fled from the capital, but he was captured on the way and killed. His wives accompanied their husband on the funeral pyre. Ratna Manikya appointed his step-brother Durjai Singha as Juvaraj, Ghanasyam as Barthakur, and Chandramani as Tripura's hostage at the Mogul durbar. Peace then prevailed at Tripura, and the people became attached to Raja Ratna Manikya.

But it was an age of personal rivalry and jealousy, and the subordination of one's interests to the greater demands of the state was not a very common feature in those days. The aggrieved parties did not hesitate to take direct and prompt action to redress real or fancied wrongs done to them. The favours conferred by Ratna Manikya upon his wife's brother Kavisekhar Narayan were not liked by Ghanasyam Barthakur; besides, Kavisekhar had once abused Ghanasyam as the son of a maid-servant. Ghanasyam cut off the head of Kavisekhar when he was offering his prayers to Chandi. Ghanasyam was further exasperated at the appointment of Rajdurlabh Narayan, the husband of the Raja's sister, as Kotwal-musib with the authority to use insignias higher in rank than those usually attached to the office.

Ghanasyam Barthakur then busied himself in finding out ways and means for the undoing of his brother Ratna Manikya Raja, and the events that followed in quick succession constitute a tragedy illustrating the operation of the immutable law of retribution, not only for one's misdeeds, but also for one's character and disposition.

The ball of impiety was set rolling by Ratna Manikya Raja himself. He made secret advances to the beautiful married sister of a Mogul in his employment, named Murad Beg, whose home was at Meherkul near Comilla. Emissaries were despatched to Meherkul to persuade Murad Beg's sister to desert her lawful husband and come with them to Udaypur to shine there in the glamour of royal patronage. The faithful lady received the messengers cordially, and asked them to wait for some days as she would require time to collect her effects and provide herself with necessary articles. Her husband, also a Mogul, was living at that time at Dacca.

Murad Beg's sister sent a secret message to her brother alluding to the visit of the emissaries of Ratna Manikya, adding,—"If the Raja takes me there you will be subjected to infamy and disgrace amongst the Moguls".

Murad Beg communicated the circumstances to Ghanasyam Barthakur who found in them an opportunity to promote his own end. Ghanasyam succeeded in inflaming the passions of Murad Beg. He agreed to leave the Raja's service, and remove his family from Meherkul and proceed with them to Dacca. Ignorant of this development the Raja asked Ghanasyam to intercept Murad Beg as he was approaching the pass of Chandigarh. Ghanasyam met Murad Beg, and they entered into a solemn pact to help each other. The Barthakur then returned to the capital, and reported that he could not meet Murad Beg.

It was the practice of the Tripura Raja to catch elephants every year at Khandal pargana, now in Feni sub-division. The Barthakur was the officer in charge of the elephant-catching operations. Ghanasyam Barthakur took with him this year more than the usual quota of men alleging the necessity to meet the increase in the Mogul tribute, and the arrears accruing since the administration of Champakrai. Ratna Manikya permitted Ghanasyam to take men as required by him, and the Barthakur left for Khandal pargana in Agrahayan 1633 *saka.*

It was during the absence of Ghanasyam that the Assamese envoys arrived at the capital of Tripura, with presents for the Raja and the Barthakur. The latter was now asked to return to Udaypur to take part in the reception of the two envoys coming from the eminent court of the Swarga-Maharaja of Assam. Ghanasyam pleaded his inability to leave the operations as some more elephants had yet to be caught.. He advised his brother to give a fitting reception to the Assam envoys promising to return before their departure from Tripura to help the Raja in deciding upon a proper reply to the Assam king.

Raja Ratna Manikya formally rceived Ratna Kandali and Arjundas on Baisakh 4, 1634 *saka* at the audience hall of the palace. The chroniclers take this opportunity to describe the durbar of the Tripura Raja as it appeared on the day of their interview. There was a gathering of about three thousand men. The equipments and costumes of the different grades of officers are fully described, and the arrival of each potentate is noted with precision. First came Juvaraj Durjai Singha with 100 attendants; then, Rajbangsi

Dharanidhar Thakur with 40 men; then the Uzir with 80 men; then, the Nazir with 60 men; then, the Karkon with 60 men; then, the Kotwal-musib with 40 shields-men, 30 burkendazes and 40 archers; then, the Dewan with 40 men; then, the Nemuzir with 60 men; then, about 30 Baruas accompanied by 1500 attendant paiks armed with shield and sword. This description runs to about ten folios of the manuscript, and it has conserved for ages the pomp and pageantry of the Tripura durbar.

In the audience given to the Assam envoys, King Rudra Singha's letter, which was in Sanskrit, was read out by the Dewan. After the customary enquiries about the welfare of the Assam monarch, and the expression of a desire for progressive friendship between the two rulers the Assam envoys were given leave to return to their camp for the present.

Ratna Kandali and Arjundas had known very well that as they would have to remain closeted inside the durbar hall they would not know what was going on outside. They directed two of their camp-followers to proceed to the place in disguise and note carefully the number of men, and the character and quantity of equipments and weapons, and of the movements of the assemblage. These two appointed observers collected the required information and transmitted the same to the two envoys. The chroniclers have also recorded the minutest details of the dress and regalia worn by Ratna Manikya Raja on this occasion.

The real object of King Rudra Singha's mission to Tripura was unfolded at the secret interview on the night of the 7th Baisakh, three days after the formal audience at the durbar hall. The second meeting was held in the throne room of the palace. Ratna Kandali and Arjundas Bairagi were secretly conducted to the presence of the Tripura Raja by Udaynarayan Biswas. The fifth man present there was the Dewan of Tripura. He took the secret letter of King Rudra Singha from the Assam envoys and read it out to the Raja. The envoys were then asked if they had anything to add to the message conveyed in the epistle. They said,—"The Barbarua Nawab has, at the instance of the Swargadeo-Maharaja, sent this message; The principal duty of a sovereign is to maintain and protect his subjects along with the cows and Brahmans in accordance with the *Dharma* or articles of faith cherished by a nation. The rulers pursuing this *Dharma* are in existence, yet the Yavanas are destroying the entire *Dharma*. Therefore, fame and *Dharma* will both be on the increase if all, being of one mind, overthrow the Yavanas and protect the *Dharma*." King Rudra Singha's own message as embodied in the secret letter, ran as follows,—"This is a secret letter, and this is the message; Popular impressions are persistent to the effect, that, on account of the hostile conduct of the Moguls, the *Dharma* propounded in the Vedas is not receiving any protection. If you consider it proper to take action for redressing this wrong, then you are requested to inform me of your strength and equipment after consultation with the leading persons whose affection and confidence you enjoy. We are all subject to God, still it is meet and proper that we should adopt measures so that we can administer our country without interference from others, and also that we may not be subject to others in the execution of our cherished course of action".

The Dewan then enquired about the way in which Mir Jumla overran Assam, and Mansur Khan occupied Gauhati. The envoys briefly described the Assam-Mogul conflicts between 1662 and 1682 A.D., attributing Assam's reverses to the treachery of Baduli Phukan and Laluk Barphukan. The Dewan, having heard the account, observed laconically,—"Oh, it is for this reason that Baduli lived at Dacca all the time".[9]

A few days after this interview there took place the celebrations connected with the spring festival Madan Puja. Robes coloured light-yellow were presented by the Raja to his nobles and officers, and the Assam Katakis also had their share. The centre of attraction was the image of Kamadeva, the god of love. An accompaniment of the festival was the Motkhela amusement on the Gomti river where the nobles including the Juvaraj sprayed water on their friends from leather syringes. Ratna Manikya sent appropriate presents for the occasion to Ghanasyam and asked him to return. The Barthakur replied that as his work was now finished he would soon return to the capital as desired by the Raja.

Behind the revelries of the season, powerful forces were working secretly for the destruction of Ratna Manikya Raja. The events occurred before the very eye of the two ambassadors of Assam. They watched

9. Assam-Mogul conflicts, 1662-1682, briefly described in S. K. Bhuyan's *Lachit Barphukan and His Times,* and *Ramani Gabharu;* and fully in his book *Atan Buragohain and His Times;* and also in Jadunath Sarkar's *History of Aurangzib,* S. N. Bhattacharyya's *History of Mogul North-East Frontier Policy* and Jagadish Narayan Sarkar's *Life of Nawab Mir Jumla.*

the developments minutely and carefully, and have left to posterity an account the like of which is rarely found in the contemporary vernacular prose literature of India.

Ghanasyam Barthakur's plans to overthrow Ratna Manikya Raja and seize the rulership for himself were being matured meanwhile. He maintained an intimate communication with Murad Beg at Dacca who sent small batches of armed men to Ghanasyam's camp at the Kheda operations. At the suggestion of Ghanasyam, Murad Beg manouvred the support of Mir Murad, an officer of consequence at the Nawab's court at Dacca, and persuaded him to depute his nephew Mamud Sapi to Tripura to take delivery of the annual tribute of elephants together with the arrears of previous years. Mamud Sapi proceeded to Tripura with an armed force, avowedly to demand the tribute; but secretly, to promote the designs of Ghanasyam Barthakur. Murad Beg's party marched simultaneously towards Tripura. Ghanasyam started for the capital after having instructed his men to continue the Kheda operations, and the adherents of the Raja who happened to be in the camp were left behind to supervise the same, and thereby prevented from opposing any *coup d'etat* against the Raja. The three parties led respectively by Ghanasyam Barthakur, Murad Beg and Mamud Sapi, advanced towards the capital by different routes, and encamped together at Mirzapore.

Ratna Manikya's devoted friends warned him of the conspiracy of Ghanasyam. But the Raja had firm faith in his brother, and he could never imagine that Ghanasyam could ever be disloyal. Ghanasyam sent messages to the Raja to disarm him of all suspicions, and explained Murad Beg's visit as being inspired by his anxiety to be received back into the good graces of his whilom master. Mamud Sapi's visit, alleged Ghanasyam, was in the usual course of business, namely, to take delivery of the current and arrear tribute. Mamud Sapi had at the outset objected to go against Ratna Manikya as he was loved by the people. But his protest was drowned in the vehemence of his two associates. The three now entered into a solemn pact to stand by each other in all emergencies.

The real intention of the trio now became clear beyond a shadow of doubt. Durjai Singha Juvaraj and Rajdurlabh Narayan Kotwal-musib proposed to attack the enemy at Chandigarh. "But Ghanasyam is my younger brother", said Ratna Manikya, "he has great love for me, why should he behave in an unfriendy manner, and why should you make unreasonable aspersions against him ? Do not entertain any suspicion whatsoever about Ghanasyam. It is desirable that he should come along with Mamud Sapi : otherwise, it will lead to harmful results." The captains retired from the presence of the Raja heart-broken and depressed.

Ratna Manikya then sent a message to Ghanasyam asking him to come with Mamud Sapi. They accordingly proceeded towards the capital, and pitched their tents near the Raja's palace. Ghanasyam informed the Raja that he would see him at an auspicious moment to be determined by the priests. The Raja sent food articles to Mamud Sapi, and betel-nut and leaf to Ghanasyam, as tokens of his good-will.

The three now realised the possibility of their plans being obstructed by the Juvaraj and the Kotwal-musib. They decided to invite the two nobles to their camp in order that they might join in persuading Murad Beg to appear before the Raja for reconciliation. The nobles saw through the game and refused to trust their persons to the mercy of the three accomplices. This development was communicated to the Raja, but he refused to believe it. They then sent the Kotwal-musib's wife to her brother Ratna Manikya Raja to explain to him the drift of the real situation. The Raja dismissed her from his presence, saying,—"You are but a woman, you do not know anything. You have read the situation in the light of their explanation".

The Raja then expressly ordered Durjai Singha Juvaraj and Rajdurlabh Narayan Kotwal-musib to meet Ghanasyam and Murad Beg in their camp. Murad Beg pretended to be repentent, and promised to see the Raja next day in the company of Ghanasyam and Mamud Sapi. The two visitors were asked to pass the night in Ghanasyam's camp and partake of the feast which had been arranged. The Kotwal-musib was taken inside where he was enchained. It was not difficult for the Juvaraj to anticipate what was coming. He promised to pay Mamud Sapi a bribe of ten thousand rupees, and escaped from the camp. The Juvaraj met the Raja that very night and told him of what had happened. He expained to the Raja that it was still possible to check the enemy. The Raja enjoyed the peoples' affection, said the Juvaraj, and they would come, one and all, if drums were beaten for a general rendezvous. The Raja simply said,—"You fail to understand anything. Ghanasyam is my brother, and he is an able man in all respects. If he is killed without an offence no happiness will ever come to me. I cannot accede to your unreasonable proposal, and you should not make it." Durjai Singha Juvaraj foresaw the inevitable doom of Ratna Manikya Raja, and took final leave of him, saying,—"You are the son of Ram Manikya Raja, and you have yourself been Raja for twenty-seven years. Still you are incapable of understanding the machinations of the enemy! This is our last meeting in this life." The Juvaraj, overwhelmed with grief, then retired to his residence.

On the following day, Ghanasyam manipulated the support of Chandramani Thakur by promising to appoint him Juvaraj, and of Jaisingha Narayan Karkon by promising to marry his daughter and make her his chief consort.

Ghanasyam Barthakur then arranged to go to the palace for the alleged purpose of an audience with the Raja. He invited Brahmans and astrologers to offer him blessings at the time of his departure. He then moved towards the palace accompanied by 200 horsemen and 700 archers. He rode on a Turkish pony and was armed with two swords hanging from his waist, a shield on his back, and a spear in his hand. Raja Ratna Manikya came out of the inner appartments and sat on the throne awaiting his brother's arrival.

Ghanasyam's followers then planted their master's standard in front of the throne room. One Pitambar Hazari, accompanied by twenty armed men, entered the room and asked Ratna Manikya to descend from the throne saying that Ghanasyam Barthakur had now become the Raja. Ratna Manikya insisted on sitting on the throne expressing his firm belief in the affection and loyalty of his brother. Pitambar Hazari then caught hold of Ratna Manikya's hand and brought him down from the throne, and sent him in a *palki* to the former residence of Ghanasyam Barthakur. Ratna Manikya's wives and the other ladies of the palace then began to cry at this sad plight of their lord.

Ghanasyam Barthakur then sat on the throne and assumed the name Mahendra Manikya. It was the morning of Monday, the 29th Baisakh, 1634 *saka*. The Brahmans chanted auspicious verses, three volleys were fired from the guns, and trumpets were blown. The soldiers declared to the inhabitants by beat of drums that Mahendra Manikya had become the Raja after having deposed Ratna Manikya Raja.

Now came the question of liquidating the possible opponents. Mahendra Manikya Raja proposed to kill Durjai Singha Juvaraj and appoint Chandramani Thakur in his place. Rajdurlabh Narayan Kotwal-musib was also to be killed. Mamud Sapi intervened, and the lives of Durjai Singha and Rajdurlabh Narayan were spared for the time being.

The deposed ruler Ratna Manikya was lodged as a prisoner in the previous residence of Mahendra Manikya. He used to pass his time in offering devotions to his tutelary deity. Pitambar Hazari who had dragged Ratna Manikya from the throne died of fever three days after as the result of the swelling of the hand responsible for the deed.

Four days after Mahendra Manikya's accession, coins were struck in his name. Rajdurlabh Narayan

Kotwal-musib was beheaded on that very day, and his widow burnt herself on her husband's pyre with the permission of her brothers Ratna Manikya and Mahendra Manikya.

On the very same day, the two Assam envoys Ratna Kandali and Arjundas were brought to the court on horseback for their interview with Mahendra Manikya Raja. There was a concourse of about eighteen thousand men on that day. The Raja sat on the throne at the appointed hour. As the Assam Katakis were waiting for being admitted to the audience hall, a fire suddenly broke out on the roof of a house at the Sona-duari Gate. The Raja despatched men to put out the fire, but its progress could not be checked owing to a powerful wind blowing at that time. The fire spread with violent speed, and engulfed and burnt all the houses including the Raja's residence and the royal stores. The Raja had to leave the throne and sit in an annexe of the Vishnu temple. He passed the night in a tent, and his necessaries were provided by Durjai Singha Juvaraj and Chandramani Thakur.

Mamud Sapi had visited Ratna Manikya who was in the house near the Raja's palace which also caught fire. Mamud Sapi, anxious for the safety of Ratna Manikya, had proceeded to his room and implored him to come out. "My house will not be burnt," said Ratna Manikya, and he continued to remain where he was. Mamud Sapi however succeeded in removing Ratna Manikya to the foot of a banyan tree. The deposed Raja asked Mamud Sapi to allow him to pass his days by listening to the *Bhagavata, Mahabharata* and the *Purana*, for which he prayed for two Brahmans. The sight of the conflagration filled the heart of Mahendra Manikya with consternation and gloom.

There lived with Mahendra Manikya an old nurse named Ganganarayani. She met the Raja at night and spoke about the fire and the damages it had wrought, "This fire," she said, "is not the doing of any man : it is an ominous portent," and she advised the Raja to put an end to Ratna Manikya who was likely to be a cause of trouble as the people were very much discontented at his disposal. She also pleaded for the promotion of Chandramani to the office of Barthakur, and for the continuance of Durjai Singha as Juvaraj.

Mahendra Manikya Raja accordingly proposed to kill Ratna Manikya. He received the support of Murad Beg ; Mamud Sapi protested against the proposed fratricide, but his counsel was a cry in the wilderness.

One Rajput named Kirtisingha Hazari was sent that night with four men to kill Ratna Manikya. The unfortunate prince was then fast asleep in his bed. The guards awoke Ratna Manikya who said to Kirtisingha, —"My brother Ghanasyam has become the Raja by removing me from the throne. The only thing I now ask is a seer of rice, by eating which I shall pass my days in religious devotions. There will be no advantage in killing an innocent Raja. You are besides a Rajput, and you understand the *Dharma* of the Hindus. If you kill me unjustly then the *Dharma* will destroy you as well." Kirtisingha went back to Mahendra Manikya and reported his inability to carry out his master's nefarious orders. The Raja then despatched four trusted men to accomplish what was left undone by the chivalrous Rajput. Ratna Manikya prepared for the event coolly and unperturbed, and after having a bath he put on a new apparel. He asked the ladies to meditate with patience on the means of salvation in the life to come. The four assassins then went near Ratna Manikya, caught hold of him, and strangled him to death.

Thus died Ratna Manikya Raja of Tripura, good-natured, simple and easy-going, but deficient in energy and enterprise, and incapable of discrimination between a friend and a foe. His death was a retribution for his imbecility, and for that unholy and unroyal attempt to disrupt the connubial happiness of a deeply attached young couple.

Arrangements were then made for the cremation of the dead body of Ratna Manikya. A pyre was erected at Muktighat on the bank of the Gomti river. Durjai Singha Juvaraj embraced the corpse and sobbed. Mahendra Manikya himself burst out in tears as the bier was lifted for the procession. The chief consort of Ratna Manikya sat by her husband's body with a *chamar* in her hand. The inhabitants of Udaypur joined the funeral procession with tears in their eyes. The wives of the dead Raja took the permission of their mother-in-law for being burnt as Satis. Mahendra Manikya constructed a brick mound on the spot where his brother's remains had been consecrated to ashes. He tried to expiate his guilt of fratricide by bathing at Dambaru Tirtha, and by offering largesses to Brahmans. He also presented one thousand rupees to the temple of Jagannath at Puri for bing spent in feeding pilgrims.

After things had settled down to some extent, Mahendra Manikya received the Assam envoys Ratna

Kandali and Arjundas on Sravan 10, 1634 *saka*, and dismissed them with epistles and presents in the company of the Tripura Ukil Aribhim Narayan.

The party reached Rangpur, the capital of Assam, on Bhadra 3, 1635 *saka*. Aribhim was received by Surath Singha Barbarua on Kartik 12, and by King Rudra Singha on Poush 24. Mahendra Manikya's letters were in Sanskrit, and they conveyed his desire for friendship with Assam, in view of the possibility of amicable relations even between distant rulers as in the case of Yudhisthira, Virata and Drupada. The Tripura Ukil was again received on Chaitra 21, 1635 *saka*, when the Barbarua communicated the Swargadeo's message : "The Tripura Raja has written to us citing the friendship of Yudhisthira and other monarchs. He should act in accordance with his assurance of friendship, and when the time for action comes he should remain steadfast by our side." Aribhim was given leave in Baisakh 1636, and Ratna Kandali and Arjundas were sent along with him to Tripura with epistles and presents for Mahendra Manikya Raja. The party proceeded on their journey not knowing that Mahendra Manikya died soon after their departure from Assam. He had sat on the throne of Tripura only for fourteen months. The envoys arrived at Tripura on Poush 24, 1636 *saka*.

Durjai Singha Juvaraj had succeeded Mahendra Manikya whereupon he assumed the name Dharma Manikya. He received the Assam envoys first on Jaistha 2, 1637 *saka*, and finally on Jaistha 20. Letters and presents were made over to them for being delivered to King Rudra Singha and Surath Singha Barbarua. Dharma Manikya said to Ratna Kandali and Arjundas, —"Please tell your Maharaja that previously to this there was no relation between us, friendly or otherwise. Friendship has subsisted since its establishment with Ratna Manikya Raja. An attempt should be made to avert the diminution of this friendship. It is not a fact that friendship can be maintained and fostered only by an exchange of Ukils, as we are always in the path of friendship. In the event of launching any notable enterprise demanding our joint exertions, we should be kept mutually informed, and action will be taken accordingly." No envoy was sent from Tripura this time, and the Assam Katakis had therefore to carry the epistles and presents from Dharma Manikya Raja.

Meanwhile, preparations for the invasion of Bengal had been going on in Assam in full swing. In Baisakh 1636 *saka*, King Rudra Singha had moved down with his army to Gauhati where it was joined by the contingents of his allies and vassal chieftains. Te total strength of the army came up to 4,00,000, which included 2,60,00 effectives. An advance body was despatched to Kandahar Choky at the mouth of the Manaha river, on the frontier between Assam and Bengal. The expedition was to march into Mogul territories in November 1714 A.D. after the harvest of Agrahayan. But, as fate would have it, King Rudra Singha was seized with a sudden illness in his camp at Gauhati, and he passed away on Bhadra 13, 1636 *saka*, August 30, 1714 A.D.[10]

10. Sawrgadeo Rudra Singha's plan to invade Mogul India : S. K. Bhuyan's English translation of *Tungkhungia Buranji*, D.H.A.S., 1933, Introduction, p. xx ; text, pp. 36-39 ; Wade's *Account of Assam*, edited by Benudhar Sharma, pp. 125-137 ; Maniram Dewan's manuscript Assam Buranji, *Buranji-vivekaratna*, II, and Assam Buranji manuscript obtained from the Bengena-ati Satra, Majuli.

Ratna Kandali and Arjundas Bairagi had been absent from Assam since Baisakh 1636, and they were thus ignorant of what had happened in their country meanwhile. After completing their mission at Tripura they left its capital in Jaistha 1637 *saka*, and reached Gargaon in Bhadra of the same year. The epistle and presents of Dharma Manikya Raja were delivered by them to Swargadeo Siva Singha Maharaj, son and successor of King Rudra Singha.

The chronicle ends with the return of the Assam envoys on the termination of their third mission to Tripura; and with it also ends the great enterprise of Swargadeo Rudra Singha to oust the Moguls from authority and power. Ratna Manikya died in May 1712, Mahendra Manikya in July 1713, and Swargadeo Rudra Singha in August 1714. Rudra Singha's successor Siva Singha, gallant and refined, was more bent upon the promotion of art and literature than upon undertaking a military expedition of the dimension contemplated by his ambitious father. The Tripura Raja Mahendra Manikya had waded through slaughter to the throne, practically with the help of the Moguls, and his consequent unpopularity would hardly enable him to marshall the resources necessary for participation in King Rudra Singha's project in an effective manner. But Mahendra Manikya's successor Dharma Manikya was noted for his boldness and integrity; and he threw enough hints to the Assam monarch about his willingness to co-operate when occasion arose. He would have been a powerful ally and comrade to fight by the side of King Rudra Singha. Raja Rup Narayan of Cooch Behar had agreed to attack the Moguls as soon as the Assam army would enter Bengal. His allies included

Raja Bhujadeb of Nischintapur and his nephew Naradeb, and also Prananath Raja of Dinajpur.

Whether King Rudra Singha's confederate forces would succeed against the Moguls will remain for ever a matter of speculation. But the greatest asset of King Rudra Singha was the vast array of disgruntled Hindu princes and subjects of Mogul India; the tenacity, resourcefulness and versatility of the Assamese; and the fighting stamina of his army consisting mainly of the martial tribesmen of Eastern India. Even the dream of such a project evokes sentiments of pride combined with a consciousness of national potentiality.

What Assam lost in military glory is compensated to some extent by this historical and literary masterpiece *Tripura Buranji* which, as a monument of Swargadeo Rudra Singha's dream, will be more enduring than triumphs of war, and will lie beyond the reach of destruction by ruffians and desperados, by fires and earthquakes, and by floods and inundations.

The manuscript of *Tripura Buranji* is deposited in the Library of the British Museum, London. It was purchased by the Museum authorities in January 1842 from one J. Rodd. Through the courtesy of the great orientalist Dr. Lionel D. Barnett, Keeper of Oriental Books and Manuscripts, a photostat copy was obtained in January 1936 by the Assam Government Department of Historical and Antiquarian Studies. The book was edited by the present writer, and published by that Department in February 1938.

The publication was well received. The Government of Tripura, under the administration of its enlightened ruler His Highness Bir Bikramkishore Manikya Bahadur at once placed orders for fifty copies. In July 1945, I met His Highness at Pynursula Inspection Bunglow on his way to Shillong. He expressed his deep appreciation of *Tripura Buranji* which contains such a vivid and accurate description of his State. He also informed me that he was engaged in translating the book into English, but the cruel hand of death snatched him away before he could complete the work.

The famous Bengali scholar the late Dr. Nalini Kanta Bhattasali wrote a detailed appreciative review of *Tripura Buranji* where he described its value as a remarkable piece of contemporary history, and exhorted Bengali dramatists and novelists to utilise its materials for their creative works.[11]

It is gratifying that this historical masterpiece of Assam has filled up a noticeable lucuna in the annals of Tripura and Bengal. Udaypur and Rangpur are both in ruins at present, but they come back to life in all their resplendent glory in this chronicle compiled by two scholarly diplomats, who looked at things with the impartiality of a judge, the accuracy of a trained observer, and the vision of a patriot and a poet, and who wrote with the consciousness of a literary artist, and the restrained embellishment of a royal historiographer.

October, 1955.

11. Nalini Kanta Bhattasali, *Rajgi,* Ananda Bazar Patrika, Calcutta, Puza Number, 1353 B.S., A.D. 1946, pp. 237-247.

APPENDIX A

AIDS TO THE STUDY OF ASSAMESE

List of books and articles relating to Assamese language and literature.

DICTIONARIES, GLOSSARIES, WORD-BOOKS, ETC.

AHOM LEXICONS, *Bar-amra,* Ahom to Assamese ; and, *Lati-amra,* Assamese to Ahom. Manuscripts and transcripts in D.H.A.S.

ASAM SAHITYA SABHA. *Chandrakanta Abhidhan.* A comprehensive dictionary of the Assamese language. First edition, Jorhat, 1933 ; Second edition, revised, Gauhati University. *In the press.*

BARUA, GOLAP CHANDRA. *Ahom-Assamese-English Dictionary.* Shillong, 1920.

BARUA, HEMCHANDRA. *Hema-kosh.* An etymological dictionary of the Assamese language. Edited by P. R. T. Gurdon and Hemchandra Goswami. 1st edition, Shillong, 1900 ; 2nd edition, Jorhat, 1941 ; 3rd edition, Sibsagar, 1955.

BHATTACHARYYA, BUDDHINDRA NATH. *The Pronouncing Anglo-Assamese Dictionary.* 1st edition, Jorhat, 1932. 3rd edition, Lawyer's Book Stall, Gauhati, 1962.

BHUYAN, SURYYA KUMAR. A Glossary of Assamese historical terms, appended to *Tungkhungiya Buranji,* English translation, Oxford University Press. Gauhati, 1933.

BRONSON, MILES. *Dictionary in Assamese to English.* Sibsagar, 1867.

BROWN, NATHAN, *Comparison of Indo-Chinese Languages.* Vocabularies in Assamese. J.A.S.B., Vol. VI, 1837.

BUTLER, JOHN. A rough comparison of some of the dialects spoken in the Naga Hills District. Vocabularies in Assamese. J.A.S.B., Vol. XLII, Part I, Appendix. Calcutta, 1873.

CHALIHA, MAKHANLAL. *English-Assamese Dictionary*. Dibrugarh, 1910.

CUTTER, MRS. H. B. L. *Phrases in English and Assamese*. Sibsagar, 1877.

DUTTA-BARUA, HARINARAYAN. *Anglo-Assamese Dictionary*. Nalbari, 1950.

Glossary of vernacular terms used in official correspondence in the Province of Assam. Shillong, 1879.

KAMRUPI, RUCHINATH. *Vocabularies of the Ashami and Camarupa languages*, compiled in 1810 A.D. Manuscript in the India Office Library, London. Transcript in D.H.A.S.

List of words and phrases showing some of the principal Aryan languages of India : Assamese language, pp. 168-185.

PEAL, S. Table of comparison of selected words and numerals in the several Assam languages. Proceedings A.S.B., 1895.

PHUKAN, ANANDARAM DHEKIAL. *Specimen of a forthcoming English and Assamese Dictionary*, from *A* to *Ablution*. Arunoday, Sibsagar, Vol. XI, No. 12, December 1856.

SAIKIA, BHRAMAR CHANDRA. *Sabdamala*. A selected vocabulary of Assamese words. Jhanji, Sibsagar, 1925, 1956.

RAJKHOWA, BENUDHAR. *Khandavakya-kosh*. A dictionary of Assamese phrases. 1st edition, Dibrugarh, 1917. Second edition, edited by Maheswar Neog, and published by Asam Sahitya Sabha, Jorhat, 1961.

SARMA, GIRIDHAR. *Asamia Abhidhan*, or Assamese-English dictionary. Shillong, 1952.

SARMA GIRIDHAR. *Anglo-Assamese Dictionary*. Shillong, 1952.

WARD, MRS. S. R. *Vocabulary in English and Assamese*. Sibsagar, 1864.

ASSAMESE LANGUAGE AND GRAMMER.

ANDERSON, J. D. *Assamese and Bengali*. Calcutta Review, July 1896.

BARUA, BIRINCHI KUMAR. *Asamia Bhasha*. Gauhati, 1949.

BARUA, HEMCHANDRA. *Asamiya Vyakaran*. 1st edition, Gauhati, 1873.

BEAMS, J. *Outlines of Indian Philology*, with a map showing the distribution of Indian languages. Calcutta, 1867.

BHARALI, DEVANANDA. *Asamiya Bhasar Maulik Bichar*. Jorhat, 1915.

— *A Manual of Assamese Grammar*. Calcutta, 1909.

— *Assamese Philology*. Jorhat, 1960.

BORA, SATYANATH. *Bahal Vyakaran*. Gauhati, 1918.

BROWN, NATHAN. *Grammatical Notices of the Assamese Language*. Sibsagar, 1848. Revised edition, Nowgong, 1893.

CHALIHA, DEBESWAR. *Assamese and Bengali compared*. Gauhati, 1909.

— *Origin and Growth of the Assamese Language and Literature*. Jorhat, 1949.

CHAKRAVARTI, JAICHANDRA. *Vyakaran-manjari*. Calcutta, 1894.

CAMPBELL, SIR GEORGE. *Specimens of the Languages of India*, including those of the aboriginal tribes of Bengal, the Central Provinces, and the Eastern Frontier. Calcutta, 1874.

Correspondence relating to the Question whether the Assamese or Bengali Language should be taught in the Schools of Assam. Calcutta, 1854.

CUST, R. N. *A Sketch of the Modern Languages of the East Indies*. London, 1878.

CUST, R. N. *Languages of the Indo-Chinese Peninsula and the Indian Archipelago*. Proceedings A. S. B., Calcutta, Nov. 1877.

CUST, R. N. *Aryan Languages of India*. Proceedings A. S. B. Jan. 1877.

GOSWAMI, HEMCHANDRA. *Asamiya Bhasha*. Jonaki, Calcutta. Vol. III.

GOSWAMI, HEMCHANDRA, AND PADMANATH GOHAIN-BARUA. *A Note on Assamese Language and Literature*, edited by S. K. Bhuyan, and prefixed to Goswami's *Typical Selections from Assamese Literature* Vol. I.

GRIERSON, SIR GEORGE ABRAHAM. The portion relating to Assamese language in *Linguistic Survey of India,* Vol. V, Part 1.

— *Assamese Literature,* Indian Antiquary, Vol. XXV, 1896. A resume of "A Few Remarks on the Assamese Language" by Anandaram Dhekial Phukan, 1855.

HAZARIKA, LAKSHESWAR. *A Primary Grammar in Assamese.* Calcutta, 1900

HUTCHINSON, C. W. Specimens of Various Vernacular Characters passing through the Post Offices in India. Contains specimens of Assamese writing. Calcutta, 1877.

KAKATI, BANIKANTA. *Assamese : Its Formation and Development.* 1st edition, D.H.A.S., Gauhati, 1941. Second edition, Lawyer's Book Stall, Gauhati, 1962.

KAKAKI, SARVESWAR. *Ancient Assamese Script.* Gauhati, 1935.

MEDHI, KALIRAM. *Assamese Grammar and Origin of the Assamese Language.* Gauhati, 1936.

MISRA, UMAKANTA. Assamese and Prakrit. Articles in Awahan, Calcutta, first series.

MOORE, REV. P. H. Revised edition of Rev. Nathan Brown's *Grammatical Notices of the Assamese Language.* Nowgong, 1893.

NEOG, DIMBESWAR. *Asamiya Bhasha aru Lipir Kahini.* Jorhat.

NICHOLL, G. F. *Manual of the Bengali Language,* including an Assamese Grammar. London, 1894.

PHUKAN, ANANDARAM DHEKIAL. *A Few Remarks on the Assamese Language.* Sibsagar, 1855. An Assamese translation by Maheswar Neog, published by Asam Sahitya Sabha, Jorhat, 1958.

RAJKHOWA, BENUDHAR. *Asamiya Bhasa Kenekoi Beleg Bhasha*? Bijuli, Vol. II, Calcutta, 1892.

— *Brochure on the Assamese Language.* Calcutta, 1898.

— *Notes on the Sylhetee Dialect.* Sylhet, 1913.

ROBINSON, WILLIAM. Notes on Languages spoken by the Various Tribes inhabiting the Valley of Assam. Grammar and Vocabulary of Assamese, etc., and also Assamese compared with Bengali. J.A.S.B., Calcutta, Vol. XVIII, Part I, 1849.

— Notes on the Languages spoken in the Brahmaputra Valley. J.A.S.B., Vol. XVII.

— *Grammar of the Assamese Language*. Serampore, 1839.

SUDMERSEN, F. W. *Notes on Assamese Language and Literature*. Shillong, 1908.

Tarkalankar, Dinabandhu. *Asamiya Lorar Vyakaran*. Published by Gunabhiram Barua, Nowgong, 1873; 10th edition, Calcutta, 1882.

WOLFENDEN, STUART N. *Outlines of Tibeto-Burman Morphology*. London, 1928.

HISTORIES OF LITERATURE :

ALL INDIA RADIO. *Modern Indian Languages*. Talks broadcast from New Delhi Centre, in the National Programme on Indian Literatures. New Delhi, 1957. Contains sections on Assamese literature, ancient and mediaeval period, and modern period.

BANERJI, SANTIRANJAN. *Adhunik Bharatiya Sahitya*. Contains a section on Assamese literature. Calcutta, 1954.

BANERJI, SUDHINDRA MOHAN. *Asamiya Sahitya*. A short treatise in Bengali. Calcutta, 1950.

BARKAKATI, RAMAKANTA, AND KANAKLAL BARUA. *Asamiya Puthir Talika*, Assamese Language Improvement Society. Calcutta, 1896.

BARTHAKUR, KUMUDESWAR. *Ratna Kaumudi*, Part I. Sketches of Assamese authors, Gauhati, 1938.

BARUA, BIRINCHI KUMAR. *Assamese Literature*. P.E.N. Publication. Bombay, 1941.

— *Asamiya Katha-sahitya*, Purani Bhag. Gauhati, 1950.

— *Studies in Early Assamese Literature*. Nowgong, 1953.

— *Modern Assamese Literature*. Gauhati, 1957.

— and Prafulladutta Goswami. *Adhunik Asamiya Sahitya.* Devanagar, Delhi, Sravan, 2010 Vikrama era.

— and Satyendranath Sarma. *Manasa Kavya.* Gauhati, 1952.

BARUA, MADHAB CHANDRA. *Bibliography of the Works of Pundit Hemchandra Goswami,* compiled under the supervision of Professor S. K. Bhuyan. Kamarupa Anusandhan Samiti. Gauhati, 1931.

BEZBARUA, DEVENDRANATH. *Asamiya Bhasha aru Sahityar Buranji.* 1st edition, Calcutta, 1912; 2nd edition, Jorhat, 1933.

BHUYAN, SURYA KUMAR. *Assamese Historical Literature.* Paper read at the Lahore session of the All-India Oriental Conference, November 1928. Published in *Indian Historical Quarterly,* Calcutta, September 1929. Incorporated in *Studies in the Literature of Assam.*

— *A Note on Assamese Manuscripts.* Prefixed to Pundit Hemchandra Goswami's *Descriptive Catalogue of Assamese Manuscripts.* Calcutta, 1930. Incorporated in *Studies in the Literature of Assam.*

— *Assamese Literature : Ancient and Modern.* A limited number of copies was printed by Assam Government in 1936. Incorporated in *Studies in the Literature of Assam.*

— *Assamese Literature : Ancient period.* Talk broadcast on April 27, 1955, from New Delhi Centre, A.I.R. Incorporated in *Studies in the Literature of Assam.*

— *Buranji-mulak Pravandhavalir Talika.* A list of articles on Assam History, published in Assamese magazines since 1846. Asam Sahitya Sabha, Jorhat, 1955.

— *Bibliography of the Works of Dr. S. K. Bhuyan.* Gauhati, 1951.

— *Studies in the Literature of Assam.* Gauhati, 1956, 1962.

DAS, BHARAT CHANDRA. *Asamiya Sahitya-buranji,* Part I. Manasa-sakha. Bharalumukh, Gauhati, 1950.

GAUHATI UNIVERSITY. *Aspects of Early Assamese Literature.* Essays, edited by Dr. Banikanta Kakati. 1953, 1959.

GOSWAMI, HEMCHANDRA. *A Descriptive Catalogue of Assamese Manuscripts*. Published by Calcutta University on behalf of the Government of Assam. Calcutta, 1930.

GOSWAMI, JATINDRA NATH. *Asamiya Sahityar Chamu Buranju*. 2nd edition, New Book Stall, Gauhati, 1962.

GOSWAMI, PRAFULLADUTTA. *Asamiya Jana-sahitya*. 1947, 1954.

— *Ei Jugar Sahitya*. Gauhati, 1950.

— *Folk Literature of Assam*. D.H.A.S. Gauhati, 1954.

— *Ballads and Tales of Assam*. Thesis approved for the D. PHIL degree of Gauhati University. Gauhati, 1961.

— ASSAMESE DRAMA. Calcutta, 1960.

NEOG, DIMBESWAR. *Adhunik Asamiya Sahityar Buranji*. Jorhat, 1937.

— ASAMIYA SAHITYAR BURANJIT BHUMUKI. Jorhat, 1940.

— ASAMIYA SAHITYAR JEUTI. Jorhat, 1950.

— ASAMIYA SAHITYAR BURANJI. 4th edition, Jorhat, 1957.

— *History of Modern Assamese Literature from 1826 to 1947*. Ganganath Jha Research Institute, Allahabad, 1955.

— *New Light on History of Asamiya Literature*. Gauhati, 1962.

NEOG, MAHESWAR. *Sankardeva and His Predecessors*. Gauhati, 1953.

PHUKAN, NILMANI. *On Assamese Literature*. P.E.N. Conference, Jaipur, 1945.

SAHITYA AKADEMI. *Contemporary Indian Literature*, containing an essay on Assamese literature. New Delhi, 1958.

SARMA, SATYENDRA NATH. *Asamiya Sahityar Itivritta*. Second edition, Bani Prakash Mandir, Pathsala and Gauhati, 1962.

— *Asamiya Natya-sahitya*. Gauhati, 1962.

ESSAYS IN CRITICISM

AGARWALA, JYOTIPRASAD. *Jyotirdhara*, essays. Collected and edited by Atul Chandra Hazarika. Tezpur, 1961.

ASSAM CHATRA SAMMILAN. *Sammilan Pravandhavali.* Collection of essays, Vols. I, II, III, IV, and V. 1918—1925.

BARUA, ATUL CHANDRA. *Sahityar Rup-rekha.* Gauhati, 1957.

— *Samalochona Sahitya.* Shillong, 1960.

— *Sahitya Drishti.* Gauhati, 1960.

BARUA, BIRINCHI KUMAR. *Kavya aru Abhivyanjana.* Gauhati, 1941.

BARUA, HEM. *Modern Assamese Poetry.* Gauhati, 1960.

— *Adhunik Sahitya.* Gauhati, 1950.

BARUA, SATYAPRASAD. *Natak aru Abhinay Prasanga.* Gauhati, 1962.

BEZBARUA, MADHAB CHANDRA. *Pravandha Sangraha.* Gauhati, 1937.

BORA, JNANANATH. *Adhunik Asamiya Sahitya.* Gauhati, 1961.

BORA, SATYANATH. *Sahitya Bichar.* Gauhati, 1889.

BHUYAN, SURYYA KUMAR. *Tripadi.* Three essays on the literature and history of Assam. Lawyer's Book Stall, Gauhati, 1959.

CHALIHA, KAMALESWAR. *Biswarasik Lakhsminath Bezbarua.* Jorhat, 1939.

CHOUDHURY, GIRISH CHANDRA. *Chinta-kosh.* Collection of essays. A.S.L. Club, Calcutta, 1936.

CHOUDHURY, RAGHUNATH. *Chinta-dhara.* Collection of essays. Pragati Samiti, Gauhati, 1939.

DAS, HARAMOHAN. *Sahitya-tatwa.* Gauhati, 1938.

GOGOI, PADMESWAR. *Chintawali.* Collection of essays. Sahitya Seva Sangha. Jorhat, 1941.

GOSWAMI, MAHESH CHANDRA DEVA. *Sahitya aru Samalochana.* Collection of essays. A.S.L. Club, Calcutta, 1941.

— NIBANDHAVALI. Collection of essays compiled on the occasion of the Asam Sahitya Sabha session held at Nowgong in April 1959.

GOSWAMI, PRAFULLADUTTA. *Bihu Songs of Assam.* Gauhati, 1957.

— *Sahitya aru Jivan.* Gauhati, 1957.

GOSWAMI, TROILOKYA NATH. *Sahitya Alochana.* Nalbari, 1950, 1961.

GOSWAMI, UPENDRA NATH. *Bhasha aru Sahitya.* Gauhati, 1961.

JORHAT SAHITYA SABHA GRANTHAVALI, Vol. I *Pancha-pallab,* five essays, Jorhat, 1956.

KAKATI, BANIKANTA. *Purani Asamiya Sahitya.* Gauhati, 1940.

— *Sahitya aru Prem.* Ramdhenu Prakash Bhavan, Gauhati, 1948.

LAKHARU, UPENDRA CHANDRA. *Asamiya Ramayan Sahitya.* Gauhati, 1949.

— RAJANI KANTA BARDOLOI. Gauhati, 1953.

MAHANTA, BAPCHANDRA. *Sahityar Swarup aru Adarsa.* Jorhat, 1959.

PATGIRI, NAVADWIP RANJAN. *Asamiya Kavitar Prabha.* Sarbhog, 1952.

SARMA, HEMANTA KUMAR. *Asamiya Sahityat Dristipat.* Gauhati, 1961.

SARMA, KAMALESWAR. *Raghunath Choudhury aru Choudhury-devar Kabita.* Asam Sahitya Sabha, Jorhat, 1961.

SARMA, SONAPATI DEVA. *Asamiya Sahityar Saj.* Revised edition, Barpeta, 1949.

SARMA, UMAKANTA. *Kavya-bhumi.* Shillong, 1948.

ANTHOLOGIES :

The books are mentioned against the names of the editors or compilers.

ASSAM ACADEMY FOR CULTURAL RELATIONS. *Sahitya Sanchayan.* An anthology of Assamese prose and verse. Gauhati, 1961.

BARUA, ATUL CHANDRA. *Kavya-prabha.* Assamese poems. Shillong, 1940.

BARUA, GUNABHIRAM. *Kavya-kusum,* poems, Part I. Published by Haribilas Agarwala. Calcutta, 1884.

BARUA, PHANINDRANATH. *Prachin Asamiya Git Sankalan.* Jorhat, 1952.

16

BARDOLOI, MADHAB CHANDRA. Assamese Selections for Intermediate and B.A. Examinations, Calcutta University. Gauhati, 1909.

BHUYAN, NAKUL CHANDRA. *Bohagi*. Collection of Bihu songs. Jorhat, 1920.

DUTTA-BARUA, HARINARAYAN. *Purani Asamiya Sahitya*. Jorhat, 1934.

— and UPARJAN SAIKIA. *Puspanjali*, poems, Nowgong, 1913.

Gauhati University. Matriculation Assamese Poetical Selections. 1950.

— Matriculation Assamese Prose Selections. 1950.

— Intermediate Assamese Poetical Selections. 1955.

— Intermediate Assamese Prose Selections. 1955.

— *Prabandhavali*. Prose selections. 1958.

GOGOI, LILA. *Bihu Git aru Banghosha*. Gauhati, 1961.

— *Asamiya Loka-git*. Gauhati University. 1956.

GOSWAMI, GOLAP CHANDRA. *Asamiya Sahityar Bachani*. Golaghat, 1916.

GOSWAMI, HEMCHANDRA. *Typical Selections from Assamese Literature*. In seven parts. Calcutta University, 1928-29.

GOSWAMI, MAHESWAR. Assamese Selections for the Entrance Examination of Calcutta University. Gauhati, 1904.

GOHAIN-BARUA, PADMANATH. *Sahitya-sangraha*. 10th edition, Tezpur, 1932.

GURDON, P.R.T. *Some Assamese Proverbs*. Shillong, 1903.

KALITA, DANDINATH. *Sahitya-muktavali*. Tezpur, 1934.

KATAKI, SARVESWAR SARMA. *Asamiya Sahitya-kosh*. Revised edition, Gauhati, 1937.

LEKHARU, UPENDRA CHANDRA. *Katha-sahitya*. Gauhati, 1940.

MALIK, SYED ABDUL. *Asamiya Jikir aru Jari*. Devotional songs of Assamese Muslims. Gauhati University, 1958.

MEDHI, KALIRAM. *Mahapurush Sankardevar Vani*. Gauhati, 1949.

NEOG, DIMBESWAR. *Kavya-pratibha*, poems, 1830-1930. Jorhat, 1935.

— *Akul Psthik*. Collection of Banghosha songs. Jorhat,

NEOG, MAHESWAR. *Sanchayan*. A collection of Assamese poetry, ancient and modern. Sahitya Akademi, New Delhi, 1958.

SARMA, JAJNESWAR, *Sata-patra*, poems. Nowgong, 1935.

SARMA, JATINARAYAN. *Adhunik Asamiya Kavita*. Jorhat, 1946.

SARMA, LAKDHESWAR. *Kavita-kunja*. Calcutta, 1938.

SARMA, TIRTHANATH. *Pravesika Katha-chaneki*. Calcutta, 1940.

MISCELLANEOUS :

AGARWALA, ANANDA CHANDRA. *Asamiya Sahityar Unnatit Tezpuriar Dan*. Awahan, Calcutta, Vol. III, No. 6, 1932.

ASSAM CHATRA SAMMILAN. *Sabhapatir Bhashanamala*. Presidential addresses delivered at the fourteen sessions of the Assam Students' Conference, 1916-1930. Edited by Atul Chandra Hazarika. Prakasan Parishad, Assam. Gauhati, 1960.

ASAM SAHITYA SABHA. *Sabhapatir Bhashanavali*. Presidential addresses delivered at the sessions of the Sabha :
Vol. I. Sessions I to XII, 1917-30. Edited by Atul Chandra Hazarika. Jorhat, 1956.
Vol. II. Sessions XIII to XXV, 1931-56. Edited by Atul Chandra Hazarika. Jorhat, 1957.
Vol. III. Fourteen sessions of the Historical Section. 1925-61. Edited by Atul Chandra Hazarika and Jatindra Nath Goswami. Jorhat, 1961.

Asam Sahitya Sabha. List of Assamese Books in the A.S.S. Library. A.S.S. Patrika, Vol. I, No. 4, Jorhat, 1927.

BARKAKATI, RAMESH CHANDRA. *Puratattwavid Sonaram Choudhury*. North Gauhati, 1955.

BARUA, BIRINCHI KUMAR. *Asamar Loka-samskriti*. A study of the popular culture of Assam. Published by Mrs. Santicchaya Barua. Gauhati, 1961.

BARUA, GUNABHIRAM. *Anandaram Dhekial Phukanar Jivancharitra*. Calcutta, 1880, 1915.

BARUA, HARAKANTA SARMA, SADAR-AMIN. *Sadar-aminar Atmajivani.* An autobiography in the form of a diary from 1834-35 to 1889-90. Edited by Kumud Chandra Bardoloi. North Gauhati, 1960.

BARUA, SIVA PRASAD, compiler and editor. *A Brochure on Assamese Literature and Culture.* Banti Sahitya Mandir, Mariani and Gauhati, December 1958.

BEZBARUA, LAKSHMINATH. *Mor Jivan Sowaran,* or recollections of my life. Collected and edited by Jatindra Nath Goswami ; General editor, Maheswar Neog. Asam Sahitya Sabha, Jorhat, 1961.

BHUYAN, NAKUL CHANDRA. *Radhakanta Handiqui Dangaria.* A biography. Asam Sahitya Sabha, Jorhat, 1961.

BHUYAN, SURYYA KUMAR. A list of Assamese manuscripts in the Library of the Kamarupa Anusandhan Samiti. Report and Conspectus of the K.A.S. Gauhati, 1927.

— List of Assamese manuscripts in the Library of the Department of Historical and Antiquarian Studies in Assam. Inserted in Bulletins I and II of the D.H.A.S. Gauhati, 1832 and 1934.

— *Ahomar Abhidhan-Sastra,* Lexicographical Literature of the Ahoms, *Bar-amra and Lati-amra.* Awahan, Calcutta, Vol. III, No. 3, 1932 ; reprinted in Tai Samskriti, Vol. I, No. I, March 1956.

— *Some Literary Reminiscences.* Gauhati, 1954.

— *Men I Have Met.* Including brief and intimate sketches of seventy Assamese men of letters. Gauhati, 1862.

BORA, ABANINDRA CHANDRA. *Satirtha.* Brief sketches of men of letters of Nowgong. Compiled for the Asam Sahitya Sabha session held at Nowgong in April 1959.

BORA, LAMBODAR. *Asamiya Bhasar Akhar-jotani.* Jonaki, Calcutta, Vol. III.

BLUMHARDT, J. F. Catalogue of the Bengali and Assamese Manuscripts in the Library of the India Office, London, 1905.

— Catalogue of the Marathi, Gujarati, Bengali, Assamese, Oriya, Pushtu and Sindhi Manuscripts in the Library of the British Museum, London, 1905.

CHALIHA, PADMADHAR. *Asamiya Sahitya aru Rangpuriar Barangani.* Sibsagar, 1956.

DUTTA, KESAB NARAYAN. *Aspects of the Heritage of Assam.* Published by the Reception Committee of the Indian History Congress held at Gauhati in December 1959.

DUTTA-BARUA, HARINARAYAN. Search for Assamese manuscripts in the Bardowa area. Asam Sahitya Sabha Patrika, Vol. I, No. 2, 1927.

— Search for Assamese manuscripts in the Majuli area. Asam Sahitya Sabha Patrika, Vol. I, No. 4, 1927.

GOGOI, LILA. *Ahom Jati aru Asamiya Samskriti.* Jeuti Prakas, Sibsagar, 1961.

GOSWAMI, NANDINATH. *Goalparia Lokar Sahitya-charcha.* Asam Sahitya Sabha Patrika, Vol. II, No. 3, 1928.

GOSWAMI, PRATAP CHANDRA. *Mantra Sahitya.* . Asam Sahitya Sabha Patrika, Vol. II, No. 3, 1928.

— Search for Assamese manuscripts in Cooch Behar. Asam Sahitya Sabha Patrika, Vol. II, No. 2, 1928.

— Search for Assamese manuscripts in Rungpore, Bengal. Awahan, Calcutta, Vol. IV, No. 2, 1932.

KESAVAN, B. S., AND AMULYA KUMAR HAZARIKA. *Jatiya Grantha-suchi,* compiled in 1959 by the Central Reference Library, Government of India. Published by Ram Goswami, State Central Library, Shillong, 1960.

NEOG, MAHESWAR. *Purani Asamiya Samaj aru Samskriti.* Bani Mandir, Dibrugarh, 1957..

— *Asamiya Giti-sahitya.* Janata Book Stall, Tezpur, 1958.

RADHANATH PHUKAN SAMBARDHANA SAMITI. *Sraddhanjali.* Containing essays on the life and work of Radhanath Phukan Vedanta-vachaspati. Compiled under the auspices of the R. P. S. Samity, Jorhat, 1958.

SABITA SABHA, GAUHATI. *Jivanimala.* Sketches of Kaliram Barua and Satyanath Bora, by Jitendra Nath Bujar-Barua. Gauhati, 1958.

SASTRI, BISWANARAYAN, AND PROMOD CHANDRA BHATTACHARYYA. *This is Assam.* Asam Sahitya Sabha, Jorhat, January 1958.

BHATTACHARYYA, TARINI KANTA. *Sahityar Gatipath.* Main trends of English and European literature. Gauhati, 1962.

APPENDIX B

BIBLIOGRAPHICAL NOTE ON ASSAMESE HISTORICAL LITERATURE

As considerable interest has been roused among students of Indian History in the indigenous chronicles of Assam, known as Buranjis, an indication is given below of the materials for the information of scholars who want to study the subject in an intensive form.

The nucleus of information will be obtained in Dr. S. K. Bhuyan's paper *Assamese Historical Literature*, read at the Fifth Session of the All-India Oriental Conference held at Lahore in November 1928, and published in the *Indian Historical Quarterly*, Calcutta, for September 1929. Fuller information can be obtained from Dr. Bhuyan's Prefaces and Introductions in English to the Buranjis edited by him, *viz.*,—

(1) *Assam Buranji*—By the late Srijut Harakanta Barua Sadar-Amin. A history of Ahom rule in Assam, 1228-1826 A. D., being an enlarged version of *Assam Buranji Puthi* by Kashinath Tamuli Phukan and Radhanath Barbarua. Published by the Department of Historical and Antiquarian Studies, Assam, in 1930.

(2) *Kamrupar Buranji*—A detailed history of the Assam-Mogul conflicts of the Seventeenth Century, with chapters on ancient Kamarupa. D.H.A.S., 1930, 1958.

(3) *Deodhai Asam Buranji*—A collection of old chronicles dealing with the earlier period of Ahom history, neighbouring tribes, Ahom customs, etc. It includes the chronicle of Assam by Atan Buragohain Rajmantri Dangaria, Prime Minister of Assam, 1662-1679. D.H.A. S., 1932.

(4) *Tungkhungia Buranji*—A history of the Tungkhungia dynasty of Ahom sovereigns from 1681 to 1806, by Srinath Duara Barbarua, Head of the Executive and the Judiciary from 1800 to 1817. D. H. A. S., 1932. The original Assamese version.

(5) *Asamar Padya-Buranji*—Two metrical chronicles of Assam dealing with the events of the period from 1679 to 1826,

by Dutiram Hazarika and Bisweswar Vaidyadhip. D.H.A.S., 1933.

(6) *Kachari Buranji*—A history of Cachar from the earliest times to the reign of the Kachari Raja Tamradhwaj Narayan and the Ahom king Swargadeo Rudra Singha. D.H.A.S., 1936, 2nd edition, 1951.

(7) *Jayantia Buranji*—A history of Jayantia from the earliest times to the reign of the Jayantia Raja Lakshmi Singha and the Ahom king Swargadeo Siva Singha, with sidelights on Jayantia matriarchal system, and the history of the Khasi State of Khyrim. D.H.A.S., 1937. Preface by Mr. S. K. Dutta.

(8) *Tripura Buranji*, or *Tripura Desar Katha*—A historical and descriptive account of Tripura with special reference to the events of 1710 to 1715, by Ratna Kandali Sarma Kataki and Arjun Das Bairagi, ambassadors of King Rudra Singha deputed to the Tripura court. From the original manuscript in the British Museum, London. D.H.A.S., 1938.

(9) *Tungkhungia Buranji*—or A History of Assam from 1681 to 1826, being an English translation of the Assamese text, with an extension of the history up to the British occupation of Assam in 1826. With a Glossary of Assamese historical terms and genealogical tables of Ahom kings. Published by the Oxford University Press for the D.H.A.S., 1933.

(10) *Assam Buranji*—Obtained from the family of Sukumar Mahanta. A history of the Ahom kings from the earliest times to the reign of Swargadeo Gadhadhar Singha. The Preface and Introduction in English cover 83 pages. The Introduction deals, among other subjects, with the ideology of the Assamese people and cites a number of illustrative anecdotes. D.H.A.S., 1945, 1962.

(11) *Padshah Buranji*—An old Assamese chronicle of the Sultans and Emperors of Delhi, from the defeat of Pithor Raja to Aurangzeb, published by the Kamarupa Anusandhan Samiti, Gauhati, in 1935. This chronicle was described by Dr. Bhuyan in a series of articles in the *Islamic Culture*, Hyderabad, Decan, in the years 1928-1929, under the heading "New Lights on Mogul

India from Assamese Sources". An English translation of *Padshah-Buranji* was also published in the same journal in 1933-34 under the title "Annals of the Delhi Badshahate".

(12) *Annals of the Delhi Badshahate*—An English translation of the Assamese chronicle *Padshah-Buranji*, with Notes. The Introduction deals with Assam's contact with the Muslim world, Padshah-Buranji manuscripts, etc. D.H.A.S., 1947.

(13) *Satsari Assam Buranji* —A collection of seven old Assamese chronicles. Gauhati University, 1960.

Reviews of the above Buranjis have been published in the Journal of the Royal Asiatic Society of Great Britain and Ireland, Journal of Indian History, Journal of the Bhandarkar Research Institute, Islamic Culture, Indian Historical Quarterly, Calcutta Review, History, Journal of the Royal Geographical Society, Indian Culture, Annual Bibliography of Indian Archaelogy, etc.

A few more Buranjis have also been published under the editorship of other authors, *viz.*,—

(1) *Assam Buranji arthat Assam Desiya Itihas*—A history of Assam, in Bengali, by Haliram Dhekial Phukan, Part 1, from the Pauranic period to the advent of the British. Printed at the Samachar Chandrika Jantra, Calcutta, 1829. Reviewed by Dr. Bhuyan in the Journal of the Bangiya Sahitya-Parishat, Calcutta, B. S. 1333, Vol. 33 No. 1. A supplementary note by Pandit Jatindramohan Bhattacharyya was published in a subsequent issue of the Parishat journal. A review of this book by Tarachand Chakravarti was published in the *Asiatic Journal and Monthly Register*, Vol. 23, 1837, and an analysis forms part of India Office Library Tract No. 166.

(2) *Assam Buranji Puthi*—A history of the Ahom kings from the earliest times to the British occupation of Assam, by Kasinath Tamuli Phukan and Radhanath Barbarua. First published in 1844 by the American Baptist Mission, Sibsagar. Reprinted and published by Authority in 1906.

(3) *Darrang-raj-vamsavali*—A metrical chronicle of the early rulers of Cooch Behar to the time of Samudra Narayan, Raja of Darrang, written about the year 1798 by Suryya Khari

Daivajna. Edited by Pundit Hemchandra Goswami and published by the Government of Assam, 1917.

(4) *Purani Asam Buranji*—A chronicle of the Ahom kings from the earliest times to the reign of Gadadhar Singha. Edited by Pundit Hemchandra Goswami, and published by the Kamarupa Anusandhan Samiti in 1922.

(5) *An Account of Assam*—Being mainly an English translation of two chronicles, one in Assamese and the other in Ahom, by Dr. John Peter Wade, who stayed in Assam in 1792-94. Edited from the original manuscript in the India Office Library, London, by Srijut Benudhar Sharma of Charing in Sibsagar, and published by Srijut Rameswar Sarma, 1927.

(6) *Ahom Buranji*—A chronicle of the Ahom kings from the earliest times to Swargadeo Purandar Singha. The original text is in the Ahom language and script, with a parallel rendering in English, by Rai Sahib Golap Chandra Barua. Published by the Government of Assam, 1930.

(7) *Assam Buranji*—A history of the Ahom kings from the accession of Swargadeo Jayadhwaja Singha in 1648 to that of Swargadeo Gadadhar Singha in 1681, with excerpts from miscellaneous chronicles. Edited by Mr. S. K. Dutta, and published by the D.H.A.S., in 1938.

Information about Assamese Buranjis is also available in the following :

(*a*) Dhekial Phukan, Anundoram,—*A Few Remarks on the Assamese Language*, Sibsagar, 1855, pp. 45-46. A synopsis of this book was published in the *Indian Antiquary* for 1896.

(*b*) Grierson, Sir George—*Linguistic Survey of India*, Vol. I, Part I, Introductory, p. 156.

(*c*) Gait, Sir Edward,—*Report on the Progress of Historical Research in Assam*. Shillong, 1897, pp. 16-24.

(*d*) Gait, Sir Edward,—Preface to his *History of Assam*, Calcutta, 1st edition, 1906 ; 2nd edition, 1926.

(*e*) Bhuyan, Dr. S. K.,—*Ahomar Din*, Jorhat, 1918, pp. 89-92.

(*f*) Bhuyan Dr. S. K.,—*History of the Reign of Rajeswar Singha*, king of Assam from 1751 to 1769. The chapter on the desecration of Buranjis by Kirti Chandra Barbarua. *Banhi*, Gauhati, Vol. XV, No. 2, Jaistha 1847 *Saka*, pp. 108-111.

There are several Buranjis, yet unpublished, in the library of the Department of Historical and Antiquarian Studies, Assam, and some of them have been mentioned in Bulletins I, II and III of the Department, and in the bibliographies appended to Dr. Bhuyan's *Lachit Barphukan and His Times, Atan Buragohain and His Times,* and *Anglo-Assamese Relations.* Copies of English translations of some Buranjis, prepared under the direction of Sir Edward Gait, were in possession of Dr. Jadunath Sarkar in their manuscript form, *Vide* his *History of Aurangzeb*, Vol. III, 1916, Foreword, and Chapters 31-32.

APPENDIX C

BIBLIOGRAPHICAL NOTES ON THE STUDIES INCORPORATED IN THE BOOK

Almost all the articles inserted in the present book *Studies in the Literature of Assam* have been printed, published or broadcast before. The details of publication, together with other relevant information, are given below :

1. ASSAMESE LITERATURE : ANCIENT PERIOD. Talk broadcast on April 27, 1955, from the New Delhi Centre of the All India Radio, in the National Programme in connection with the series of talks on Indian literatures. Published in *The March of India*, for March 1956.

2. ASSAMESE LITERATURE : ANCIENT AND MODERN. A limited number of copies was printed by the Government of Assam in 1936 for official use, with a list of important Assamese books, both ancient and modern. This essay was recommended by the University of Gauhati for study for the M.A. Examination in Assamese, in the paper on the History of Assamese Literature. An Assamese translation by Shri Liladhar Sarma Kataki was published in *Awahon*, Calcutta, Volume VIII.

3. ASSAMESE HISTORICAL LITERATURE. This paper was read at the fifth session of the All-India Oriental Conference held at Lahore in November 1928. It was also published in the *Indian Historical Quarterly*, Calcutta, for September 1929. The article was recommended by the University of Calcutta for study for the M.A. Examination in Assamese, in the paper on the History of Assamese Literature. An Assamese translation by Shri Bipin Kumar Bargohain and Shri Harendranath Sarma was published in *Awahon*, Volume I.

4. ASSAMESE MANUSCRIPTS. It was prefixed as Introduction to Pundit Hemchandra Goswami's *Descriptive Catalogue*

of Assamese manuscripts, published by the University of Calcutta on behalf of the Government of Assam, 1930.

5. HEMCHANDRA GOSWAMI. This biographical sketch was prefixed to Pundit Hemchandra Goswami's *Typical Selections from Assamese Literature,* published by the University of Calcutta, Volume I, 1929. A detailed sketch in Assamese of Pundit Hemchandra Goswami's life was published in *Milan,* Calcutta, Volume VI, which has been inserted in the present writer's *Jonaki,* 3rd edition, 1955. Republished in Hemchandra Goswami Commemoration Volume, K.A.S., 1962.

6. MODERN KHASI LITERATURE. It was originally inserted as Introduction to *Ki Khasi* Poetry, containing a collection of the poems of U Soso Tham of Shillong, and was afterwards published in *The Assam Review,* Silchar, for October 1928, which was then edited by the late Rev. W. H. S. Wood.

7. MANIPURI SAHITYA PARISHAD. This essay was written for being delivered in inaugurating the general session of the Manipuri Sahitya Parishad held at Imphal on October 10, 11 and 19, 1952. As the writer could not attend the session personally owing to unfavourable weather conditions between Gauhati and Manipur, a summary was given at the meeting by the Secretary of the Parishad. The speech is incorporated in the Proceedings of the session published in February 1954, with the following note from the publisher: "The Sahitya Parishad has now the pleasure to publish the entire speech of Dr. Bhuyan under the title 'Assam and Manipur', in view of his valuable suggestions to guide the activities of Manipuri scholars and litteratures, and to stimulate investigations and research works into the relations of Manipur with its eternal neighbours". An Assamese translation by Shri Kamaleswar Chaliha was published in the *Asam Sahitya Sabha Patrika,* issue for Baisakh to Sravan, 1876 *saka,* Volume XIII, No. 1. Partly published in *This is Assam.*, 1958.

8. BANIKANTA KAKATI. Talk broadcast from the Gauhati Centre of the All India Radio on the evening of November 15, 1952. It was published in *The Assam Tribune*, Gauhati, on November 17, 1952. An Assamese translation by Shri Birendra Kumar Bhattacharyya was published in *Ramdhenu*, Gauhati, for Agrahayan, 1874 *saka*, Volume V, No. 8; another version was published in *Santi Doot*, Gauhati, of Agrahayan 29, 1359 B.S.

9. INDIAN HISTORY CONGRESS. This speech was delivered as President of the Modern History Section of the Indian History Congress, held at Gwalior in December 1952.

10. ASAM SAHITYA SABHA. It is a summary in English of the original Assamese speech delivered as President of the twenty-second session of the Asam Sahitya Sabha, held at Shillong, in November 1953.

11. AN ASSAMESE CHRONICLE OF TRIPURA. This article describes the chronicle *Tripura Buranji*, the original manuscript of which is deposited in the Library of the British Museum, London. The text, edited by the present writer, was published by the Assam Government Department of Historical and Antiquarian Studies in Assam, Gauhati, in 1938. The book was reviewed by Shri Krishnakanta Handiqui in the *Oriental Literary Digest*, Poona, for November 1938; by Shri Jatindramohan Bhattacharyya in the *Ananda Bazar Patrika*, Calcutta, in the issue of September 9, 1945; and by Dr. Nalini Kanta Bhattasali of Dacca, in the same paper, Puza Number, 1353 B. S., 1946 A.D. *Tripura Buranji* has been prescribed by the University of Gauhati as a text-book for the B.A. Honours Examination in Assamese. A slightly abridged version of the study has been published in *The Oriental Review*, Calcutta, for March 1957.

APPENDICES

A. AIDS TO THE STUDY OF ASSAMESE. The nucleus of this bibliography was appended to *Assamese Literature: Ancient and Modern*, printed by the Government of

Assam in 1936. The list has since been enlarged and brought up to date.

B. BIBLIOGRAPHICAL NOTE ON ASSAMESE HISTORICAL LITERATURE. This note was appended to the author's book *Annals of the Delhi Badshahate,* D.H.A.S., 1947. Since revised.

C. BIBLIOGRAPHICAL NOTES ON THE STUDIES INCORPORATED IN THE BOOK. Full details and particulars.

THE END

BOOKS BY DR. SURYYA KUMAR BHUYAN

Published by Lawyer's Book Stall, Panbazar, Gauhati, Assam.

ENGLISH :

STUDIES IN THE LITERATURE OF ASSAM. With a Foreword by Shri Sri Prakasa, formerly Governor of Assam, Madras, Bombay and Maharastra. Second edition, 1962. Price Rs. 8.

ATAN BURAGOHAIN AND HIS TIMES. Or, A History of Assam, 1662-1696, mainly centering round the career of the great statesman and patriot Atan Buragohain Rajmantri Dangaria, Prime Minister of Assam from 1662 to 1679. Published in 1957. Price Rs. 12.

MEN I HAVE MET. Brief and intimate sketches of 152 contemporaries. Published in 1962. Price Rs. 2·50 nP.

ASSAMESE :

JAIMATI UPAKHYAN. A longer narrative poem. Second edition, 1954. Price Rupee 1.

ANUNDORAM BOROOAH. A biography of the eminent Sanskritist. Second edition, 1956. Price Rs. 3.

JONAKI. Life-sketches of eminent men. Third edition, 1956, illustrated. Price Rs. 3.

BURANJIR VANI. Sixteen essays on different aspects of Assam History. Fourth edition, 1961. Price Rs. 3.

MIR JUMLAR ASSAM AKRAMAN. An account of the Mogul invasion of Assam in 1662-63. Published in 1956. Price Rs. 3.

KOWANR BIDROH. Revolt of Assam princes during the reign of Swargadeo Lakshmi Singha, 1769-80. Second edition, 1956. Price Rs. 1·50 nP.

GOPAL KRISHNA GOKHALE. A short biography of the great Indian statesman and patriot. Second edition, 1956. Price Rs. 1·50.

TRIPADI. Three essays on aspects of Assam's literature and history. 1959. Price Rs. 2.

HARIHAR ATA. Life-sketch of a great Vaisnava saint of Assam, and a devoted follower of Mahapurush Madhabdeva. 1960. Re. 1.

N.B. Other books by Dr. S. K. Bhuyan are also stocked by us for sale. For the complete hand list of Dr. Bhuyan's works, please write to —

BICHITRA NARAYAN DUTTA-BARUA, B.L.,
Proprietor, **LAWYER'S BOOK STALL,**
PANBAZAR, GAUHATI, ASSAM.